Security in Vehicular Networks

To my beloved parents,
my cherished brothers,
my dear sisters
Leila Benarous

To Afaf, Nada, Nour, and Rami
Salim Bitam

To my beloved young daughter Intissar
Abdelhamid Mellouk

New Generation Networks Set

coordinated by
Abdelhamid Mellouk

Volume 1

Security in Vehicular Networks

Focus on Location and Identity Privacy

Leila Benarous
Salim Bitam
Abdelhamid Mellouk

WILEY

First published 2022 in Great Britain and the United States by ISTE Ltd and John Wiley & Sons, Inc.

ISTE Ltd
27-37 St George's Road
London SW19 4EU
UK

www.iste.co.uk

John Wiley & Sons, Inc.
111 River Street
Hoboken, NJ 07030
USA

www.wiley.com

Library of Congress Control Number: 2022941634

British Library Cataloguing-in-Publication Data
A CIP record for this book is available from the British Library
ISBN 978-1-78630-848-1

Contents

Preface

Vehicular networks are formed by connected vehicles. They were initially developed to ensure the safety of their users and extend Internet services to the road. They offer various types of services and applications to road users to make their trips more enjoyable and more comfortable. However, cyber activity can result in the creation of new types of risks, such as blackmailing, data trading or profiling. Worse still, they may have an impact on the safety of on-board users and may lead to road accidents. The risks arise from tracking and privacy violations through the interception of messages, the exchange of which is necessary for participation in the network. Privacy and security are the major issues that need to be resolved in order for vehicular networks to be implemented in real-world applications.

This book proposes privacy-preserving solutions that protect the user's identity and on-road location to prevent tracking from occurring. Our solutions have been tested experimentally and analytically to evaluate their performance against a strong attacker model. Initially based on the work conducted by Leila Benarous as part of her PhD thesis, this book has developed into a resource to facilitate the understanding of vehicular networks and the technologies they employ, as well as their various types. It highlights the significance of their associated privacy and security issues and their direct impact on the safety of users. Furthermore, it includes two anonymous authentication methods that preserve identity privacy, as well as five schemes that preserve location privacy in vehicular ad hoc networks (VANETs) and cloud enabled Internet of vehicles (CE-IoV) respectively. The design of a new privacy-aware blockchain-based pseudonym management framework is also included. The framework is secure, distributed and public, ensuring revocation, non-repudiation, authenticity and integrity, which are the fundamental security requirements. The proposal was developed as a potential replacement for the vehicular public key infrastructure (VPKI).

To give a complete historical account of the research that led to the present form of the subject would have been impossible. It is thus inevitable that some topics have been covered in less detail than others. The choices partly reflect personal taste and expertise, and also a preference for the very promising research and recent developments in the field of technology-based security in vehicular networks.

This book is a start, but many questions remain unanswered. We hope that it will inspire a new generation of investigators and investigations. This book would not have been possible without the hard work of the following people: Professor Bouridane Ahmed, Professor Guizani Mohsen, Professor Kadri Benamar, Professor Belabbaci Youcef, Professor Ouinten Youcef, Dr. Saadi Boudjit, Dr. Bensaad Mohammed Lahcen and Dr. Oubbati Omar Sami. We give particular thanks to Mr. Djoudi Mohamed as well as the late Dr. Yamani Ahmed for their endless support. Finally, we thank everyone who has contributed to the success of this work. The authors hope that you will enjoy reading this book and get many helpful ideas and overviews for your own study.

June 2022
Leila BENAROUS
Salim BITAM
Abdelhamid MELLOUK

List of Acronyms

AASS	Average Anonymity Set Size
ASS	Anonymity Set Size
AVISPA	Automated Validation of Internet Security Protocols and Applications
BAN	Burrows, Abadi and Needham
BB	Big Brother
BC	Blockchain
BCN	Beacon
CA	Certifying Authority
CaaS	Cooperation-as-a-Service
CE-IoV	Cloud Enabled Internet of Vehicles
CIoV	Cognitive IoV
CL-atSe	Constraint Logic-based Attack Searcher
CLPPS	Cooperative-based Location Privacy-Preserving Scheme for Internet of Vehicles

CM	Cloud Manager
COO	Cooperation
CPS	Certified Pseudonyms
CPU	Central Processing Unit
CRL	Certificate Revocation List
CS	Content Store
CSLPPS	Concerted Silence-based Location Privacy-Preserving Scheme for Internet of Vehicles
CVD	Change VMID
CVDNN	Cloud-enabled Vehicle Data Named Networks
DataPk	Data Packet
DC	Do the Change
DDoS	Distributed Denial of Service
DoS	Denial of Service
DRL	Data Reliability
DSRC	Dedicated Short-Range Communications
EDGE	Enhanced Data rates for GSM Evolution
ERGS	Electronic Route Guidance System
FCC	Federal Communications Commission
FIB	Forwarding Information Base
GPA	Global Passive Attacker
GPRS	General Packet Radio Service

GPS	Global Positioning System
GSM	Global System for Mobile
HLPSL	High-Level Protocol Specification Language
HMI	Human–Machine Interface
HSDPA	High-Speed Downlink Packet Access
HVC	Hybrid Vehicular Cloud
IC-NoW	Information Centric Network on Wheels
InaaS	Information-as-a-Service
IntPk	Interest Packet
IoT	Internet of Things
IoV	Internet of Vehicles
ITS	Intelligent Transport System
LBS	Location-Based Service
LTCA	Long-Term Certification Authority
MANET	Mobile Ad hoc Network
MITM	Man in the Middle
MSC	Message Sequence Chart
NaaS	Network-as-a-Service
NDN	Named Data Networks
NoW	Network on Wheels
NRV	New Reputation Value
NS	Network Simulator

OBU   On-Board Unit

OFMC   On-the-Fly Model Checker

ORV   Old Reputation Value

PCA   Pseudonym Certification Authority

PIT   Pending Interest Table

PKI   Public Key Infrastructure

PoS   Proof of Stake

PoW   Proof of Work

PRA   Pseudonym Resolution Authority

PROMETHEUS Program for European Traffic with Highest Efficiency and
                   Unprecedented Safety

PSD   Pseudonym

PUF   Physically Unclonable Functions

QoS   Quality of Service

RA   Regional Authority

RCA   Root Certifying Authority

RCP   Resource Command Processor

RDC   Ready to Do the Change

RFID   Radio Frequency Identification

RS   Registration Server

RSU   Road Side Units

SATMC   Satisfiability-based Model Checker

SC   Service Continuity

SDN	Software-Defined Networks
SDVN	Software-Defined Vehicular Networks
SF	Selfishness
SIG	Signature
SPAN	Security Protocol Animator
StaaS	Storage-as-a-Service
TA	Trusted Authority
TA4SP	Tree Automata for Security Protocols
TMN	Testimony
TPD	Tamper Proof Device
Tx	Transaction
UMTS	Universal Mobile Telecommunication System
V2H	Vehicle-to-Human
V2I	Vehicle-to-Infrastructure
V2N	Vehicle-to-Network
V2S	Vehicle-to-Sensors
V2V	Vehicle-to-Vehicle
V2X	Vehicle-to-Everything
VANET	Vehicular Ad hoc Network
VC	Vehicular Cloud
VCS	Vehicular Cloud Services
VIN	Vehicle Identification Number

VM	Virtual Machine
VMID	Virtual Machine Identifier
VN	Vehicular Networks
VPKI	Vehicular Public Key Infrastructure
VS	Verification Server
VuC	Vehicle using the Cloud

Introduction

I.1. Introduction

Vehicles are continuously evolving, from a simple means of transport to a powerful computer on wheels. The overwhelming concerns about reducing road causalities and protecting the environment are pushing researchers and the industry to develop smart vehicles that are safer and more eco-friendly. Extending the Internet and networking concepts to the road is becoming a necessity rather than a luxury.

Vehicular networks (VNs) are formed by vehicles, road infrastructures, on-road devices and sensors. They were originally created to safeguard on-roads users and reduce the number of accidents and casualties. They are now developed to provide high-quality infotainment services. The broadcast of real-time road information such as construction work, traffic, accidents, weather and road conditions helps road users to easily and safely plan their trips. VNs offer various applications, including autonomous driving. In fact, autonomous driving can be achieved by smart vehicles independently, and can also be realized via VNs, where road data is exchanged over the network to make automatic adaptive driving decisions. The vision of researchers and the industry is not limited to offering on-road safety-related applications, but also aims to extend the Internet infotainment to road-edge. As VNs manage vehicular traffic in a smooth way, they result in reducing fuel consumption and emitted toxins and gases. Therefore, they help in protecting the environment.

However, although VNs are developed to save users' lives and offer them various on-road services, and despite the benefits they bring in protecting the environment, they result in breaching the privacy of road users. This is due to their nature that requires the broadcast of real-time spatio-temporal identifying data. This identifying data can be used to perform profiling and tracking attacks on users.

Therefore, security and privacy are two fundamental issues that must be preserved and ensured to safely deploy these networks.

I.2. Motivation

The damage caused by cyber-system security breaches is significant in terms of moral and financial implications, as well as the impact on human life. The technology news reports devastating security violation launched against top high-tech corporations yearly. VNs extend computers and the cyber world to roads. Therefore, fatalities resulting from security and privacy violation on-road are even more tremendous because they are directly related to the user safety.

A vehicle should not be tracked via its on-road cyber activity. Its user's identity should not be known nor extracted from the vehicle's exchanged messages. If a vehicle is successfully tracked from its cyber activity by an attacker, they may learn its driver's routines, parsed trajectories, hideouts and frequented places. The attacker may track (stalk) the vehicle to trade its user's data for profit, out of personal interest or to blackmail the vehicle owner using collected secrets. The consequences of leaking trajectory data about the user may give rise to serious risks, such as planning traffic congestion or accidents along frequented routes. Even worse, a malicious attacker may even execute on-road assassination. To avoid these serious consequences and ensure the safe use of VNs, we concentrated our research on developing security and privacy solutions. These solutions reduce the tracking risks for VN users.

I.3. Objectives

Our research aims to preserve the privacy and security of VN users. More precisely, our interest lies in protecting identity and location privacy as they are interconnected. Exposure of one results in the violation of the other, leading to the aforementioned fatalities. The cause of privacy vulnerability in VNs is the broadcast of periodic state messages needed for safety applications, which are sent wirelessly in clear with high frequency. Moreover, they contain accurate, real-time identity and spatio-temporal information. Their easy interception results in vehicle trajectory tracking. Furthermore, VNs also demand the assurance of non-repudiation (accountability), authentication and revocation of mischievous nodes to maintain their reliability. In fact, these requirements go against privacy demands. Therefore, when developing a solution, both privacy and security requirements should be guaranteed in a balanced way. The existing solutions to protect location privacy use temporal identities known as pseudonyms. These pseudonyms are frequently updated through change strategies aiming to reduce their inter-linkability. Unlinkability between updated pseudonyms also protects location (trajectory) privacy. Moreover, the use of pseudonyms ensures anonymity. Therefore, the majority of existing solutions are designed to protect anonymity and limit linkability to prevent tracking.

Identity privacy may be further exposed if repeatedly used to authenticate the vehicle to infrastructures, authorities and service providers. Consequently, we concentrate on developing privacy-preserving authentication schemes, also known as anonymous authentication methods. While designing these solutions, we intended to make them resilient to security attacks that target VNs, such as Sybil attacks, and authentication systems.

Currently, VNs are authority-based, i.e. vehicle registration and the issuance of certificates are done by the authority. This authority ensures the correct functionality of the network through the revocation of misbehaving nodes and the tracing of honest nodes. This means that privacy is conditional in VNs; it is preserved from other vehicles and exposed to the authority when the vehicle misbehaves and disrupts the functionality of the network. Moreover, the authority provides the vehicle with security parameters, keys, certificates and algorithms. The authority-based system is known as the vehicular public key infrastructure (VPKI). The VPKI is preferred over the self-generated key system because it satisfies the main requirements needed in VNs, such as preventing Sybil attacks, guaranteeing conditional privacy, ensuring non-repudiation and revocation, etc. Therefore, most of the existing solutions for safeguarding privacy in VNs are built over the VPKI.

In the following, we explain the aims of this book:

– Our first objective is to understand VN characteristics and types, alongside a review of their security issues and sources. Our focus is on authentication and privacy issues.

– Our second objective is to ensure authentication without any violation of identity privacy. Nevertheless, privacy-preserving authentication methods, also known as anonymous authentication methods, may instigate other security infringements. Being anonymous may enable untraceable network exploitation. It may also disrupt network functioning. Furthermore, it contradicts non-repudiation and revocation requirements. Consequently, when developing anonymous authentication methods, we first thought of how to resolve the issues mentioned above.

– Our third objective relates to the development of infrastructure, crowd and road-map independent location privacy-preserving schemes for vehicular ad hoc networks. The solutions discussed are pseudonym update strategies, which maintain correct network functionality while reducing linkability. The solutions are designed to protect location privacy, even when used on low density roads where tracking is likely to occur.

– Our fourth objective is to design location privacy-preserving schemes for Internet of vehicles (IoV) road users. Our target is to reduce the linkability achieved from matching IoV location-based service queries with periodic beacon safety applications. Reducing linkability in turn reduces tracking. Developed solutions must not negatively interfere with network functionality nor cause service interruption.

– Our final objective is to propose a potential replacement for the central-based VPKI. The VPKI is secure and most of the existing solutions discuss its robustness from the researcher's perspective. However, certificate issuance is most likely to be a paid service. Furthermore, the fact that it is centralized makes it prone to a single point of failure and the target of attacks. Lastly, VPKI deployment costs to cover and satisfy all the needs of the network vehicles' pseudonyms are extremely high. We therefore design a distributed, cost-free blockchain-based pseudonym management framework as a potential replacement for VPKI. This framework ensures the security requirements of authenticity, privacy, non-repudiation, integrity and revocation. It relies on the network nodes (vehicles and infrastructures) to self-generate the pseudonyms and add them to the blockchain. The aim is to decrease the cost of the VPKI, provide a secure, distributed pseudonym management framework and prevent the single point of failure problem.

I.4. Book structure

This book is organized into nine chapters. The first four chapters are dedicated to a literature review. The remaining five chapters are based on some of our past contributions. A brief outline of each chapter is given below.

Chapter 1 aims to clarify the basic concepts related to VNs: their evolution, technology, architecture, characteristics and challenges. It also lists their standards, applications and real-world implementations. This chapter also includes public opinions about these networks. Most importantly, it enumerates the various types of VNs and highlights the key differences between them.

Chapter 2 introduces the reader to the privacy and security issues in VNs; particular attention is paid to identity and location privacy, as well as to authentication as a security issue. This chapter explains the privacy issue and sheds light on its importance and the potential consequences of its violation. It also answers the questions about why privacy is threatened, when, by whom and how. Similarly, the authentication issue is explained and its contradiction with privacy requirements is highlighted. This chapter also surveys prominent existing solutions for each issue separately.

Chapter 3 explains the security and privacy evaluation methodology, metrics and tools. We mention the key methods used in the literature and then explain our chosen methodology and our reasons for using it.

Chapter 4 studies security issues against an attacker model that deploys various types of attack, in order to evaluate performance in terms of its resilience to those attacks. In this chapter, we explain the security objectives and properties that should be maintained in VNs. We also mention key security challenges in these networks that are subject to research. Finally, we explain our attacker model for both authentication and privacy issues. We clarify its aims, types, means and attacks.

Chapter 5 defines the model for cloud-enabled vehicle data named networks where vehicles may share their resources with one another on the road. Resource sharing happens upon successful authentication and is done while ensuring privacy. To preserve privacy between the resource requester and the service provider, an anonymous reputation-based authentication is performed. The proposed mutual authentication method is proved to achieve its underlying aims using the BAN logic.

Chapter 6 includes privacy-preserving anonymous authentication that ensures privacy as well as security. The solution is used as the initial phase to request on-road pseudonym/certificate refilling. This process is repetitive and may lead to tracking if the identity is used repeatedly in the request, even if the communication is secure. The proposed authentication method ensures authenticity, integrity, non-repudiation and revocation. Furthermore, it is resilient to man-in-the-middle attacks, replay attacks, impersonation, brute force and Sybil attacks. We use the BAN logic to prove its correctness and SPAN and AVISPA to prove that it is safe, ensures the authentication aims and is resilient to well-known attacks.

Chapter 7 deals with location privacy in VNs, which is a critical issue. Trajectory tracking is risky, and results from accurate linkability between updated pseudonyms. The consequences of tracking may vary from stalking and blackmailing to assassination. Various solutions exist in the literature, aiming to reduce the linkability and tracking ratio. In this chapter, we propose two solutions that are road-, crowd- and infrastructure-independent. Both aim to reduce the linkability ratio, even when the vehicle is within low density roads. The solutions were analyzed by simulation against the attacker model defined in Chapter 4. The first proposal reduced the tracking ratio to an average of 27%. The second proposal was even better, with an average tracking ratio of 10.4%.

Chapter 8 presents the Internet of vehicles, which is the evolution of VANET. It relies on cloud computing to provide a wider range of more stable and global services. Consecutively, the risks to privacy come from linking the location-based services used by the vehicle through the IoV. Also, its safety-related application participation is necessary to maintain the correct functionality of networks. In this chapter, we propose three location privacy-preserving solutions that take the above risks into account. The solutions are tested through simulation against the attacker model defined in Chapter 4. Each solution is the amelioration of its predecessor. These ameliorations aim to reduce the tracking ratio: the lower this ratio, the higher the level of privacy provided by the solution. The ratios obtained are 30%, 16% and 10% on average for the three proposals respectively.

Chapter 9 proposes a potential replacement framework to the vehicular PKI that suffers from a single point of failure and is costly to deploy. The framework is based on the blockchain. It preserves privacy even though it is public. It ensures authentication, revocation, non-repudiation and integrity. It inherits the security strength of blockchains, prevents alterations and ensures availability. The framework is a blockchain of two public blockchains. The first blockchain is permissionless, and contains vehicle-generated pseudonyms. The second blockchain is permissioned, and contains revoked pseudonyms. Our framework provides the same requirements ensured by the VPKI, while ensuring a higher level of security.

It is worth noting here that some of the work presented in these chapters has already been published in several journals and featured at numerous conferences.

Vehicular Networks

1.1. Introduction

Vehicular networks are at the core of the intelligent transport system (ITS). Interest in these networks is constantly growing due to the need to reduce road fatalities, which result in immense yearly losses in terms of human lives, physical and mental health repercussions, property damage and financial losses. They were initially developed to ensure the safety of road users by providing them with accurate prior knowledge about the traffic, road conditions and shortcuts. They were also intended to provide users with safe, comfortable trips in their autonomous vehicles. Moreover, vehicle networks help to lower fuel consumption by reducing traffic jams and streamlining the driving experience.

In this type of network, the vehicles are the main nodes. They are also referred to as computers on wheels in the literature. The vehicles are equipped with various types of sensors for external and internal roles such as sensing proximity or engine heat. They also contain a global positioning system (GPS) to localize the vehicle, cameras, radar and lidar to sense the surroundings and detect obstacles and road conditions. The on-board unit (OBU) is the brain of the vehicle and computer controlling it; it ensures the vehicle's correct functioning and processes the sensed data. The OBU gives the vehicle the trait of smartness, which is the same reason they are known as "smart vehicles". They also have network interfaces that are used to communicate, alongside a storage space to save sensed data, security programs and received messages.

The vehicular networks encompass several types of networks in which the main type of node is a vehicle. It comprises the autonomous vehicles, Vehicular Ad hoc Networks (VANETs), vehicular data named networks, vehicular cloud computing, Internet of vehicles, etc. The appearance of these types is due to the evolution of the on-road users' service demands and corresponding answering applications. The earliest applications of VNs were safety-related, oriented towards assisting the driver. Then, the infotainment applications became a necessity later on. Lastly, the Internet and cloud computing were extended to road-edge in order to provide road users with their services.

This chapter reviews vehicular networks, their evolution and their applications. It depicts the yearly fatalities caused by vehicle causalities and the assessments of the benefits of using the vehicular networks to ensure safety, alongside the evaluation of their market value. It describes the vehicular networks' evolution as part of the intelligent transportation systems and road automation projects. It also explains the components of intelligent vehicles and the architectures of vehicular networks. It describes the main distinguishable characteristics of the vehicular networks. It enumerates the issues and technical challenges halting the vehicular networks' real implementations. Furthermore, it lists the wireless technologies that could potentially be used in vehicular networks. It outlines the vehicular networks regulating standards and explains the vehicular network's different existing types along with its test beds. Lastly, it reviews the public opinion and acceptance of the technology.

1.2. Motivation by numbers

The following statistics emphasize the importance of vehicular networks (Contreras-Castillo et al. 2018):

– approximately 1.3 million people die every year;

– more than 7 million people are injured;

– nearly 8 million traffic accidents are recorded;

– estimated wasted time because of traffic jams and accidents is over 90 billion hours;

– vehicles produce 220 million tons of carbon;

– the expected global market of the Internet of Everything may reach 14.4 trillion dollars by 2022 (Bonomi 2013) and the value of the Internet of vehicles (IoV) alone was estimated to be 115.26 billion Euros by 2020 (Contreras-Castillo et al. 2018);

– more importantly, autonomous vehicles usage would eliminate 80–90% of vehicles' accidents and crashes (Maglaras et al. 2016);

– a rough estimation (Bai and Krishnamachari 2010) states that 100% market penetration by vehicular networks would take 14–15 years from its initial deployment date.

With these statistics, it is abundantly clear that vehicular networks are most likely serving the purposes they were developed for in reducing car accidents, injuries, mortalities, pollution, etc. Academics and industry are doing their best to concretize and market this technology. What is left is to convince the public and draw attention to its benefits.

1.3. Evolution

Automated roads and the creation of self-driving vehicles have been the dream of various researchers and industry sectors. General Motors was the leader in exhibiting the basic concepts of road automation, known as "Futurama", at the 1939 World Fair. In 1970, a follow-up proposition came from the United States, which is the Electronic Route Guidance System (ERGS). It pilots the drivers to their destination by decoding and transmitting routing instructions to and from roadsides at intersections. In Japan, between 1973 and 1979, the Comprehensive Automobile Traffic Control System was launched. The project aimed to reduce air pollution and traffic congestion and prevent accidents. It also aimed to provide the driver with appropriate route directions thanks to the accurate information and warnings received (Gerla et al. 2014). In Europe, the PROMETHEUS (Program for European Traffic with Highest Efficiency and Unprecedented Safety) framework was introduced in 1986 and launched in 1988.

The term vehicular ad hoc networks was first coined by Ken Laberteaux in the first International Workshop on Vehicular Ad hoc Networks (VANET) held in Philadelphia in 2004 (Hartenstein and Laberteaux 2010). VANET is considered to be the first commercialized version of Mobile Ad-hoc Networks and one of its most promising applications, aiming to automate the roads and ensure user comfort and safety. It draws the community nearer to realizing the self-driving vehicles' vision (Gerla et al. 2014).

Ever since the VANET became a hot topic, various related consortiums and projects were launched yearly. We mention a few of them as an example: FleeNET, CarTalk2000, Car2Car consortium, PReVENT, Network on Wheel (NoW), MobiVip, etc. (Meraihi et al. 2008).

Starting from 2010, a new vehicular networks type appeared, the vehicular cloud (VC) concept, which combines cloud computing with vehicular networks. The VC takes advantage of the vehicles' sensing, calculation and storage capacities to extend the clouds that offer various kinds of stable services (Gu et al. 2013). As of 2014, researchers focused on the Internet of vehicles (Gerla et al. 2014; Yang et al. 2014), which is the evolution of VANETs and an instantiation of the Internet of Things.

In 2009, Google's first autonomous vehicle project started. It continued its tests and trials until 2015, when it first hit the public road. In 2016, the project became independent and was named Waymo under Alphabet, a self-driving technology company. Meanwhile, major car companies such as Renault, Mercedes, Tesla and Audi have been competing to launch their own self-driving vehicles (top companies for self-driving vehicles).

1.4. Architecture

Autonomous vehicles, also known as self-driving vehicles, are smart. They have two types, illustrated in Figure 1.1. The first type is the self-dependent (self-contained) vehicle, relying only on its smarts and computational capacities to process sensed data, execute instructions and make decisions. The second type is the interdependent vehicle, where a vehicle either exchanges data and instructions with a control server via Vehicle-to-Infrastructure (V2I), or, it is connected to other network nodes (vehicles) via Vehicle-to-Everything (V2X) to interchange sensed data. The second type is denoted as vehicular networks. Although the types differ, the design and components of the smart vehicles are similar (Glancy 2012).

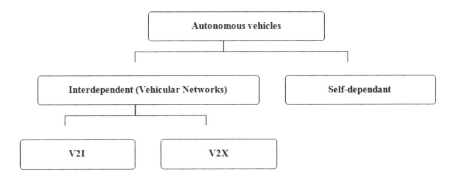

Figure 1.1. *Autonomous vehicles*

Vehicular networks in general are built upon the VANETs basic architecture. They are composed of vehicles as mobile nodes known as on-board units (OBU) and road side units (RSU) as static infrastructures. The OBU stores, locates, calculates and sends messages over a network interface (Gerla et al. 2014). It is composed of a read/write memory used to store/fetch information, a Resource Command Processor (RCP), a user interface and a network device using IEEE 802.11p radio technology for short-range wireless communication (Al-Sultan et al. 2014).

The RSUs broadcast advertisement and road information; they also spread data sent by OBUs (Gerla et al. 2014). They are equipped with network interfaces using IEEE 802.11p radio technology for a dedicated short-range communication, and wired interfaces for communication with the other infrastructures in the network (Al-Sultan et al. 2014). The basic components of a smart vehicle were initially summed up into the use of GPS, radar, sensors, an on-board computer (for processing and storage), network interfaces and a human-friendly interface.

However, the technology is constantly developing, with numerous carmakers competing on intelligent vehicles' implementations and testing. Therefore, the components are more sophisticated, refined and advanced. For illustration purposes, we study the components of a Google smart car as an example of the current design and technology in use.

A Google vehicle uses a distinguishable set of hardware and software technologies, and we mention a few of them (national):

– laser range finder (lidar, 360° camera), which can create 3D images of objects within a 200 m range and calculate the distances;

– front camera for near vision, which can detect front objects, pedestrians, obstacles, traffic lights, road signs, etc.;

– bumper-mounted radar, which are mounted on the front and rear of the vehicle to avoid bumps and crashes with vehicles, pedestrians and obstacles;

– an aerial on the rear of the vehicle that reads precise geo-location; this is done by matching the GPS location received from the satellite with the sensed location and internal map to render the location more accurately;

– ultrasonic sensors on rear wheels, which are used to keep track of the wheel's movement and detect the obstacle on the rear of the vehicles;

– the altimeters, gyroscopes and tachymeters inside the vehicle give precise information about its position;

– synergistic combining of sensors. The vehicle has a set of sensors for various purposes, all of the sensed data is combined and processed by the on-board unit to help achieve safe self-driving;

– in-built programmed maps, human behavior, data processing and decisional algorithms.

1.5. Characteristics

Vehicular networks have a particular nature and characteristics that differentiate them from other networks:

– their topology is highly dynamic due to the vehicles' high speed;

– predictable patterned movements defined by the roads and paths the vehicles run through;

– frequently disconnected networks causing a delay and potential loss of messages;

– the use of different types of external and internal sensors for various purposes;

– unlimited battery power and large storage capacity (Kumar et al. 2013);

– variable network density in roads (in rural areas, in the city, during daytime, during nighttime, etc.) (Al-Sultan et al. 2014);

– the various obstacles on road and surrounding it, such as trees and tall buildings;

– security and privacy threats (Guo and Balon 2006);

– availability of the vehicles' accurate real-time geographic positions (Sivasakthi and Suresh 2013);

– geographical communications using location information (Da Cunha et al. 2014).

1.6. Technical challenges and issues

Few technical issues and obstacles that need to be resolved confront the real-world implementation of vehicular networks. We mention some of them in this section:

– signal fading due to large distance between vehicles in case of a sparse network and/or the existence of the multiple obstacles in the case of urban areas;

– limitation of bandwidth, which engenders congestion when excessive simultaneous applications are being used in dense urban areas. Therefore, even the fair use of bandwidth increases latency in a dense environment;

– connectivity fluctuation and frequent fragmentation due to the high mobility of vehicles and the small effective diameter of the network;

– balancing and satisfying security and privacy requirements in VANETs;

– the rapidly changing topology hardens the task of researchers aiming to design a reliable routing protocol for VANETs. These protocols are responsible for delivering packets in the shortest possible time, even in a dense network (Al-Sultan et al. 2014);

– VANETs inherit the problems of exposed and hidden terminals from MANETs;

– the high cost of the deploying roadside units and infrastructures, IT-management issues and connectivity are among the leading reasons holding the real-world implementation of VANET back (Hartenstein and Laberteaux 2010).

1.7. Wireless technology

Various wireless technologies may be used to ensure the connectivity between the VANET components, among which are:

– **Cellular systems**: can be used as a communication solution for VANETS to exchange messages and data. Among the reused systems are: the Global System for Mobile (GSM), also known as 2G, the General Packet Radio Service (GPRS), also known as 2.5 G, Enhanced Data rates for GSM Evolution (EDGE), also known as 2.75 G, the Universal Mobile Telecommunication System (UMTS), also known as 3G, High-Speed Downlink Packet Access (HSDPA), CMDA2000, LTE 4G and 5G.

– **WLAN/Wi-Fi**: may also possibly be used to provide wireless access enabling V2I or V2V communications.

– **WiMAX**: Worldwide Interoperability for Microwave Access, also known as IEEE 802.16e. It covers a wide transmission range, achieves high data rate and has a high quality of service.

– **DSRC/WAVE**: licensed spectrums of 75 MHz at 5.9 GHz in the United States and at 5.8 GHz in Japan and Europe. It can be used solely for vehicle-to-vehicle and vehicle-to-infrastructures communications.

– **Combined wireless access technology**: combines various wireless technologies, such as GPRS, GSM and 3G (Al-Sultan et al. 2014).

1.8. Standards

To specify the operation of vehicular networks from the physical to the application layer, a group of protocols were standardized. The standards are primarily developed in Japan, Europe and North America. There are two major standardization groups: the ETSI ITS-G5 and IEEE WAVE stack protocols in Europe and North America respectively (Boualouache 2016).

The vehicles communicate with each other and with road side units (RSU) through dedicated short-range communications (DSRC). The DSRC provides low communication latency and high data transfer rate in small communication zones. In

1999, the United States Federal Communications Commission (FCC) allocated 75 MHz of spectrum in the 5.9 GHz band to be used for a service called DSRC. The DSRC is a licensed free spectrum divided into seven channels that are 10 MHz each, among which only one channel is for safety communications, while four are service channels and the remaining two channels are reserved for special purposes (Boualouache 2016). The data rate varies between 6, 9, 12, 18, 24 and 27 Mbps for the 10 Mhz channel. It may increase to 54 Mbps for 20 MHz channels.

1.8.1. *IEEE WAVE stack*

The WAVE IEEE standards define the standards set for each layer. It has a stack for safety and for non-safety applications. Figure 1.2 illustrates the IEEE WAVE standards (Sjöberg 2011), and Figure 1.3 shows a simplified view of it.

	Safety applications	Non-safety applications
	Safety application sublayer	Application
Security IEEE1609.2	Message sublayer SEA J2735	Transport (TCP/UDP) IETF RFC 793/768
	WSMP (IEEE 1609.3)	Network (IP V6) IETF RFC 2460
	LLC sublayer IEEE 802.2	
	MAC sublayer extension IEEE1609.4	
802.11P	MAC sublayer	MAC layer
	PHY sublayer	PHYSIC layer

Figure 1.2. *IEEE WAVE standards (Sjöberg 2011)*

– **IEEE 802.11p**: IEEE 802.11p mac protocol for VANET extending the 802.11e.

– **IEEE1609.1**: defines the formats of messages and their responses.

– **IEEE 1609.2**: defines the secure messages' formatting, processing and exchange.

– **IEEE 1609.3**: defines the transport and routing layer services.

– **IEEE 1609.4**: describes the multichannel operations (Rawashdeh and Mahmud 2011).

Security IEEE1609.2	Resource manager	IEEE 1609.1
	Networking services	IEEE 1609.3
	Multi-channel operations	IEEE 1609.4
	Phys./MAC IEEE 802.11P	

Figure 1.3. *A simplified WAVE standard view (Rawashdeh and Mahmud 2011)*

1.8.2. ETSI standards

The ETSI standards is the European equivalent of the US IEEE WAVE standards for vehicular networks and ITS. The access technologies layer adapts IEEE 802.11p standards on the European version, defining its physical and MAC layer protocols. The network and transport layer defines the IP-based and geo-networking protocols, in addition to the transport layer protocols. The facilities layer manages the services and messages supporting information, applications and communications. The application layer basically defines the applications related to traffic efficiency and road safety. The management layer is a cross-layer that plays a pivotal role in controlling all of the layers. The security layer defines the protocols, ensuring the integrity, privacy, authentication and non-repudiation (Sjöberg 2011). Figure 1.5 illustrates the ETSI ITS layers.

Management	Applications	Security
	Facilities	
	Network and transport	
	Access technologies	

Figure 1.4. *ETSI TC ITS protocol stack (Sjöberg 2011)*

1.8.3. The 3GPP standard

The 3GPP V2X leverages traditional cellular networks to enhance the DSRC to double range for V2V communications. It also functions both in and out of cellular networks coverage via V2V communications. Moreover, it offers robust V2I and vehicle-to-network (V2N) communications (Lucero 2016). Compared with IEEE 802.11p, cellular-based V2X provides better quality of service (QoS), higher data rate and larger coverage for moving vehicles. Additionally, V2X is synchronous, while IEEE 802.11p is asynchronous. Although V2X services may coexist with IEEE 802.11p-based radio access in adjacent channels, V2X is additionally advantageous for being scalable and evolvable (Wang et al. 2017). The 3GPP V2X standard supports a frequency of up to 10 messages per second and variable payloads of 50–300 bytes; event-triggered messages have payloads up to 1,200 (3GPP (2017-03)).

1.9. Types

Vehicular networks characterize various types of networks in which the vehicles on the roads are the main type of nodes. Usually, people's familiarity with the VANET confuses them to think that all vehicular network types are VANETs. Although it is true that the VANET is the first type introduced, as time has passed, the concept has continuously evolved with the introduction of new purposes, needs and applications. VANET may now be considered as the building block of more global, sophisticated and advanced vehicular technologies and networks. Figure 1.6 depicts, in an encapsulated illustration, the vehicular networks, which are explained in the following sections.

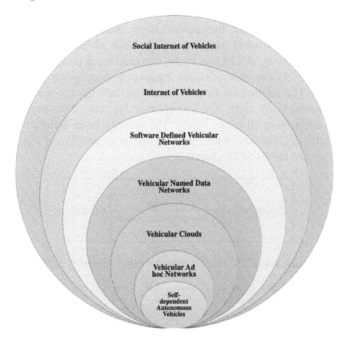

Figure 1.5. *Vehicular networks. For a color version of this figure, see www.iste.co.uk/benarous/vehicular.zip*

1.9.1. *The autonomous vehicle (self-dependent)*

The self-contained (self-dependent) autonomous vehicles rely solely on their processing abilities, artificial intelligence and sensing powers. Vehicles that are equipped with GPS, maps, cameras and radars make decisions locally. No instructions or commands are sent from distant servers or control units. Also, no network is used in the process (Glancy 2012).

1.9.2. *VANET*

The VANET or Vehicular Ad hoc Network refers to the vehicular networks composed of vehicles (OBU) and RSU as their main nodes. The communication between the vehicles is wireless through DSRC, and is known as the vehicle-to-vehicle (V2V). The DSRC is also used between the vehicle and the infrastructure (RSU), and is known as vehicle-to-roadside (V2R). The VANETs were developed primarily for safety applications to decrease road causalities, in addition to offering infotainment applications. Hence, the vehicles engender three classes of messages, which are: safety messages, also known as periodic state beacons, event-based alert messages and non-safety messages or service messages, related to information, entertainment and comfort applications (Hartenstein and Laberteaux 2010; Al-Sultan et al. 2014).

1.9.3. *Vehicular clouds*

The vehicular cloud is the road edge extension to conventional clouds. Due to this fact, each vehicle has an on-board unit that senses its surrounding environment, stores the sensed data and processes it. The sensing, processing and storing capacities may be made use of to form clouds known as VANET clouds or vehicular clouds.

Gerla (2012) suggested benefiting from vehicle storage and sensing capacities to improve traffic management. They proposed a vehicular cloud-based urban surveillance system and navigation system that saves sensed data from the road. It uses the vehicles' cameras to film roads and read the number plates of other cars. These videos and data are locally saved in the vehicle, while their descriptive meta-data saved on the Internet enables police forensic investigators to harvest them. The videos may record proofs against criminals, especially in assaults, hit-and-run accidents or bombings.

Whaiduzzaman et al. (2014) cited different applications that the vehicular clouds could offer, such as:

– **The network-as-a-service (NaaS)**: vehicles with Internet access offer it as a service to other road nodes that require it.

– **The storage-as-a-service (StaaS)**: vehicles may lease their storage capacity as a service to other road users to provide them with storage for large files.

– **The cooperation-as-a-service (CaaS)**: vehicles cooperate to gather and broadcast the data based on the interest. In other words, the data is routed based on its content to interested parties faster. Consequently, the vehicular cloud is formed of content-based clusters.

– **Computing as a service**: vehicles have sophisticated processing units that handle calculations and data treating. Unfortunately, these capacities are not exploited when vehicles are idly parked for hours each day. Hence, computing as a service was thought of to resolve this issue and benefits from the vehicles on-board units.

– **Photography-as-a-service**: vehicles with high-resolution cameras may offer better and wider road-vision than static infrastructures due to their mobility. They could deliver recorded proof on road crimes to the police and may send real-time updates on road conditions.

– **Information-as-a-service (InaaS)**: vehicles generate and process a variety of road information related to the driver's safety or entertainment. They can exchange this data on the road as a service.

The same authors classified vehicular clouds (VCs) into three types: static, dynamic and infrastructure-based. In static VCs, vehicles unify their resources and capacities while static, such as in parking lots, to offer services to users like in conventional clouds. Dynamic VCs are formed on-road by moving adjacent vehicles that combine their resources. Infrastructure-based VCs are suitable for urban areas with infrastructures distributed over roads that can form clouds with the passing vehicles. The infrastructure or RSU becomes the cloud coordinator, bridging the VC and conventional clouds.

Hussain et al. (2015) stated that vehicular clouds are more appropriate to provide infrastructure and software as services rather than offering platform-related service, noting that in clouds offering the platform as service, the user is provided with a development platform enabling them to develop remote applications. Likewise, they considered that the VANET clouds have three types, which they denoted as: vehicular clouds (VCs), the vehicle using the cloud (VuC) and hybrid vehicular clouds (HVCs). In VCs, the vehicles that are either static or dynamic combine their resources, forming a cloud offering paid services. In the VuC, the on-road vehicles use conventional cloud services, and, in HVCs, VC vehicles use conventional cloud services, i.e. HVCs combine both VCs and the VuC.

1.9.4. *Internet of vehicles*

The Internet of vehicles (IoV) is a vital part of the Internet of Things (IoT) and one of its promising instantiations (Gerla et al. 2014; Yang et al. 2014). It is the extension and evolution of VANETs. It incorporates vehicles, things, humans and the environment. The humans are people in vehicles (passenger, driver) and people in the surrounding environment, such as pedestrians and cyclists. The things refer to other entities and devices that are neither human nor vehicles, such as access points or traffic signs. The environment englobes humans, vehicles and things (Yang et al. 2014).

The IoV uses vehicular clouds as its basic technology (Gerla et al. 2014) and may rely on diverse kinds of wireless communication technologies, such as the DSRC, WIMAX, cellular networks (3G, 4G, 5G) and satellite networks. Therefore, it is able to offer more stable and global real-time and asynchronous services (Yang et al. 2014).

Mainly, the IoV has two technology directions. The first is the vehicle's networking consisting of the vehicle telematics (exchange of data), VANET and mobile Internet. The second is the vehicle's intelligence, reflecting the combination of the vehicle and the user's, as well as the use of artificial intelligence, cognitive computing and deep learning (Yang et al. 2014). Note that the IoV's vehicle is regarded as a swarm of sensors collecting road-related data, the vehicle's inner condition and its surrounding environment. The IoV's vehicle also has large storage capacities and sophisticated processing units (Bonomi 2013).

Contreras-Castillo et al. (2018) illustrated the IoV's seven-layer model, and each of these layers is briefly explained below:

– *the user interface layer*: facilitates the interaction between the vehicle and the user. They may query the on-board system, receive notifications and use the IoV services through this layer;

– *the data acquisition layer*: collects the data that are either sensed by the vehicles sensors or received from other vehicles and infrastructures;

– *the filtering and pre-processing layer*: pre-processes and filters the data based on their validity, utility and used service;

– *the communication layer*: enables the broadcast of communication and messages using different types of technologies, such as DSRC, WiMax, WiFi, 3G, 4G and 5G;

– *the control and management layer*: uses various packet inspections and traffic management policies methods to process the received information;

– *the processing layer*: uses the conventional clouds along with vehicular clouds capacities to store and process the received and collected data;

– *the security management layer*: is a transversal layer that handles and ensures security properties for all other layers.

Owing to the intelligence of the autonomous vehicle and the deep learning algorithms it uses, a new paradigm has appeared, which is the cognitive IoV (CIoV), the evolution of the IoV (Chen et al. 2018). It amalgamates the intelligence of autonomous vehicles with the vehicular networks, cellular networking and cloud computing. It is more precise in terms of perceptive ability concerning the vehicle's interactions and surrounding environment. It makes more reliable decisions, and uses its resources more efficiently.

The architecture of C-IoV has five layers:

– *sensing layer*: responsible for collecting data;

– *the communication layer*: includes interactions related to the cloud along with communications required for the functioning of conventional vehicular networks;

– *cognition layer*: uses data mining, machine learning, deep learning and pattern recognition to process sensed and collected data;

– *control layer*: makes decisions in a distributed manner to ensure the vehicular networks expected QoS and faster responses;

– *application layer*: provides a variety of applications and stable global services.

1.9.5. *Social Internet of vehicles*

After the social media networks emanation usage and knowing that the vehicle is most likely the third place people spend the majority of their time after their home and office, combining the social network with the vehicular network is now a necessity, in which passenger and drivers share road-related real-time events such as accidents, road works, café and restaurants offers, new gyms and shops or beautiful sceneries (Lequerica et al. 2010). This procreated a social vehicular network, more precisely, the social Internet of vehicles (IoV), which is a special case of Social IoT.

The social IoV is described as the social interactions between drivers and vehicles. It is also stated as a network created by the drivers within the same area with similar interests. Likewise, it is defined as the interactions between autonomous vehicles and interchange services and data (Maglaras et al. 2016). Alam et al. (2015) defined the social IoV as "a cyber-physical application over the physical vehicle networks of WAVE", in which the home, RSU and OBUs exchange data over cyber-physical formed social networks. The data interactions form a social graph where the graph nodes represent the entities and the graph links represent the exchanged data (Alam et al. 2015).

Nevertheless, Maglaras et al. (2016) asserted that in the future the social IoV will be defined as the social interactions of passengers, drivers and vehicles. It will allow the ranking of vehicles based on a set of characteristics. The ranking will help in making interaction decisions, and may be used to build trust and reputation, which are essential security properties in vehicular networks.

1.9.6. *Data named vehicular networks*

An information-centric network on wheels, or IC-NoW, is a vehicular network in which the data routing is based on information content rather than the usual IP addressing methods. The scope of information is defined by its time, space and user's interest relevance. It is referred to as a vehicular NDN, or named data vehicular network (Bai and Krishnamachari 2010).

The exchanged packets between roadside units and vehicles are information-centric, which means that they are shared among users with similar spatiotemporal and interest scope. However, these networks are still not completely independent of the IP-based networks. The IC-NoW encapsulates the packets exchanged via V2V, V2I within IP packets before sending them over the Internet (Bai and Krishnamachari 2010).

Note that each NDN node possesses three types of data structures: content store (CS), pending interest table (PIT) and forwarding information base (FIB). A vehicle interested in a packet sends an interest packet (IntPk). If the CS has the requested content, the requester receives a DataPk. Otherwise, the IntPk is added to the PIT to be forwarded to a potential CS from the FIB (Chen et al. 2014; Bouk et al. 2017).

1.9.7. *Software-defined vehicular networks*

In software-defined vehicular networks (SDVN), the centralized control plane logically controls the data communication. The difference between the SDVN and vehicular NDN is that the latter focuses on content-based routing of data, while SDVNs separate the control and data plane to make various services manageable without physical interference with switches and routers. Note that the vehicles in SDVN have multiple interfaces (Ahmed et al. 2017).

The SDVN consists of:

– an SDN controller, which has an overall view of the networks. It coordinates its elements to perform the NDN operations, which are intelligent interest, cashing, data forwarding and so on;

– cashing, which is an ultimate task performed by forwarding nodes. The forwarding nodes selection and the format of the cashed content are essential to ensure instant query/response. The content formats are compressed, non-compressed and chunked, saved entirely in a single or multiple node(s);

– content naming, which is another fundamental component that labels the contents and their chunks. This labeling smoothes the data search upon the vehicle's reception of an interest request, noting that each content has a specific spatiotemporal frame validity;

– intelligent forwarding: the FIB maintains the content communication. With this in mind, a face is ranked every time some content is satisfied through it. The face rank is dropped each time it does not satisfy an interest. If no interest is satisfied through this face, it gets purged from the FIB. If the FIB is empty, the requests are forwarded to the controller to be satiated;

– push-based forwarding, which delivers warnings constantly to potentially interested nodes;

– intrinsic data security: data messages are digitally signed. The SDN controller spreads the content security policies to interested vehicles;

– congestion control: congestion occurs because of certain contents' popularity. Thus, to alleviate congestion, each node has to send the traffic status at every face to evenly distribute the traffic over diverse cashing points;

– a topology indicator: each vehicle postulates its position, direction and speed to the control manager so that it can settle on the forwarding rules and disseminate them;

– a content prefix manager: every node sends its content store (cashed data) with its validity and expiry to the controller to help in forwarding the interest requests;

– the vehicle calculates state information at each interface. It sends a report about the requests and satisfied queries so that the controller can improve the cashing/forwarding policy (Lutterotti et al. 2008).

1.10. Test beds and real implementations

Middlesex University in the United Kingdom built the Middlesex VANET Research Testbed located at Hendon Campus in London. It has four RSUs fixed on different buildings. The test bed evaluates studies done by the developing team on VANET[1].

The Porto Living Lab in Portugal built a couple of independent test beds for VANET: harbor and urban, sited in the harbor and city of Porto respectively. In both

1 See: https://mdxminds.com/2016/01/11/the-future-of-driving-is-here/.

urban and harbor test beds, vehicles are equipped with OBUs, GPS receivers, DSRC, cellular and Wi-Fi communication interfaces. Vehicles connect to the Internet using cellular communications or through RSUs. The DSRC is used in V2V and V2I communications. In the urban test bed, most of the deployed RSUs were mounted on traffic light poles, control camera poles and buildings managed by the University of Porto[2].

The C-VeT vehicular test bed has been developed by UCLA-USA to evaluate MAC and network layer protocols and models. The CarTel and Cabernet test beds were developed by MIT-USA. Massachusetts Amherst-USA also developed two projects named Dome and DieselNet (Lutterotti et al. 2008). In 2008, Microsoft established its VANET Test bed called VanLan[3]. ITS corridor is another in-progress project from Amsterdam, passing by Germany to Vienna[4].

Among the European accomplished projects are SimTD (2013)[5], DRIVE C2X (2014)[6] and Compass4D (2016)[7]. Similarly, over 200 ITS-related projects are ongoing in Canada, two of which are at the Universities of Alberta and British Columbia (Lawson et al. 2015).

1.11. Services and applications

The vehicular networks aim to safeguard users' safety, ensure comfortable driving, maintain sleek traffic, reduce consumption of fuels and pollution of air, etc. They offer varied services and applications such as (Meraihi et al. 2008; Kumar et al. 2013; Al-Sultan et al. 2014; Seuwou et al. 2014):

– **Safety application**: has the top priority due to its role in preventing accidents and saving human lives. Among its examples are:

- accident alerts: prevent road causalities engendered from accidents that have already occurred. It speeds up the response by rescue services (Ambulance, Police). It facilitates the evacuation of the road and assists secondary roads and detour planning,

- cooperative driving: improves traffic management and reduces fuel consumption. It is known as vehicle platooning,

---

2 See: http://cordis.europa.eu/result/rcn/188104_en.html.

3 See: https://www.microsoft.com/enus/research/project/vanlan-investigating-connectivity-from-moving-vehicles/.

4 See: http://c-its-korridor.de/?menuId=1&sp=en.

5 See: http://www.simtd.de/index.dhtml/enEN/news/Presse.html.

6 See: http://www.drive-c2x.eu/project.

7 See: http://www.compass4d.eu/.

- collision avoidance: to avoid crashes and bumps, vehicles detect road obstacles by using their in-built sensors, lidars and radar and swiftly respond. Furthermore, vehicles disseminate accurate real-time information about current position, headings and speed, in order to avoid the collision, especially when doing U-turns, changing lanes, suddenly braking, etc.,

- security distance warning: the vehicles maintain a safety distance that is either preliminarily set as a few meters or dynamically adequate to vehicles' sudden brake response time. This distance also depends on the speed of the vehicle. The warning is sent when the vehicles do not keep to the defined security distance,

- lane changing: the vehicle alerts other vehicles when it is changing its lane to avoid collisions and accidents. This alert emulates the turn sign in manual driving,

- navigation and map location: the majority of recent vehicles come with a navigation system that corrects the users' location obtained from GPS with their in-built map so that they can plan their trajectories,

- traffic jam and road work alerts: these event-based messages propagate in the network to assist users in planning secondary routes,

- public safety (SOS, post-crash warning, nearing emergency vehicle, etc.),

- vehicle diagnostic and maintenance: vehicles can have on-road diagnosis. If an issue is detected, early reports are sent to the closest car care center for more efficient and prompt service provision.

– **Comfort application**: ensures the users' entertainment and comfort, such as:

- Internet access, chat between car users, video streaming, network games and other advanced stable services,

- weather forecasts and alerts,

- advertisement messages regarding close, affordable or ranked hotels, gyms, restaurants, gas stations or tourist spots, etc.

– **Driver assistance**: assists the driver through the provision of crucial warnings and aid information. A few examples of its applications are:

- parking spot reservation and parking management,

- automatic parking,

- self-driving vehicle (driverless cars): a vehicle is totally autonomous when it is driven solely by its system; it is semi-autonomous if the driver's intervention is still needed in driving. Figure 1.7 depicts the automated driving levels that are explained below (Maglaras et al. 2016; Wang et al. 2017):

– *level 0*: a human driver is needed to drive and monitor the vehicle's surrounding environment,

– *level 1*: the driving system assistance is either in steering *or* acceleration/deceleration based on the actual driving environment,

– *level 2*: the driving system assists both acceleration/deceleration *and* steering based on the actual driving environment,

– *level 3*: the driving system interferes in the dynamic driving tasks based on the surrounding environment, while drivers sort and respond to the requests of intervention they receive from the system,

– *level 4*: the driving system interferences in the dynamic driving tasks are with or without the driver's approval, based on the driving environment,

– *level 5*: the driving system executes the entire dynamic driving tasks, emulating the human driver.

Human Driver Monitors the driving environment	**0**	**No Automation**
	1	**Driver Assistance**
	2	**Partial Automation**
Automated driving System Monitors driving environment	**3**	**Conditional Automation**
	4	**High Automation**
	5	**Full Automation**

Figure 1.6. *Automated driving levels (Litman 2018)*

1.12. Public opinion

In the report presented by Schoettle and Sivak (2014), the public's opinion about autonomous and self-driving vehicles was surveyed in the United States, the United Kingdom and Australia. The plurality of respondents were acquainted with the technology or at least acknowledged its existence. While most of them showed their high expectations about it, they also voiced their concerns about it in terms of security, privacy and reliability, in addition to their concerns about the vehicle's self-dependency and absence of human intervention, questioning whether it can emulate human driving skills. Unlike the men, the women expressed more concerns about this technology and were more cautious about it. Lastly, at the time of the survey, the majority of respondents were reluctant about paying extra fees to obtain it, despite being interested in it.

The Office of the Privacy Commissioner of Canada conducted a similar survey where over one-third of Canadians expressed their concerns about their privacy if they were to use these connected cars. Similarly, over half of the respondents preferred their privacy over the advantages of connected car services. In a more recent poll conducted in the United States, Spain, Germany and the United Kingdom (Lawson et al. 2015), the respondents also voiced their concerns about their privacy and personal data, insisting that the vehicle is their private space, emphasizing the importance to protect them.

1.13. Conclusion

This chapter explains vehicular networks, their purpose, underlying technologies and offered applications. Moreover, it stated the vehicular networks evolutions and types. It concluded with a survey of public opinion illustrating the users' hesitation about VN technology and concerns about their confidentiality, as well as the VN reliability from a technical perspective.

Indeed, it is an undeniable fact that both privacy and security are equally important in vehicular networks. Likewise, they are also among the key issues hindering vehicular network market penetration and they top the end-users' concerns. The following chapter explains these issues and surveys the existing solutions to preserve them.

2

Privacy and Security in Vehicular Networks

2.1. Introduction

In the previous chapter, we outlined vehicular networks with their characteristics and types. In this chapter, we concentrate on the two essential issues halting the actual adoption of vehicular networks on a greater scale. These issues are the security and the privacy. Both are crucial in ensuring road users' safety. The slightest tampering in the vehicle's security system or in the network may imply devastating causalities. Among the security issues that exists, our focus is on authentication due to its influences on identity privacy. In vehicular networks, identity and location privacy are entangled. Revealing one of them leads to the disclosure of the other. The vehicle constantly broadcasts non-encrypted heartbeat messages containing the vehicle state information such as positions, velocity and its identity represented by a temporal public key known as a pseudonym. It could also emit event-based messages to report road accidents. In addition, it sends messages to obtain infotainment services. However, the resolve behind using anonymous certified pseudonyms (identity-less) is protecting identity privacy. If the pseudonyms are linked successfully upon their change and the attacker efficaciously tracks the location of the vehicle, resolving its owner's identity is just a matter of time. Using social engineering techniques, the attacker can match their collected tracks with each visited location specificity to identify the vehicle owner. For example, when a vehicle departs from location A and during weekdays frequents location B, noting that A is a house address and B is a workplace, even though multiple individuals may live in A, it is most likely that only one of them works at B. Therefore, the attacker may presume it is the vehicle owner thanks to social engineering. Similarly, if the user's identity is published in the network, its use is traceable, which leads to the exposure of location privacy. In vehicular networks, the security and more precisely the privacy are imperilled because the communications in VN are wireless, making the attacker's intrusion easier. They can either be passive simply eavesdropping on the communications or be active and launch packet alteration, injection or dropping attacks. We emphasize that in our research, we concentrate on studying the privacy issue and developing protective schemes that preserve it on the network level where the vehicle is tracked by its cyber-activity level. Henceforth, in the rest of this chapter, we only cite related research works working on this perspective. Other means of violating privacy such as physical stalking and the use of road surveillance camera are beyond the scope of this book. They are well known threats that may endanger the user's privacy regardless of whether they are driving a regular or smart vehicle or whether they participate or not in VN. Noting that, in this chapter, we do not specify the attacker's means or executed attacks in detail, instead we describe them generally. The technical details about the attacks are found in Chapter 4. This chapter explains the privacy issue in vehicular networks and highlights its importance in preserving the user's safety for both moral and physical threats. It also lists the types of threats and answer the questions about who is threatening privacy, when, how and what the consequences of such a threat are. Moreover, it reviews, classifies and analyzes the existing state-of-the-art location privacy-preserving schemes and evaluates their advantages and disadvantages. Furthermore, it explains the authentication issues in vehicular networks, explains what is being authenticated and lists the authentication types. It also highlights how the authentication risks privacy. Lastly, it gives a brief review of identity privacy preservation authentication solutions.

2.2. Privacy issue in vehicular networks

Privacy is generally crucial. People are by nature secretive, and they like to keep parts of their lives private. They prefer to keep some of their matters confidential. They incline to be selective of what, when and with whom a secret is to be shared. They abhor being on another person's radar. They dislike being spied on. They hate being pestered by any means, and they strongly object to stalking. These requirements were consecutively inherited by the cyber world. With the same mindset, users of the cyber world loath their cyber activities being tracked because they feel that the cyber world gives them more freedom in expressing their minds and voicing their opinions. The users are undoubtedly more truthful in front of their screens; they write comments honestly, they unrestrictedly ask questions and send queries and they also benefit from varied online services. Despite the fact that the users may willingly publish their daily pictures, updates and videos on their social media profiles, they strictly object to the implicit data retrieval or collection from their devices by unknown parties such as hackers, without their knowledge and consent.

In vehicular networks, the shared data type, accuracy, frequency and impact adds to how crucial privacy protection is. Moreover, the jeopardy of leaking this data by an attacker targeting the cyber-tracking of the vehicle's owner on the road is emphasized.

So far, we have written about the importance of privacy and the necessity of protection without properly explaining it. In 1890, Warren and Brandeis first defined privacy as "the right to be let alone" (Warren and Brandeis 1890). Then, in 1967, Alan Westin defined it as "the right to control, edit, manage, and delete information about themselves and decide when, how, and to what extent information is communicated to others" (Eduardo Cuervo n.d.; Westin 1967). In his paper, Adrienn Lukács (2016) reviewed the history of privacy and its various definitions through the eras following the evolution of society and technology. In the context of vehicular networks, Petit et al. (2015) defined it as the capability of the vehicle's user to control and select the type, lifetime and content of information sent by the vehicle even when forwarding.

2.2.1. *Types*

In vehicular networks, there are three types of privacy (Lim and Chung 2012):

– *identity privacy*: identifies the vehicle user through their cyber activity. This is done by their public key, network addresses or real identity;

– *location privacy*: past and current locations of the vehicle are tracked upon sharing its actual on-road location needed by the network safety requirements (Beresford and Stajano 2003);

– *data privacy*: concerns the content of exchanged messages, used and requested services, shared images, videos and files. It pertains more to infotainment services.

Privacy was classified into three types by Buttyán (2009), which are syntactic, semantic and robust. Syntactic privacy requires vehicles to periodically update their pseudonyms. Semantic privacy implies that vehicles broadcasting beacons should not lead to the tracking of the vehicle nor to the reconstruction of their trajectories. Robust privacy is about the resiliency to internal attackers and their impact on the system.

Since encryption protects confidentiality, also known as data privacy, researchers concentrate more on resolving identity and location privacy issues in vehicular networks. They are intertwined in their effects, both causing vehicle tracking by its on-road cyber activity with direct consequences on the user's safety.

2.2.2. *When and how it is threatened?*

The identity and location are essential to ensure the network's correct functionality. The location data assists other vehicles in making decisions guaranteeing safe driving, such as preventing accidents triggered by sudden lane change, slow down, braking, U-turn, etc. It ensures the vehicles' cooperation for smooth driving. The identity, which is the vehicle's certified public key, is used to avert false data injection by external attackers. It confirms the messages' authenticity, as well as the behavior non-repudiation and accountability. The vehicle is held responsible and is revoked when it misbehaves or injects false data in the network. The misbehavior may be caused by a hardware failure, the vehicle being an internal attacker or the vehicle being compromised by an attacker. The revocation stops honest vehicles from interacting and trusting the misbehaving nodes. Note that the accountability ensures undeniable evidence that can be used against the malicious user if they are prosecuted judicially.

The importance of the location and identity render their usage indispensable, and eliminating them is impossible. Still, their usage threatens privacy and can lead to vehicle tracking, which is the cyber equivalent of stalking. The risk comes from intercepting the vehicle's safety messages and when receiving the user identity sent in the network during authentication, and when using location-based services.

2.2.3. *Who is the threat?*

We have previously explained *how* and *when* privacy is threatened. Now, we discuss *who* is interested in violating and risking the user's confidentiality. The attacker may be an organization or an individual entity. They may target a particular user or track the network looking for possible prey. They may be a location-based service provider or authoritarian entities like the police. Regardless of the attacker's identity, they are anyone who can implicitly track the vehicle without the approval and knowledge of its user. The tracking is established through the interception and linking of the wirelessly broadcasted messages. Further details regarding the attacker, their means, executed attacks and types are explained in Chapter 4.

2.2.4. *What are the consequences?*

Tracking is as irritating as stalking. It is even more perilous because it happens without us noticing and it is hard to detect. The attacker tracks a vehicle either out of a personal grudge or motivated by the profits to make from trading users' private road-related data. Collecting tracks of vehicles can be used to achieve diverse purposes:

– it can be used to issue parking violation tickets or speeding tickets, if pursued by the police;

– it assists in sending targeted advertisements basing on the users' habits and likes, if gathered by service providers;

– if collected by a malicious attacker, the consequences could become more brutal and perilous; they may use it to:

- change and direct the user's planned routes,

- threaten, blackmail and manipulate the user,

- deliberately delay the users or hinder them from reaching their destinations,

- instigate traffic jams,

- stimulate road causalities and accidents,

- plan on road kidnaps, traps and assassinations.

These are just a few examples of the potential resulting risks of vehicle tracking.

2.2.5. *How can we protect against it?*

To protect identity privacy, the IEEE 1609.2 standard (Kurihara 2013) recommended the usage of pseudonyms, which are certified temporal keys. The certificates ensure non-repudiation despite being anonymous. They are revocable guaranteeing they are not used after their expiry or after detecting a vehicle's misbehavior. Moreover, being managed and issued by the authorities prevents the vehicle from having several valid pseudonyms at the same time, and thus prevents the execution of Sybil attacks. This mechanism guarantees conditional privacy, which means that the privacy of the vehicle is protected as long as it behaves correctly and is exposed otherwise.

To achieve full privacy protection instead of a conditional one, some methods have suggested that the vehicle self-generates its keys and signs them. Indeed, these propositions do preserve privacy even from the authorities; however, it also covers the traces of misbehaving vehicles and allows Sybil attacks. Moreover, the generated keys are non-revocable and the vehicle's actions can be repudiated in this case. Another approach suggests that the vehicles form groups where members have the same public key (Group Leader Key) to verify the message authenticity while each vehicle has its own distinct private key to sign the message. On the other hand, the hybrid approach proposes that each vehicle generates its pair of temporal private and public keys individually and requests their certification from the Group Leader (GL) (Emara 2016).

The use of symmetric instead of asymmetric cryptography is another approach aiming to replace pseudonym usage, in which the vehicles sign and verify the authenticity of messages using a shared key. This method is not commonly acknowledged or used in the literature due to the importance of the usage of pseudonyms in ensuring security requirements. Henceforth, we continue reviewing asymmetric-based solutions (Hussain et al. 2009; Boualouache 2016).

Regardless, the usage of identity within safety applications is protected through the use of pseudonyms. However, identity privacy may be violated upon authenticating to authorities and service providers to request refilling of pseudonyms. As a recap, it may be a risk in on-road use. Furthermore, the service providers are not necessarily dependable. They may trade the data of users or track them while benefitting from the location-based services. Even if the end party the user is authenticating themselves to is trustworthy, as we assume the authorities to be, the frequent identity usage even through encrypted communications may lead to the vehicle's tracking. The repetitive use of the same encrypted pattern of the identity enables tracking by pattern matching. Cisco has already begun developing solutions to discover threats in real time found in encrypted traffic without decrypting it (Cisco White Paper 2019). Similarly, the attacker may use the same techniques to track identity usage even within encryption-secured traffic. Henceforth, the identity-based authentication methods should be replaced by an anonymous authentication method, satisfying the same security requirements.

Although the use of pseudonyms instead of long-term public key or real identities protects identity privacy, it does not resolve the location privacy issue or preserve it from tracking. When the pseudonyms get updated hastily and randomly in adverse contexts, they may provide the same privacy level as when using a single pseudonym. An adverse context is one enabling the attacker to link the updated pseudonyms of the same vehicle, allowing them to track its movements and parsed trajectory; see Figures 2.1 and 2.2 for illustration.

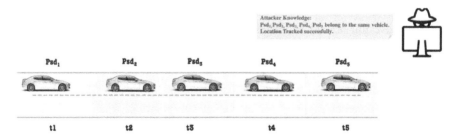

Figure 2.1. *Vehicle tracked successfully even with a pseudonym change. For a color version of this figure, see www.iste.co.uk/benarous/vehicular.zip*

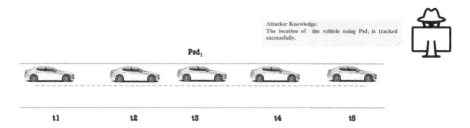

Figure 2.2. *Vehicle tracked successfully when no pseudonym update is done. For a color version of this figure, see www.iste.co.uk/benarous/vehicular.zip*

To impede linkability and prevent tracking, the update of pseudonyms should be strategic to confuse the attacker and fluster their tracks. These strategies are known as pseudonym change mechanisms. The literature is rich with different methods serving this purpose. Some researchers have proposed to prevent vehicle linkability in an independent manner where each vehicle runs its update strategy irrelatively with surrounding environment. The vehicles may apply a silent period after the pseudonym change to confuse the attacker and disrupt their predictions. Other suggestions recommend that the vehicles synchronously change their pseudonym; these propositions are often referred to as change within a cooperative crowd or hiding within the crowd. This category of solution consists of the mix-zone-based methods and hybrid methods combining multiple mechanisms to decrease linkability.

To preserve location privacy, another approach was proposed relying on the obfuscation of the location field. Yet, this approach needs extra caution as it may affect location-based services and safety applications, which depend on accurate positions. Figure 2.3 gives a broad classification of privacy preservation methods. This will be explained in more detail in the next section.

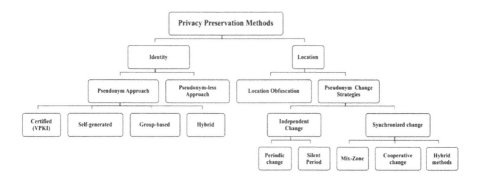

Figure 2.3. *Privacy preservation methods when using safety applications*

2.3. State-of-the-art location privacy-preserving solutions

This section reviews the existing pseudonym change strategies, which are commonly used to preserve not only identity privacy but also the location privacy of the users from tracking. They were subject to the ETSI ITS pre-standard technical report ETSI (2018-04), in which the privacy solution parameters and the trade-off between the privacy and security as well as the important issues related to pseudonym usage and change were studied. Also, the location privacy evaluation metrics were specified. Herein, we classify the prominent existing solutions into: cooperative (infrastructure or infrastructure-less), non-cooperative, silence and hybrid approaches. We discuss the advantages and disadvantages of each solution in each category after explaining its principle. We conclude with a recapitulative study evaluating the pros and cons of each category in overall.

2.3.1. *Non-cooperative change*

These change strategies include solutions that are executed by the vehicles independently. The vehicle does the pseudonym update without any cooperation or synchronization with neighbors. Table 2.1 resumes the advantages and disadvantages of schemes belonging to this category.

2.3.2. *Silence approaches*

This is one of the earliest approaches proposed to break the attacker's continuous tracks. Instead of just changing the pseudonym periodically upon its expiry, the vehicle goes on silence, and then it continues its cyber activity using the new freshly updated pseudonym. The silence refers to the vehicle ceasing its message emitting and broadcasts. The silence serves as mystifier to puzzle the attacker. In Table 2.2, we cite relevant works that have proposed using the silence method and highlight their advantages and disadvantages.

2.3.3. *Infrastructure-based mix-zone approach*

This approach is inspired by the network-mix proposed first by Chaum (1981). He proposed anonymizing the communication by relaying the messages through a sequence of trusted intermediaries defined as mixes to prevent the eavesdropper from identifying the sender (Danezis 2003). In the vehicular context, various solutions relied on the use of mix-zones to prevent the linkability of pseudonyms upon their updates. A mix-zone is defined as a zone where the attacker cannot track the vehicle's activity (Freudiger et al. 2007, 2009). In the initial proposal, it was supposed to be an uncovered region where the eavesdropper has their receivers on its extremities (its borders) but not within it. Thus, they are able to know the order and time of vehicles entering and exiting it. In later proposals, the mix-zone is created, maintained and advertised by the infrastructure (Road Side Unit). It is independent of the assumption of the attacker having uncovered areas. Instead, the mix-zones are becoming areas that even if the attacker reaches, they cannot eavesdrop on the communications within them because the vehicles exchange encrypted messages or cease their broadcast (apply silence) within them. This approach is infrastructure-dependent. The placement of these zones (Sun et al. 2015), the number of vehicles within them and the time spent inside them are critical criteria to study in order to achieve a good unlinkability level. Table 2.3 resumes the various existing solutions of this approach.

Solution	Year	Principle	Advantages	Disadvantages
Song et al. (2010)	2010	The vehicle senses within a specified delay its neighbors; it keeps actual tracks of the vehicles within its vicinity from their broadcasted messages. The vehicle changes its pseudonym upon its expiry when it is sure that it is within k other vehicles.	The vehicles keep actual track of vehicles in its neighborhood. This step prevents changing the pseudonym when the anonymity set size is less than k because of one of the vehicles exiting the communication range or changing direction.	– Being within a crowd does not necessarily ensure unlinkability. If the vehicle changes its pseudonym by itself, the attacker may still like this change as the other vehicles did not update their pseudonyms. – The solution is trigger-based, where the trigger is the density of the vehicles. – The solution is crowd-dependent and cooperation-independent.
Kang et al. (2016)	2016	The authors proposed a location privacy-preserving solution in the Internet of vehicles where the vehicle has a pseudonym used in beaconing and a virtual machine identifier (VMID) used to satisfy the location-based service queries. The solution suggests a synchronized identifier change (VMID and pseudonym).	The synchronized change of identifier prevents the mapping of the safety application activity and the location-based services. Thus, it stops the linkability by the VMID and/or pseudonym.	– The identifiers are changed synchronously, yet, this is not enough to prevent the linkability. The non-cooperation between the vehicles when executing the update process leads to tracking by the attacker. – The solution adds extra overheads caused by the long synchronization process between the cloud manager and the vehicle to validate the VMID update.

Table 2.1. *Non-cooperative change strategies*

Solution	Year	Principle	Silent period	Advantages	Disadvantages
Huang, L. et al. 2005	2005	Uses silent periods (constant and variable) to thwart linkability.	Random from min and max bounds.	Reduces linkability.	Unfixed silent period.
Sampigethaya et al. (2005, 2007)	2005 and 2007	The silent period is used to thwart the linkability of pseudonyms; the group concept is added to extend the silent period and prevent linkability when using LBS. The group leader plays the role of proxy or a mix that sends messages on behalf of the group member vehicles.	– Silent period < safety application beaconing frequency. – Extended silent period not determined but expected to be longer.	Reduces linkability by confusing the attacker and interrupting their tracks even when using LBS.	– The silent period is too short to reduce the linkability. – The reliance on the group leader could create a vulnerability, if they are malicious. All vehicles' communications are then read by them. They may not mix requests, or they may track the vehicles. – If the group leader is honest, then their privacy is sacrificed for the privacy of the group. – The attacker relies on the safety messages to track the vehicle because they are more frequent and sent in clear. The solution does not reduce linkability in this case as the extended silence does not apply to safety applications and the after-change silence is too short. – If the vehicle is alone, or not in the range of other vehicles, then the group cannot be formed.

Solution	Year	Principle	Silent period	Advantages	Disadvantages
Chaurasia et al. (2009)	2009	The random silent periods are used to thwart linkability. The solution is neighbor-aware, and it also relies on the variation of transmission power. The RSU broadcasts the number of vehicles in its range, and the vehicles listen for broadcasts to estimate the number of neighbors. It updates its pseudonym after applying silence when the number of neighbors is above a threshold value.	The silent period is random and undefined.	The solution is crowd aware. It tries to take advantage of the neighborhood changes to hide within them, also from varying the transmission power to confuse the attacker.	– The use of random silent periods is an open issue. The impact of using large silent periods on safety applications is known to be negative. While using short periods is known to be inefficient to thwart tracking. – The authors tried to fix this in simulation by min and max bounds, which if known to the atracker may lead to successful tracking. – Just being within a crowd does not protect privacy when doing an update. The attacker may be confused only if all the neighbors change simultaneously.

Table 2.2. *Silence-based change strategies*

Solution	Year	Principle	Advantages	Disadvantages
Freudiger et al. (2007)	2007	The authors suggested the use of CMIX, a symmetric cryptography protected mix-zone at intersections maintained by the RSU. All the entering vehicles obtain the session key from the RSU. The communications within the mix-zone are encrypted using this key.	The attacker is unable to track the vehicle, which is exchanging encrypted beacons. This reduces the linkability ratio of the attacker as the vehicle may change its speed, lane or direction when exiting the CMIX.	– The solution is infrastructure-dependent. It is also road-dependent where in the straight part of the road with no intersections or no infrastructure, the change will not happen undetectably. – The encryption may add extra processing and overheads because the keys are obtained after checking the vehicle's authenticity. Also, because of their updates and extension processes. – The communication with vehicles outside of the mix-zone cannot be read unless the vehicles exchange the session key with other vehicles. – The solution is resilient to global passive attackers, but, if the attacker happens to be physically there in their vehicle, they can obtain the key and track the vehicles. However, this case may not be redundant with all mix-zones or else it would be stalking.
Buttyán et al. (2007)	2007	The mix-zone is uncovered by the attacker. They have knowledge about vehicles entering and exiting it but cannot intercept communications within it. The vehicle is assumed to change its pseudonym frequently enough to maximize the chances of having a change occurring within a mix-zone.	The change within uncovered zones is unlinkable by the attacker.	– The mix-zone is attacker-dependent. The user has no knowledge of when they are being tracked or not. – The solution relies on the assumption that the attacker is weak leaving uncovered places. – The vehicle that is frequently changing pseudonym may never enter an uncovered area (mix-zone). Thus, it may be tracked all along by the attacker. – From the solution design perspective, this proposal is the standard pseudonym update strategy. No extra measures were added to ensure that the vehicle updates its pseudonym within a mix-zone.

Solution	Year	Principle	Advantages	Disadvantages
Palanisamy et al. (2011, 2012)	2011, 2012	The solution studied the impact of vehicles' velocity, road restrictions, movement pattern and statistics, in creating mix-zones where pseudonym tracking is reduced.	– The rectangular mix-zone at intersections may cause the vehicle pseudonym update to be linked as the attacker may calculate the time spent within the mix-zone types because they can match the vehicle speed and direction with road restrictions and observations. – The authors continued proposing various mix-zones until they proposed the time window bounded non-rectangular mix-zones. It starts from the center of the outgoing road segments of the junction, taking into consideration the vehicle's speed and entering time. This type outperformed all the other mix-zone types studied in ensuring unlinkability.	– The authors did not explain the process of creating the mix-zone or its placement. – The mix-zone information is implicit from the user, so is its shape. – The attacker spreads their receivers across the road. Achieving the proposed shape may not be plausible because this attacker is targeting privacy. Thus, they may put extra efforts on junctions as it is a place of confusion.
Lu et al. (2011, 2012) Mathews et al. (2014)	2011, 2012, 2014	The solution proposed suggests the pseudonym update to be done at intersections and traffic signals upon light color change. They named these as small mix-zones. Or, it may happen at parking lots also denoted as hot spots or large mix-zones.	The randomness of entering and exiting the spot and the time spent within it helps in confusing the attacker and achieving a higher privacy protection.	– Although the vehicles at intersections all change simultaneously, their position such as the lane they are within may help in the attacker's predictability and linkability. Especially, these vehicles do not cease beaconing while stopping at intersections. – The hot spot may have various entering and exiting points, and the random time spent does confuse the attacker. However, if the attacker has their receivers at the hot spot, they may locate the vehicle's parking spot before and after the update.

Solution	Year	Principle	Advantages	Disadvantages
Liu et al. (2012)	2012	The authors suggested the use of multiple mix-zones. They studied the best placement of these zones to reduce their cost and achieve a higher privacy protection level. They considered both the road map and traffic density.	The mix-zones placed at the appropriate dense road junctions reduce the linkability and enhance the privacy, because the crowd of vehicles changing directions and speed enhances the attacker's confusion.	The mix-zones are (infrastructure, road-map) dependent.
Ying et al. (2013)	2013	A vehicle with a pseudonym that is about to expire sends a request to the authority through the nearby RSU informing it about its readiness to update its pseudonym, providing both its old and new pseudonyms. The RSU is commanded to create a mix-zone to the vehicle; other vehicles receiving the mix-zone announcement also change their pseudonyms. The safety beacons are encrypted after the successful update of pseudonyms to avoid linkability.	– The use of encryption after the pseudonym update prevents the attacker from linking old and new pseudonyms. – The mix-zones ensure that the change happens within at least k vehicles. – The mix-zones are at intersections and road junctions where the chance of changing direction is higher.	– The encryption of beacons adds extra overheads related to the secure key exchange and additional computations. – The solution is (infrastructure, road) dependent.

Solution	Year	Principle	Advantages	Disadvantages
Boualouache et al. (2016)	2016	The authors suggested that the vehicle changes its pseudonym within infrastructure-based mix-zones at toll booths or service stations. Each zone has a router, which is the entering point of the mix-zone; the vehicle once it reaches the router ceases its broadcast and enters silence. The vehicle is assigned a lane and stays in the zone depending on its service period, and the zone also has one aggregator, which is the mix-zone exit point. The vehicles resume their broadcast with a new pseudonym once it surpasses this aggregator.	– The solution uses the silence to prevent the attacker from intercepting the messages exchanged within the mix-zone. – It uses the aggregator and depends on the random service time to ensure that the order of vehicles entering the mix-zone and exiting it is different. This prevents the attacker from linking the old and new pseudonyms using position prediction and linking attacks.	– The solution is infrastructure- and road-dependent. – The toll booths and service stations may not have high vehicle densities all the time. Also, the vehicles may enter and exit with the same order and after a short service time. – The vehicle frequency of pseudonym update is in the order of minutes/few kilometers. Therefore, the vehicle cannot enter every toll booth and service station on road just to ensure its privacy.
Kang et al. (2018)	2018	The authors suggested a pseudonym change strategy for fog-based Internet of vehicles. The strategy relies on the local authority ensuring the cooperativeness of the stable neighbor vehicles (synchronized change at hot spots).	– The solution reduces the linkability when executing the update process within a cooperative crowd. – The local authority encrypts the synchronization messages and records the change.	– The encryption and synchronization processes add extra overheads and computations. – The solution is infrastructure- and crowd-dependent.

Table 2.3. *Infrastructure-based mix-zone change strategies*

2.3.4. *The cooperation approach (distributed mix-zone)*

In this approach, vehicles synchronize with each other to change their pseudonyms at the same time to thwart the linkability and confuse the attacker's tracks. This is also known as distributed mix-zones. They do not rely on the infrastructure to synchronize their change by creating and advertising the existence of such a zone. The vehicles may achieve cooperativeness implicitly without explicitly sending synchronization messages, such as when the vehicle changes its pseudonym when within a traffic jam. Table 2.4 resumes the distributed mix-zone-based solutions.

2.3.5. *Hybrid approach*

The hybrid approach mixes one or a set of methods from the previously mentioned approaches. The various possible resulting combinations make the contribution open in this category. It can even include new unclassified solutions based on new criteria of change. It may also combine location obfuscation techniques with a pseudonym change strategy to get a more secure solution that is resilient to tracking. Table 2.5 resumes existing solutions in this category.

In Table 2.6 we present an overall evaluation of existing solutions according to the categories as a recapitulative overview stating the principle, advantages and disadvantages of each category. The aim of such a recap is to highlight the key concepts to understand and keep in mind, as well as to overcome, the fundamental drawbacks in developing a new solution.

Solution	Year	Principle	Advantages	Disadvantages
Liao et al. (2009)	2009	Every vehicle informs its neighbors that it is changing its pseudonym. If the vehicle has k (threshold) neighbor vehicles willing to change and having a similar state, the vehicles update their pseudonyms simultaneously. Otherwise, it waits. If the maximum lifetime of the pseudonym is reached, then the vehicle updates its pseudonym regardless of its neighbors.	– The solution is infrastructure-less. The vehicles cooperate on the road by themselves to perform the pseudonym change. The attacker is confused as the k vehicles execute the update simultaneously. The higher the k, the more the attacker is confused. – The solution does not need to send specific messages for the synchronization. It just uses one bit from the beacon header (flag) to achieve the same aim.	– The solution is resilient to syntactic linking attacks but not semantic attacks. The attacker may form knowledge about the vehicle's distributions and positions. This knowledge helps them predict the vehicle's future state. The predictions may be used to link old and new pseudonyms after the update. – The vehicle changes its pseudonym upon expiry (max lifetime) even when it has fewer than k neighbors making this update linkable. – The vehicles inform each other about their readiness to execute the change strategy. The attacker intercepting these messages is able to know that a change is about to happen. They may take extra measures to make their predictions more accurate.
Pan et al. (2012, 2013, 2017)	2012, 2013, 2017	The vehicles inform each other about their readiness to update their pseudonyms. Once a vehicle receives K confirmations from another K vehicles within its radius R, the vehicle initiating the change and all other K vehicles change their pseudonyms simultaneously. Even if among them are vehicles that do not have K neighbors.	– The change is infrastructure-less. The vehicles cooperate among themselves to synchronize their pseudonym update on the road. – The larger the crowd of the cooperating vehicles, the higher the attacker's confusion.	– A vehicle may change its pseudonyms in cooperation with other vehicles even when it has fewer than K neighbors. It is scarifying its privacy level to help other vehicles achieve their desired protection level. – Just by being within a crowd does not necessarily mean that the cooperation may be achieved, and vehicles will not participate in the change if they have updated their pseudonyms recently. – The attacker can link the change by using position-prediction techniques if the vehicles change their pseudonyms only without changing their physical disposition.

Solution	Year	Principle	Advantages	Disadvantages
Emara et al. (2015)	2015	The authors suggested that the vehicle tunes to its neighbor's. It changes its pseudonym when it is about to expire and when it notes that one or more neighbors are turning silent. If so, it turns silent for a minimum period as well and updates its pseudonym. The vehicle checks if its current position is closer to one of its silent neighbor's predicted track. Or, if it is out of the gate of its original track before it resumes its activity with the newly updated pseudonym.	– The cooperative silence confuses the attacker, especially as nodes will not resume their activity unless they have broken the attacker's linkability. – The solution does not need any extra message exchange for the synchronization process.	– A silent neighbor does not necessarily mean it is changing its pseudonym. A vehicle may turn silent if it stops its engine or the vehicle fails to receive its messages when it exits its range. – The silence negatively impacts the safety applications. – The gating process executed by the vehicle to resume its activity after the pseudonym update adds extra computations. – The solution is crowd-dependent. If the vehicle is not within a crowd, the silence will not be sufficient to prevent the tracking.
Ying et al. (2015)	2015	The vehicle creates distributed mix-zones by sending requests to its neighbors within a set radius (n-hop vehicles). Upon reception of the requests, the vehicles change their pseudonym in the designed slot.	– The vehicles choose from the location candidate list the best time to change their pseudonym. They change when their pseudonym approaches its expiry time. If the vehicle receives multiple mix-zone join requests, it changes its pseudonym once only within the right zone. – The cooperation reduces the linkability.	The synchronization messages and location candidate list verification for establishing and joining the mix-zone adds extra computations and network overheads.

Table 2.4. *Cooperative change strategies*

Solution	Year	Principle	Advantages	Disadvantages
Li et al. (2006)	2006	**The swing protocol**, the vehicle updates its pseudonym when it has neighbors from which it may receive an update message. It changes its direction after going on silence for a random period. **The swap protocol** suggests exchanging the pseudonyms between the wireless nodes instead of updating to a new identifier. It is not applicable in vehicular networks as the pseudonym is a pair of public/private keys. Therefore, if exchanged with another vehicle, it exposes past messages encrypted with the pseudonyms.	The linkability of the attacker is reduced because the vehicle changes its pseudonyms when changing direction. Then, it goes on silence for a random period confusing the attacker.	– The solution is theoretically plausible. However, the vehicle is assumed to change its pseudonyms every 1–5 minutes, changing directions every few minutes just to preserve privacy annoys the user, delays them and may cause them to enter unnecessary loops. – In Swing, the vehicles only update when it is within a group of vehicles. At least one neighbor is present. No condition obliges the vehicles to update their pseudonyms simultaneously. This reduces the anonymity set size. Also, if no group exists, the vehicle continues using its expired pseudonym. – Lastly, if the road has a restriction such as no direction change is possible within X kilometers, then the change using this method is not plausible. – Swap cannot be applied in a vehicular network because it violates the accountability and data privacy.
Burmester et al. (2008)	2008	The authors suggested that the vehicle updates its pseudonym only when it crosses junction points where a crowd of vehicles is expected to be. Prior to the update, each vehicle enters a random silent period.	The linkability is reduced because the vehicle is more likely to be within a crowd when it changes its pseudonym. Furthermore, the random silence and the possible change of direction at junctions confuse the attacker.	– The solution is road-map-dependent. – Junctions are not necessarily crowded all the time. – The silence may impact safety applications.

Solution	Year	Principle	Advantages	Disadvantages
Buttyán et al. (2009)	2009	SLOW or Silence at Low Speed proposes that vehicles should update their pseudonyms when their speed is less than or equal to 30 kmph after ceasing beaconing for a silent period. This ensures that a group of vehicles change their pseudonyms collaboratively without the need to do the synchronization such as when being at traffic signals or in traffic jams.	– The cooperative silence and change thwarts the linkability. The silence when the vehicle is slow does not impact the safety applications as the probability of accidents or road causalities is small when at a low speed. – The vehicles' cooperation is achieved without causing the overheads of synchronization. – At traffic jams, the vehicle has a similar state. When they cease beaconing, they reduce the overheads caused by signature verification and prevent broadcast storming.	The solution depends on the vehicle's speed. If the road traffic is smooth, the vehicle may continue to use the same pseudonym for long periods causing it to be tracked.
Hang et al. (2009)	2009	The solution combines the group signature, mix-zone and silent periods concepts into one solution. The vehicle is supposed to be a member of a group whenever it can. All members share the same public group key and each has its private key. When the vehicle approaches a mix-zone announced by the RSU, all entering vehicles cease their broadcast within the mix-zone (enter silence period). The group keys and the vehicle individual keys (pseudonyms) are changed upon exiting the mix-zone (end of silence).	The attacker confusion is higher as the solution requires vehicles to change cooperatively. Also, the silence breaks the attacker's predictability and accuracy.	– The solution is infrastructure-dependent. The coverage of infrastructure may not be global due to its high deployment cost. In uncovered areas, the solution is not applicable. – The scheme assumes that the group managers are authority vehicles. Having available groups means that authority vehicles must be parsing the roads all the time. This may not be plausible due to its high cost and potential unacceptability by the public. – The placement of mix-zones is road restricted (at intersections). In road sections with no intersections, the solution is not applicable. – The silent period must be well studied to balance between the privacy and safety requirements.

Solution	Year	Principle	Advantages	Disadvantages
Boualouache et al. (2014)	2014	The solution suggests infrastructure-based mix-zones at traffic signals. The vehicles enter silence from beaconing when the light is red. They can, however, exchange encrypted messages with the RSUs managing these zones to manage the pseudonym swapping protocols between the mix-zone vehicles. When the light turns green, the vehicles resume their beaconing with their newly updated pseudonyms.	– The solution relies on asymmetric cryptography. It reduces the overhead caused by the key generation and exchange protocols executed in symmetric cryptography-based mix-zones. – The silence prevents the attacker from tracking the vehicle location within the mix-zone. – The pseudonym swapping confuses the attacker who has mapped the vehicles and their lanes disposition when entering the zone and again when they exit it. The swapping with vehicles from different lanes and positions confuses the attacker, who may keep following the same pseudonym thinking that they are tracking the old target vehicle which they are not. – The RSU broadcasts encrypted messages about the vehicles' disposition at each lane. This replaces the beaconing process by delivering the same information the vehicles need. – It reduces the over-consumption of pseudonyms and allows their reuse.	– The solution computational cost of asymmetric cryptography is higher than that of symmetric cryptography. Thus, it is slower. – The swapping does confuse the attacker; however, it threatens the privacy of the user, when exchanging the pseudonym, which is the pair of public and private keys used to sign and encrypt the messages. The user exposes their past confidential messages encrypted with these keys. – The pseudonyms are certified. They cannot be used beyond their lifetime. Also, if their lifetime is expended to match the protocol requirements, the possibility of the vehicles keeping using its past and newly obtained pseudonyms to execute Sybil attacks is higher. – The swapping protocol contradicts the non-repudiation and accountability needs in vehicular networks. Furthermore, if a misbehavior occurs using a pseudonym, it would be hard to revoke the appropriate node and hold it responsible. – The solution is applicable only if the pseudonym was an identity or an address and not the pair of keys used to sign and encrypt messages.

Solution	Year	Principle	Advantages	Disadvantages
Xingjun et al. (2014)	2014	The authors suggested that the vehicle synchronizes its pseudonym update with its neighbors using the RSU to forward the update request message. The vehicle sends its request when it confirms that it has k neighbor vehicles, where k is the minimum threshold needed. The vehicles may choose to cooperate or not with the vehicle when it updates its pseudonym.	The cooperative change reduces the linkability, as the anonymity set of the vehicle is increased.	– The solution does not oblige neighbor vehicles to cooperate in the update process. Instead, they have the choice not to. This means that the level of privacy obtained by this change strategy may be lower than expected, if one or more vehicles decide not to participate in the change. – The solution is infrastructure-dependent. – It is vulnerable to position-based linking attacks.
Ying et al. (2015)	2015	The authors suggested that the vehicle dynamically forms infrastructure-aided mix-zones whenever it needs to update its pseudonym, the zone is formed when the vehicle requests it to be and vehicles within the requester's vicinity cooperate to make the change simultaneously. The vehicles are encouraged to participate in the change by the increase of their reputation value, which gets decreased by the authority (control server) otherwise. Vehicles with low reputations will not receive the cooperation of others when they need to update their pseudonyms and their anonymity is reduced. To overcome the pseudonym over-consumption caused by the repetitive cooperation participation, the number of successive changes (to cooperate) is limited.	– The cooperative change reduces the linkability. – The mix-zones are formed on-demand. – The inclusion of reputation as criteria in the cooperation reduces the chances of having selfish vehicles that reduces the anonymity.	– The dependency on the control server. – The reputation computing, verification and update cost and overheads. – Although the reputation value helps in reducing the selfish behavior by not cooperating with the selfish node when it does its pseudonym change. However, the vehicle can control when to be selfish and when not. It can actively cooperate when its reputation is low and be selfish upon its decision. The alteration between the cooperative and selfish behavior is still possible, and it does not help in guaranteeing that the anonymity set size of the mix-zone is as high as intended to be. To make the reputation usage more impactful, selfish nodes reducing the anonymity set size need to be punished more severely. Also, the reputation value should depend on history logs.

Solution	Year	Principle	Advantages	Disadvantages
Eckhoff et al (2016)	2016	The authors suggested using time-slotted pseudonyms which if changed within a crowd of vehicles achieves a similar protection level as the cooperative approach. The authors avoided the impact of pseudonym change on safety applications by briefly including the old pseudonym after the change. This causes the linkability of pseudonyms by neighbor vehicles. The authors claimed that if the attacker is close enough to the vehicle then it is more likely stalking it. The privacy would be violated either way. They also slowed the safety beaconing frequency and included location noise to confuse the local attacker.	– The time-slotted pseudonyms ensure cooperation without adding extra synchronization overheads when the vehicle is within a crowd. – The addition of noise and the change of beaconing frequency creates a blind spot to the weak local attacker studied, reducing their tracking ability.	– The solution is not studied against a global passive attacker with full coverage. – The addition of the old pseudonyms clearly causes the linkability by the global attacker. – The inaccuracy caused by noise addition negatively impacts the safety applications, so does the change of beaconing frequency.
Boualouache et al. (2017)	2017	The solution proposed is traffic-aware. The vehicle detects that it is within traffic congestion (low speed). It broadcasts a message that it is within congestion. A vehicle is then elected to be the silent mix-zone creator. The vehicle ceases its safety beacon broadcast, changes its pseudonym and sends periodical anonymous congestion notification. All vehicles are silent until the initiator (mix-zone creator) informs them about the end of traffic congestion. Then, they all resume their activities with new pseudonyms.	– The combination of cooperative crowd and extended silence weakens the attacker's prediction and linkability abilities. The attacker is more confused if the vehicle changes its lane within the congestion. – The mix-zones are dynamically created.	– The solution is congestion-dependent. – The silence negatively impacts the safety application, especially if the vehicle is changing lanes. – The synchronization process, elections, silence-period extension and end traffic congestion notification add overheads both in terms of computation and message exchange. – The privacy is not preserved in non-congested roads where the update of the pseudonym is linked.

Solution	Year	Principle	Advantages	Disadvantages
Wang et al. (2018)	2018	The authors suggested an RSU-based pseudonym exchange strategy. The vehicle checks its neighbors when it finds trigger vehicle(s) with the same headings that is closer than threshold value and with similar speed. If one trigger vehicle or more is found, the vehicle sends an exchange request to the RSU. When the RSU accepts the vehicle's request, both vehicles are informed and the exchange happens and is recorded by the RSU to ensure revocability and traceability. If the RSU receives multiple requests for the same trigger, it chooses one randomly.	– The exchange of pseudonyms with vehicles of similar state confuses the attacker. – The valid pseudonym exchange allows their traceable reuse and reduces their over-consumption. – The RSU-aided pseudonym exchange between willing vehicles ensures the security and confidentiality.	– The pseudonym exchange violates the privacy of the users. All past messages encrypted using these pseudonyms become readable by the new pseudonym owner. – The pseudonyms are lifetimed. They cannot be used beyond their validity period. – Allowing pseudonym exchange gives the possibility that each node has multiple pseudonyms (old and new) that could be used to launch Sybil attacks.
Memon et al. (2018)	2018	The authors suggest that the vehicle cooperatively changes its pseudonym with its neighbors and then enters silence to avoid linkability. The cooperativeness is within infrastructure mix-zones. The authors investigated the impact of cheating attack on the privacy and defined a mechanism to detect this attack.	The mix-zones and silence combination reduce the linkability.	– The cheating attack is executed by an active internal attacker. This assumption in itself is theoretical. If the attacker is able to hack a vehicle, then hacking the victim vehicles is more logical. If the attacker is able to deploy their vehicle on all mix-zones, then it is better to just stalk the vehicle. It is cheaper and more targeted. – The solution is infrastructure- and crowd-dependent. – The silence impacts the safety applications negatively.

Solution	Year	Principle	Advantages	Disadvantages
Khacheba et al. (2017, 2018)	2017, 2018	The authors suggested that the vehicle creates distributed mix-zones where vehicles cooperate to change their pseudonyms simultaneously. The initiator vehicle enters random silence as soon as it receives a ready-to-change flagged message from k vehicles. Neighbor vehicles enter silence upon the reception of the flagged message. If no message is received until the expiry of the pseudonym's maximum lifetime, the vehicle enters silence then changes its pseudonym. The authors investigated the impact of a cheating attack on the anonymity level and proposed a mechanism to detect it.	– The combination of mix-zones and silence reduces the linkability. – The mix-zone is distributed and infrastructure-independent.	– The vehicle may not find cooperative neighbors and change the pseudonym alone after applying silence. The change is then linked. – The solution is crowd-dependent. – The silent period is random. Thus, the vehicles exit the silence individually and if their chosen silent period is short, their linkability is higher. – The silence impacts the safety applications negatively. – As we explained in Memon et al.'s (2018) proposal, the cheating attack is not plausible in practice due to its cost.
Belal (2018)	2018	The author suggested an infrastructure mix-zone-based change strategy where the zone has receivers on its lanes emulating the vehicle's behavior and engaging in virtual pseudonym change. All communication within these zones is encrypted to prevent eavesdropping.	– The solution is crowd-independent. The virtualization and emulation of the vehicle's behavior help in reducing the attacker's linkability and increase their confusion. – The vehicle is always with k other virtual crowd of vehicles when it updates its pseudonym in mix-zones.	– The solution is costly both computationally and financially. – The virtual vehicles and their broadcasted messages increase the overhead. – The solution is infrastructure-dependent. – In areas not covered by the infrastructure, the solution cannot be applied.

Solution	Year	Principle	Advantages	Disadvantages
Guo et al. (2018)	2018	The authors suggested independent mix-zones where every vehicle with a pseudonym approaching expiry checks for a distributed mix-zone (cooperative crowd). If the number of vehicles in the mix-zone is less than the desired threshold *k*, then the vehicle randomizes fake pseudonyms emulating virtual vehicles to reach the threshold *k*. All the exchanged messages are encrypted to prevent the attacker from eavesdropping on the communications.	– The independent mix-zones are self-made by the vehicle. – The randomized pseudonyms before and after the change reduce the linkability and confuse the attacker. – The solution is not crowd-dependent. – The solution is distributed and dynamically created. – The encryption prevents the leakage of sensitive contents.	– Although mix-zone creation messages are piggybacked in the beacons, still the solution adds extra computational cost and overheads caused by encryption, creation of fake crowd, synchronization and change of pseudonym. – The attacker may detect that the vehicle is the one sending fake messages if the road restrictions do not support this assumption. For example, on a straight road with no intersections, if the attacker that has been tracking the *l* vehicles on the road suddenly detects *l+s* active vehicles, then it is clear that the additional *s* messages come from fake identities. If the vehicle is alone on the road, it is even worse as it is clear that it is the initiator of these fake messages. Also, if the attacker detects such a case, they can locate the message sender from the signal strength to confirm their assumption and tracks.

Table 2.5. *Hybrid change strategies*

Category	Principle	Advantages	Disadvantages
Non-cooperative	The non-cooperative change includes methods that are executed by the vehicles independently without synchronizing with their neighbor vehicles.	– The update process is fast. – It is road-, crowd- and infrastructure-independent.	– The frequent-independent change does not necessarily reduce the linkability. – Those schemes are not resilient to syntactic linking.
Silence	The silence-based approaches rely on ceasing the broadcast of safety messages which are beaconed with high frequency until after the pseudonym update.	– The silence breaks the vehicle tracking and prevents the linkability between the old and newly updated pseudonyms. – Silence-based schemes are more likely to be resilient to semantic linking (position-based linking) if applied correctly and adequately.	Silence negatively impacts the safety applications, which are the fundamental incentive behind the creation of vehicular networks. Impacting safety applications implicates risking the lives of users on-board the vehicles.
Infrastructure-based mix-zone	Changing within mix-zones created, maintained and advertised by the RSU (infrastructure) is more secure. The mix-zone includes cooperative vehicles simultaneously updating their pseudonyms. It is usually placed at intersections and junction where the vehicles change their direction after the update. Within a mix-zone, the vehicles either stay silent or exchange encrypted communication.	The linkability is reduced when the change happens within a cooperative crowd. The attacker's confusion increases as the number of cooperative vehicles does, especially when they change their directions and speed after the change.	– These schemes are road-, crowd- and infrastructure-dependent. – To create and maintain the mix-zone extra calculation and overheads are added. – The mix-zone using silence or encryption impacts safety applications' efficiency.

Category	Principle	Advantages	Disadvantages
Distributed infrastructure-less mix-zone	This type of mix-zones is self-formed by the vehicles dynamically on roads. When they need to update their pseudonym, the vehicles synchronize with each other to update their pseudonyms simultaneously.	– The cooperative change strategy reduces the linkability. – This type of mix-zone is infrastructure- and road-independent.	– The synchronization between vehicles and the use of silence as well as encryption may add extra overheads and impact safety applications. – The solution is crowd-dependent. – Even if the vehicles simultaneously update their pseudonyms, road restrictions may lead to linkability.
Hybrid	This category includes various solutions that combine existing approaches together to overcome their lack. Also, it combines new contexts that reduce the linkability. It is the category that may include different new solutions.	The combination of various strategies is for the aim of reducing the linkability.	Unless the combination of schemes is done carefully, their drawbacks may be inherited to the new used method.

Table 2.6. *Pseudonym change strategies – recap*

2.4. Authentication issues in vehicular networks

Authentication is a fundamental property in security. It protects against intrusion and helps in ensuring accountability. It is the essential step to identify the internal users, organizing their correct access rules and tracing their activity. Furthermore, it prevents non-registered users from accessing the system or the network.

2.4.1. *What is being authenticated in vehicular networks?*

In vehicular networks (VN), there are two types of authentications:

– The authentication of users to access VN services

This authentication is between the vehicle's user and a server, which can be a service provider, authority or RSU to obtain a service, pseudonyms and certificates. It is preceded by a registration phase where the user registers to this server by providing the essential needed information, agreeing on the rights provided as well as on the identification information and parameters. Once authenticated, users benefit from the authorized services and continue their secure queries with the server. Naturally, all the exchanges, messages and actions done by this user are mapped to their account, ensuring accountability on the one hand, and the possibility to revoke the users if a misbehavior or role abuse is detected on the other hand.

– The authentication of messages

In this authentication, the messages are authenticated. This is a fundamental operation in VN to accept or reject a message, especially those required by safety applications. This is a security measure to prevent an external attacker from injecting bogus messages.

Before we continue explaining this type of authentication, we remind the readers that every vehicle signs its safety messages also known as beacons with its pseudonym. The latter is a certified pair of temporal public and private keys. They are certified by the authority and are temporal because they have a short validity time and space where they can be used. Also, to avoid Sybil attacks, every vehicle has a unique valid pseudonym at a given time slot. The certificates of these pseudonyms are identity-less, in another word anonymous. This is essential in ensuring privacy and avoiding tracking. Therefore, the authentication aims are to check that the message comes from an authentic node without identifying it. The identification is required only when a misbehavior occurs and the misbehavior is held accountable and then revoked.

When a vehicle receives a message from another vehicle, it first checks the certificate validity, i.e. it is still fresh and not expired. Then, it checks that this certificate is signed by the authority's key and that it has not been tampered with. Once the certificate checking is done, the receiving vehicle checks that the certified pseudonym is not in the freshly updated revocation list (CRL), i.e. not revoked/blacklisted. Upon the end of pseudonym verification, the receiving vehicle checks the integrity of the message by checking the digital signature. This operation not only proves that the message was not altered but also that the pseudonym used for the verification belongs to the same owner who signed the message with the private pair of this pseudonym.

2.4.2. Authentication types

The authentication is commonly classified into three types, which are based on the way the user is identified into by what they *know*, what they *have* or what they *are*. We explain each type below (Benarous et al. 2017):

– *Knowledge-based authentication* also known as authentication with something the user knows. This is one of the most commonly used methods. A famous example is password-based authentication where the user only needs to provide their identifier or username and password assigned to them upon registration. The username and password are also referred to as credentials (Egan and Mather 2004; Pfleeger 2006; Stolfo et al. 2008).

– *Possession-based authentication* or authentication with something the user has. This is one of the preferred authentication methods at workplaces and hotels. The user possesses a dongle, smart card or badge that they use to authenticate to a system (Stolfo et al. 2008).

– *Physiology-based authentication*, the user uses their unique features to identify themselves to the system. It is also known as biometric authentication; famous examples are authentication by iris, fingerprint and face. It also includes behavioral authentication methods such as handwriting, gait and signature analysis (Pfleeger 2006).

In Table 2.7, we compare these methods and highlight their advantages and disadvantages.

Authentication type	Advantages	Disadvantages
Knowledge-based	– Easy implementation – Commonly accepted and used – Can be saved in cookies	– May be forgotten easily – Vulnerable to cracking and guessing attacks
Possession-based	– Practical and convenient for industrial usage – Does not require memorizing anything, mastering any technology or having IT background	– Costlier than knowledge-based methods – Can easily be forgotten or lost
Physiology-based	More secure and harder to emulate or crack	– Costlier than the other approaches – Prone to light and noise – Vulnerable to injuries, burns and cuts

Table 2.7. *Advantages and disadvantages of authentication types*

2.4.3. *How does authentication risk privacy?*

The above-explained types of authentication risk privacy. The user who needs to access a system or a service must provide the required information to establish the authentication. They may have to provide their identity and biometric data in the registration phase. Most service providers emphasize their respect for privacy policies. However, we often hear in the news that these data are exchanged for profit, have been leaked by hackers or provided to judicial systems when asked for cooperation. Furthermore, vehicular networks are sensitive because they are related to the user's safety. The vehicle may use various services requiring authentication. Also, they may frequently ask for pseudonym refilling from the authorities on roads. The repetitive authentication using the same credentials (data) may lead to vehicle tracking on the road even if the communication is secured.

Here, to highlight the importance of privacy, we list some famous privacy leaks and breaches from prominent service providers (Friesland 2018):

– the Facebook and Cambridge Analytica scandal, which caused the leak of about 50 million accounts (2018);

– in 2016, Uber was hacked; 57 million users were impacted by this attack;

– Yahoo suffered from attacks in 2013–2014, it was reported in 2016 that 3 billion accounts were hacked;

– Ebay was attacked in 2014 and the privacy of 150 million accounts was breached.

These examples prove that not all service providers can be trusted. Although they claim to be and even when we want to believe them to be trustworthy, attacks targeting them may lead to the exposure of our private data we entrusted them with. The more you share, the greater the risks. For example, if a user uses their fingerprint to unlock their phone and uses it to access their home and office, then any breach or leak in one of the systems storing their fingerprint leads to the vulnerability of other systems where the fingerprint is used.

However, to use a system, we need to provide proof that we are who we claim to be and that we are authorized to use this system. At the same time, we need to preserve privacy. Therefore, there needs to be a balance between privacy and authentication. We need to provide the minimum required information to ensure authentication and at the same time preserve privacy. This is what led to the appearance of a new set of authentication mechanisms. They are known as anonymous authentication, privacy-preserving authentication or also as challenge (zero-knowledge) authentication methods. In the next section, we give an overview of the usage of these authentication methods in vehicular networks.

2.5. Identity privacy preservation authentication solutions: state of the art

We explained in section 2.4.1 that in vehicular networks, the authentication is used either to identify the user or to check the authenticity of the message. The second is usually done by the verification of the pseudonym used in the signature. The pseudonym verification phase examines whether this pseudonym is certified by the authority, or is a group key. Some have even suggested the use of symmetric keys to sign the beacons (Hussain et al. 2009; Emara 2016). Regardless of the method, as long as it relies on the use of temporal keys (pseudonym) and not the identity of the user, then it preserves privacy. The studies emphasize this requirement when developing any solution. It is the main aim behind the introduction of pseudonyms in VN. In our work, we concentrate on user authentication as it requires identity exchange. Moreover, it is repetitive as the vehicle on the road may periodically request pseudonym refilling from the authorities or request services from service providers. In this section, we review existing solutions belonging to a new type of authentication methods that balances the privacy and security properties by ensuring the successful identification of the users without exposing their identity privacy.

For pseudonym refilling and/or certifying in vehicular networks, many proposals exist among which is the work of Khodaei and Papadimitratos (2016) where the authors used one-time tickets issued by the Long-Term Certification Authority (LTCA) to request the certification of self-generated pseudonyms from the Pseudonym Certification Authority (PCA). Similarly, Alexiou et al. (2013) also used the tickets to obtain pseudonym certificates from the PCA, but the difference was that the same valid anonymous ticket may be used for multiple requests. In both works (Alexiou et al. 2013; Khodaei and Papadimitratos 2016), the tickets are obtained upon the vehicle's successful identity-based authentication to LTCA. Schaub et al. (2010) suggested the token usage to request the pseudonym provider to certify the vehicle's generated temporal keys (pseudonyms). To obtain these tokens, the vehicle authenticates itself to the certifying authority using its identifier. The multiple token requests using the same identifier are linkable leading to the vehicle's tracking on the road. Khodaei et al. (2014) suggested the use of anonymous tickets to request the certifying of the vehicle's generated pseudonyms, which are obtained after a successful authentication using the long-term certificate. The solution preserves the privacy, but the repetitive use of a long-term certificate to obtain tickets leads to tracking. Also, because the tickets are anonymous, they may be vulnerable to impersonation attack where the tickets are used by this attacker to certify their keys. This further violates the accountability propriety.

Weerasinghe et al. (2010) suggested an anonymous service request using the group concept and the pseudonym certificates. They suggested that when the vehicle is issued a pseudonym certificate, this certificate is to include all the services that the vehicle is registered to, in other words, the service provider register to the Regional Authority (RA) and the vehicle register through the RA to these service providers. When it does, the information about the registered services is included in the pseudonym certificate using a blind signature. This way each service provider is able to verify if the vehicle is registered or no to use their service. To further improve the solution, they suggested that the vehicles request services from within a group to avoid linkability. The solution preserves the identity privacy but requires the vehicles to know all of their needed services before requesting pseudonyms. It is commonly known that the pseudonyms are short-lived, which means that the process of inserting the registered services is repetitive adding more computational cost on the RA. Also, the certificate size will grow linearly as the number of service registrations increases. Jiang et al. (2017) proposed a random identity-based authentication. In their proposal, they used a one-time randomly generated identity for each authentication. The user registers to the registration server using their real identifier. Then, an initial random identity is created and sent to both the vehicle user and the verification server. The vehicle may then use it to generate its own random identifiers. To authenticate itself to a service provider or other vehicles, the user sends their random identity in an authentication request to the verification server then to the other interacting party denoted as P. P sends a request to the verification server, which has already received an authentication request from the vehicle. The server acknowledges the request and confirms to P that the user is the real owner of the used random identity. To ensure traceability, the cooperation of the Verification Server (VS) and Registration Server (RS) is needed. Note that only RS knows the real identity of the vehicle user. Also, only it keeps the records of authentication history. The VS does the verification only and discards the old identity once the new one is proved. Lastly, both the RS and the vehicle have a time interval seed list, which is used by the vehicle to generate a new identity at every time interval. Also, it allows the RS to keep track of the vehicles' identities without the need to be constantly informed of every identity generation. The proposal ensures authentication while preserving privacy; it is also secure against replay and man-in-the-middle attacks. However, it is server-dependent, and the authenticating parties need initially to check with the VS to be able to finish the authentication. This may be a drawback, and attacks on the availability (single point of failure) of the server hinder the authentication. Also, as the number of the users grows and authentication requests increase, the server's response may be slow.

2.6. Conclusion

In this chapter, we highlighted the privacy issue in vehicular networks with its importance and types. We also answered key related questions such as what are the privacy violation risks, who is threatening privacy, how and why. We also reviewed existing privacy-preserving solutions proposed in the literature, shedding more light on their advantages and drawbacks. We ended with a categorical comparison and analysis to help guide the reader interested to develop a privacy-preserving solution to avoid the lacks in the existing schemes. The chapter also concentrated on authentication issues and included a brief review on existing privacy-preserving authentication methods.

In the next chapter, we study the evaluation, analysis, proofing tools and methods used to study and examine the performance and robustness of privacy and security solutions in vehicular networks.

Security and Privacy Evaluation Methodology

3.1. Introduction

In the previous chapter, we explained the privacy and security issues in vehicular networks, reviewed state-of-the-art solutions and analyzed their advantages and drawbacks. In this chapter, we cite existing vehicular network security and privacy evaluation methods and metrics. As mentioned in the previous chapter, we focus on the privacy-preserving authentication methods as a security issue. Furthermore, we concentrate on identity and location privacy-preserving strategies for vehicle network users on roads.

Before explaining the proofing process, we illustrate the process of resolving a security and/or privacy issue in Figure 3.1. It starts by understanding the issue and its causes. It also analyzes what the existing solutions lack and their drawbacks. Then, it brainstorms how to overcome what is lacking and how to out-do the existing solutions, in order to propose a robust solution. It ends by implementing the solution, testing it and proving that it fulfills the desired aims, is resilient to attacks and outperforms the existing ones.

Figure 3.2 illustrates the various proof and analysis methods. Descriptive discussion and analysis is one of the primal methods used that helps in understanding the solution and highlighting its advantages and drawbacks. Unfortunately, although essential, it is not enough to prove the robustness of a given security solution. It is usually either accompanied by simulations or by mathematical (analytical) or logical proofs. The same applies for comparative studies. They are fundamental in analyzing and synthesizing the existing solution and also convincing the reader about the advantages of a new solution compared to state-of-the-art works and how it overcomes what is lacking. However, they are not enough to illustrate the robustness and performance of the solution. Game theory, on the other hand, helps study the feasibility of a given solution before testing it through simulation or real implementations (test bed). The combination of the various methods helps in the understanding of the security and privacy solutions, alongside the demonstration of correct functionality, robust performance and resiliency to attacks in an irrefutable manner. In this book, we used various combinations of proofing and analysis methods for different purposes and applications. Before we continue explaining their usage in the rest of the coming chapters, we will first explain each method separately.

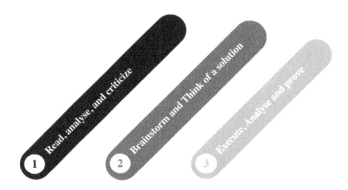

Figure 3.1. *Process of security/privacy issue resolution*

This chapter explains the evaluation methodology for both security and privacy issues.

– For security issues, the following methods are explained in a separate section:

- BAN logic;

- SPAN and AVISPA;

- attack trees;

- discussion and analysis.

– For privacy issues, the following methods are explained in a separate section:

- simulation and its tools;

- analytical models;

- game theory;

- comparative studies.

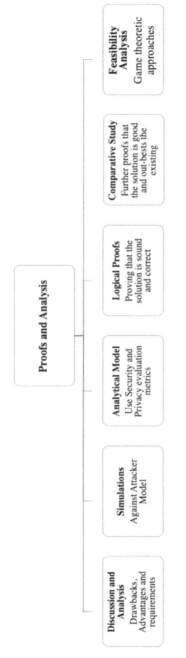

Figure 3.2. *Privacy and security proof and analysis methods*

3.2. Evaluation methodology

In this section, we explain the various existing evaluation, testing and proofing methods and tools for security and privacy issues.

3.2.1. *Security*

In this book, we consider studying the privacy-preserving authentication security issue with its properties to be ensured and its potential threatening vulnerabilities. In this section, we explain the various methods of proving the robustness of a security solution.

3.2.1.1. *BAN logic*

BAN logic is a belief-based logic introduced by Burrows, Abadi and Needham (Burrows et al. 1989) to formally write authentication protocols and analyze their security. The logic is used to prove the correctness of a protocol on one hand, and prove that it achieves the underlined aims it was developed to fulfill on the other. The demonstration starts by first writing the protocol in terms of its exchanged messages between entities. These messages are then idealized. The demonstration starts from using the idealized messages, the set of protocol assumptions and logic postulates to arrive at the specified goals. In this section, we give an overview of the logic idealization, notations and postulates.

– **The notation**

Table 3.1 resumes the notations used in the BAN logic (Burrows et al. 1989).

To analyze a protocol, the steps given in Figure 3.3 are essential and recapitulate what we have explained.

The BAN protocol (Burrows et al. 1989) analysis is often composed of:

– *The message idealization*: is used to idealize the authentication protocols which are usually described by the list of exchanged messages between the participating entities. These informal string messages are rewritten using the above-given notations to be formal so that it can be analyzed using the BAN logic postulates.

– *The assumptions*: are the set of assumptions on the authentication system and its entities, such as defining the initial beliefs and jurisdictions.

– *The objectives*: are the final goals of the authentication. For example, that both authenticating entities believe each other or believe that the emitted messages come from the intended source.

– *The demonstration*: is the process that uses the BAN logic postulates to attend the final objective from the initial assumptions on the system and the exchanged messages.

Symbol/construction	Meaning
P, Q, R	Denotes a principal or an entity
K_a	Public key of A
K_a^{-1}	Private key of A
K_{ab}	Shared key between A and B
X	A message or a formula
P **believes** X	P considers X to be true
P **sees** X	P can read X
P **said** X	P sent the message X
P **controls** X	P has jurisdiction (authority) over X
Fresh (X)	X is fresh, and has not been sent in any previous message. It is helpful in the verification of a nonce
$P \overset{K}{\leftrightarrow} Q$	K is a secret key shared, known and only used by principals P and Q
$\overset{K}{\mapsto} P$	K is the public key of P, its corresponding secret key K^{-1} is known to P only
$P \overset{X}{\rightleftharpoons} Q$	X is a secret known only to P and Q. They use X to authenticate each other
$\{X\}_K$	X is encrypted using X
$\langle X \rangle_Y$	The presence of the secret Y combined with X proves the identity of the sender of X and owner of Y

Table 3.1. *BAN logic notations*

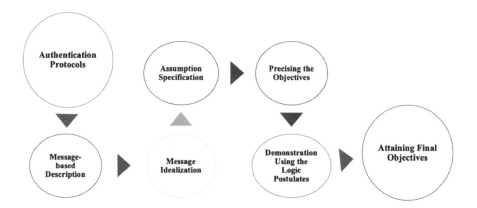

Figure 3.3. *Protocol analysis process using the BAN logic. For a color version of this figure, see www.iste.co.uk/benarous/vehicular.zip*

– The postulates

– Postulate 1: Meaning of the messages

"For shared keys, if P believes that the key K is shared with Q and sees X encrypted under K, then P believes that Q once said X" (Burrows et al. 1989).

$$\frac{P \text{ believes } \ Q \overset{K}{\leftrightarrow} P, \quad P \text{ sees } \{X\}_K}{P \text{ believes } Q \text{ said } X}$$

"For public keys, if P believes that the secret K is the public key of Q and X encrypted under K^{-1}, then P believes that Q once said X. Note that K is a public key and K^{-1} is a private key" (Burrows et al. 1989).

$$\frac{P \text{ believes } \ \overset{K}{\leftrightarrow} Q, \quad P \text{ sees } \{X\}_{K^{-1}}}{P \text{ believes } Q \text{ said } X}$$

"For shared secret, if P believes that the secret Y is shared with Q and sees $<X>_y$, then P believes that Q once said X" (Burrows et al. 1989).

$$\frac{P \text{ believes } \ Q \overset{Y}{\rightleftharpoons} P, \quad P \text{ sees } \langle X \rangle_Y}{P \text{ believes } Q \text{ said } X}$$

– Postulate 2: Nonce verification

"If P believes that X could have been uttered only recently and that Q once said X, then P believes that Q believes X" (Burrows et al. 1989).

$$\frac{P \text{ believes fresh}(X), \quad P \text{ believes } Q \text{ said } X}{P \text{ believes } Q \text{ believes } X}$$

– Postulate 3: Jurisdiction

"If P believes that Q has jurisdiction over X, then P trusts Q on the truth of X" (Burrows et al. 1989).

$$\frac{P \text{ believes } Q \text{ controls } X, \quad P \text{ believes } Q \text{ believes } X}{P \text{ believes } X}$$

– Postulate 4: Sees

"If a principal sees a formula, then they also see its components, provided they know the necessary keys" (Burrows et al. 1989).

$$\frac{P \text{ sees } (X, Y)}{P \text{ sees } X}, \quad \frac{P \text{ sees } \langle X \rangle_Y}{P \text{ sees } X}, \quad \frac{P \text{ believes } Q \overset{K}{\leftrightarrow} P, P \text{ sees } \{X\}_K}{P \text{ sees } X},$$

$$\frac{P \text{ believes } \overset{K}{\mapsto} P, P \text{ sees } \{X\}_K}{P \text{ sees } X}, \quad \frac{P \text{ believes } \overset{K}{\mapsto} Q, P \text{ sees } \{X\}_{K^{-1}}}{P \text{ sees } X}.$$

– Postulate 5: Freshness

"If one part of a formula is fresh, then the entire formula must also be fresh" (Burrows et al. 1989).

$$\frac{P \text{ believes fresh}(X)}{P \text{ believes fresh}(X, Y)}$$

3.2.1.2. *SPAN and AVISPA*

AVISPA is the Automated Validation of Internet Security Protocols and Applications and SPAN is its Security Protocol Animator. They are used to analyze the security protocols that are specified using the high-level protocol specification language (HLPSL) (Glouche et al. 2006–2017).

AVISPA checks the validity of security protocols, while SPAN graphically illustrates the exchange sequence of messages using a Message Sequence Chart

(MSC). It also includes an active attacker implementation to build attacks on the security protocols, detect their weakness and analyze their performance robustness and resiliency to commonly known attacks. The tool comes with a set of libraries of pre-specified known security protocols, which helps both in understanding and learning the language logic and instructions. Furthermore, it may help academics to do comparative studies and ameliorate the existing solutions (AVISPA 2002).

The HLPSL specification is first translated using HLPSL2IF to the intermediate format IF, which is a lower-level language used by AVISPA. This step is automatically done by the tool and is transparent to the user. The IF will then be processed by the back-end to check the validity of the protocols and the satisfaction of the desired security goals.

The back-end of AVISPA is OFMC, CL-atSe, SATMC or TA4SP, each of which is explained below (A. Team 2006a, 2006b):

– OFMC (On-the-Fly Model Checker): this is the default model used by AVISPA. It is used to quickly detect attacks on the security protocol and verify its correctness on a bounded number of sessions and unbounded number of messages generated by the intruder.

– CL-atSe (Constraint Logic-based Attack Searcher): provides the translation of IF transition relations into a set of constraints that can be used to find protocol attacks. The constraints are on the attacker's knowledge or, in other words, from their perspective. The honest legitimate message is seen as a forgeability constraint from the attacker's perspective. The protocol specification is first simplified to reduce its steps that are translated to constraints and verified to evaluate the security performance by detecting the presence or absence of vulnerability (attacks un/found).

– SATMC (Satisfiability-based Model Checker): creates the propositional formula of the IF transition relations starting from the initial state to the states representing the security violations. It checks that the security protocol satisfies its underlined requirements, and discovers the attacks on this protocol (Compagna 2005).

– TA4SP (Tree Automata for Security Protocols): calculates, from an initial state, the under- and over-approximations of the attacker's knowledge by using a tree library that contains knowledge of prior attacks. This back-end checks the secrecy property of a given solution and does not handle the conditions, sets, etc.

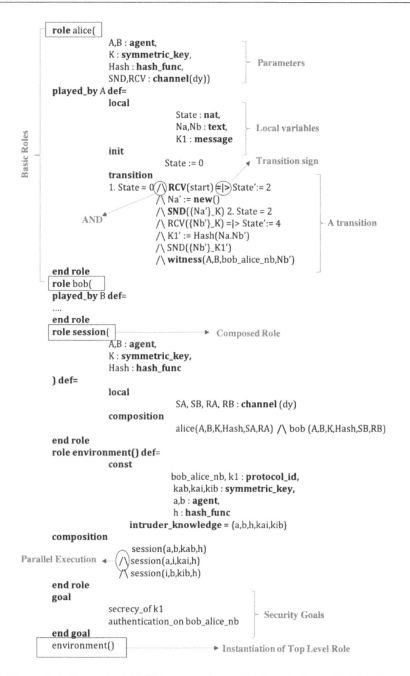

Figure 3.4. *Example of HLSPL protocol specification (A. Team 2006a). For a color version of this figure, see www.iste.co.uk/benarous/vehicular.zip*

The HLPSL is a role-based language, which means that each participant is defined by the role they play and the code they execute in the protocols. Each role definition specifies the participant's used parameters, initial state and transitions that define the rules to change from one state to another.

Figure 3.6 shows an example extracted from the HLPSL tutorial (A. Team 2006a). The content of the example and its meaning is not of any significance to us. It is only for illustrative purposes of the organization and basic elements of a protocol specification. Each protocol is composed of basic roles that define the participants' codes, and a complex role, which is composed of a set of basic roles. The environment represents the top-level role that combines the regular sessions with the intruder's injection. The goal part defines the final desired security goals, which are ensured by the use of security properties such as "witness" instruction. The above-explained sections are the definition of the participant codes, and the last line is the instantiation of the top-level role that would call the roles and the intruder using the specified code (A. Team 2006b).

The output of the analysis is the trace of the attack if it exits upon the end of the verification. If no attack is found, the protocol is considered safe.

Table 3.2 gives a summarized user guide on the usage of HLSPL, in which we list the reserved constant names and keywords, the security goal predicates, the variable declaration rules and the used operators.

Variables	**Naming**	Has a unique name. Starts with a capital letter. Can be a mix of letters and digits.
	Types	Nat, set, text, symmetric_key, public_key, message, hash_func, agent, bool, channel(dy) Dy: Dolev-Yao channel type
	Assigning new fresh values	New()
Constants	**Naming**	Starts with a lower-case letter.
	Reserved constant names	apply, attack_state, attack_states, contains, crypt, dummy_agent, dummy_bool, dummy_chnl, dummy_chnl_dy, dummy_chnl_ota, du mmy_hash, dummy_msg, dummy_nat, dummy_nonce, dummy_pk, dummy_set, dummy_sk, equal, equations, initial_state, inits, intruder, leq, pair, properties, property, rules, scrypt, section, step, types.
Operators	:=	Assignments
	=|>	Transition
	∧	Within a transition, it means "AND". Within a composed role, it means "executed in parallel"
	.	Message concatenation
	,	separator
	;	Sequel execution

Operators (cont'd)	**in**	Checks if an element is part of a set
	xor	Exclusive OR
	exp	Exponentiation
	not	Logical negation
	'	X' refers to the newest value of X.
	=	Equality test
Instructions and symbols	**accept**	Indicates the end of a role and the beginning of the next in sequential execution
	inv	Inverse of the public key which is the private key
	delete	Deletes an element from a set
	SND()	Sends message
	RCV()	Receives message
	init	Precedes the initialization of the variables
	intruder_knowl edge	Defines the intruder's knowledge
	Def=	Starts the definition of the role
	local	Local variable section
	played_by	Specifies which agent is playing the basic role
	composition	Begins a composed role definition
	transition	Precedes the definition of transitions
	End role	Indicates the ending of role definition
	%	Comments
Security properties	**witness**	Used along with wrequest to check authentication
	request	Used to check strong authentication
	wrequest	Used to check weak authentication
	secret	Used to check the secrecy
	owns	Ownership of a variable. Only the owner can change the value of this value (edit it)
Reserved keywords	accept, agent, authentication_on, bool, channel, composition, cons, const, def=, delete, dy, end, exp, goal, hash, hash_func, iknows, in, init, intruder_knowledge, inv, local, message, nat, new, not, ota, played_by, protocol_id, public_key, request, role, secrecy_of, secret, set, start, symmetric_key, text, transition, weak_authentication_on, witness, wrequest, xor.	

Table 3.2. *HLPSL simplified user guide (A. Team 2006a; 2006b)*

3.2.1.3. *Attack tree*

Attack trees (Schneier 1999) are a method to describe the security systems, evaluate them in terms of resiliency to attacks and therefore improve them. The attacks on a security solution are represented as a tree, where the root node is the goal of the attack and the leaf nodes are the attacks executed. The OR nodes represent the various possible ways to execute an attack, while the AND nodes represent the different needed steps to execute an attack. If attack A can be executed using either method A1 or A2, then the combining node is OR, as illustrated in Figure 3.5(1). If both A1 and A2 are required to happen for attack A to be successful, then AND is used, as illustrated in Figure 3.5(2). Each leaf is then assigned a value or a set of values depending on a set of criteria. A simple example would be a Boolean value indicating the possibility of executing an attack, such as 1 if it is possible and 0 if it is not. The node values are then calculated based on the leaf values from bottom-up by applying the calculation rules for the "AND" and "OR". This operation is recursive until the value of the top-level node known as the security objective is found. The value presents the likability of the attack goals to be achieved and therefore gives an overview of the security level of the solution. It illustrates the system weaknesses and vulnerabilities. Then, it helps the analyst in improving it. It may also be appended by the counter-measure implemented against each attack. It also presents the system assumptions and allows the comparison of security systems, after rigorously evaluating and analyzing them. Several tools exist that build the attack trees of systems and calculate the possibility of achieving the underlined attack goal of a system, such as Isograph (Attack Tree, Isograph) and ADTool (Attack Tree, ADTool).

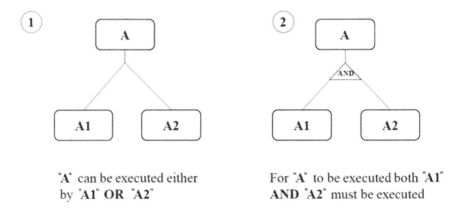

Figure 3.5. *Attack tree example (AND/OR nodes)*

3.2.1.4. *Discussion and analysis*

Discussion and analysis are usually done descriptively to highlight the security issue and its proposed solution. It includes a study on the set of potential vulnerabilities or attacks on a given method and the suggested counter-measures. This analysis concerns the conception and design of a protocol, the issue it treats and the weaknesses it may have or prevents. It requires knowledge of vulnerabilities concerning various types of security solutions. It also helps in better explaining the solution in natural language. However, although necessary, it cannot be sufficient to prove its robustness or evaluate its performance level.

In this book, we used discussion and analysis to illustrate the potential vulnerabilities and preventative counter-measures taken.

For the privacy-preserving authentication issue, we considered the following security properties: anonymity, unlinkability, forward security, non-repudiation and message integrity, alongside a set of attacks, such as replay attacks, session hijacking, man-in-the-middle, impersonation, guessing, brute force and Sybil attacks.

For location privacy issues, we considered the eavesdropping and linkability attacks (semantic, syntactic mapping and observation linking). Identity privacy is analyzed in terms of anonymity and non-repudiation. The security properties and attacks are explained in the next chapter.

3.2.2. *Privacy*

In this book, we also studied location and identity privacy preservation in vehicular networks. In this section, we explain the various existing methods for privacy-preserving schemes, proofing and analyzing empirical and analytical methods.

3.2.2.1. *Simulation*

Simulation is one of the most used methods to test protocols and analyze them before their real-world implementation. It is less costly in comparison with real test beds. It allows the general evaluation of a given solution under different scenarios, which helps in detecting its abnormalities and improving them. To simulate the vehicular networks, two types of simulators are used: the first one is the mobility simulator, which generates maps and traffic, and the second one is the network simulator, which simulates vehicle behavior. There exist various tools for each type. In this section, we give a non-exhaustive list of the commonly used tools for each type of simulator. Then, we specify the tools we used in our works and explain why we chose to use them.

– **Mobility simulators**

Various mobility simulators exist that generate mobility models for ad hoc networks in general, and for vehicular networks in particular. Herein, we list a few existing tools that are preferred by academics. They export map traffic traces in a compatible format with widespread network simulators.

– Sumo

Sumo is a free and open traffic simulator including road vehicles and maps. It is used to generate the mobility models to be used by the network simulator for simulating vehicular networks. It can import real maps from OpenStreetMap and generate mobility models of moving vehicles that follow the roads and traffic patterns on the map. The user specifies the number of vehicles (low, medium and high densities) and the duration of the simulation. Sumo-generated mobility files can be imported to NS2, NS3 and OMNET.

– MobiSim

MobiSim (Mousavi et al. 2007) is a free mobility model generator for ad hoc networks; it generates mobility scenarios that can be used by network simulators. It is directly compatible with NS2, and may also export the mobility traces as text or xml files to be imported by other simulators. It is a cross-platform java-based tool with easy-to-use graphical interface and available documentation (Javadi 2006).

– VanetMobiSim

VanetMobiSim is a free java-based mobility trace generator compatible with various network simulators such as NS2. It is the extension of CanuMobiSim for the simulation of vehicular networks. It can import or generate maps and traffic following roads restrictions.

– Network simulators

The previous tools simulate the vehicle's movements on roads, but they do not simulate their behavior or executed codes. To simulate the vehicle's cyber activity on the network, other sets of tools are used, known as network simulators. The tools take the traffic traces and embed them with the vehicle executed codes. There exist various tools, and we mention here only a few of the most famous ones in the literature.

– MATLAB

MATLAB is used by scientists and engineers to analyze and design systems. It has various application fields thanks to its various offered toolboxes. It is mathematically rich and allows the graphical illustration of data. Most importantly, it is actively updated, documented and has a large community. This facilitates its usage and the exchange of expertise between its users. It can be used to simulate vehicular networks,

MAC, networking and security protocols. The repository presented in Gupta (2022) was developed specially for VANET simulation. However, the literature is not rich with studies on the use of MATLAB as a simulator for these networks.

– NS2

NS2 or Network Simulator is a free discrete event simulator for wired and wireless networks. It is commonly used to simulate ad hoc networks such as mobile networks (MANET) and vehicular networks (VANET). It is documented and has a large active community, making its learning and usage easier. Being commonly used helps when doing comparative studies. The tool is made using C++ and so the developed protocols. The configuration files are written in Otcl. The tool accepts external mobility models generated by other tools such as MobiSim or Sumo for the simulation of vehicular networks[1].

– NS3

NS3 is also a free discrete event simulator for Internet systems, but not exclusively. It may be used to simulate other types of networks. It is suitable for educational and research purposes with an active community and available documentation. Note that NS3 is not the extension and evolution of NS2. It is a completely independent project, and it is not backward compatible with NS2 simulation files. It is written in C++ for both simulation code and scenarios (with optional usage of Python) and visualized using NetAnim. Unlike NS2, where the simulation is written in C++ and the scenario is written in OTcl scripts, the output is visualized in NAM (NS3 Tutorial).

– OMNET

OMNET is a discrete event extensible and modular network simulator. The tool uses the C++ language to write the nodes codes, which are defined using the NED language. It also uses the "ini" configuration files. The concept of components and modules facilitates the exchange and re-usage of modules in various simulation and codes. It may be extended with various libraries to allow the simulations of different types of networks. It is used to simulate vehicular networks when extended with the veins framework (Veins), which connects the traffic traces generated by Sumo with the vehicle code written in OMNET during parallel simulation. The tool is free and has an active community and available documentation.

---

1 See: https://www.isi.edu/nsnam/ns/doc/index.html.

Criteria	MATLAB	NS2	NS3	OMNET
Core component	MATLAB	C++	C++	C++, NED
Scenarios	MATLAB	OTcl	C++	Ini configuration
Graphical interface	Tool interface	NAM	NetAnim	IDE
Documentation	Available for subscribers	Available	Available	Available
Ease-of-use	Easy for mathematics-oriented users	Easy for network simulations	Easy for network simulations	Requires the manipulation of various types of files as modules
Used since	1994	1989	2009	1997
Community	Large	Large	Large	Large
License	Proprietary software	Free software	Free software	Free software
Platform	Cross-platform (Windows, Linux and Mac OS)	Linux and Windows (via Cygwin)	Cross-platform (Windows, Linux and Mac OS)	Cross-platform (Windows, Linux and Mac OS)

Table 3.3. *Comparative study of simulation tools*

Kim et al. (2014) conducted an earlier investigation on vehicular network simulators. In their paper, they considered MATLAB, NS2, NS3 and OMNET simulators and analyzed each tool's weaknesses and strengths, while also conducting a statistic on the use of each tool in the literature. The authors found that NS2 is the most favored and used by researchers for vehicular simulation. Table 3.3 resumes the comparison we elaborated between these tools.

In our works, we used MobiSim for the generation of mobility models and NS2 for vehicular network simulations. We chose the tools taking into account the above criteria, besides our familiarity with the tools, their ease of use, their extensive utilization in related works, their stability, their large community and the availability of tutorials and documentation.

3.2.2.2. *Analytical model*

Liu et al. (2018a) defined five privacy analytical evaluation metrics:

– The certainty

The certainty metrics measure the attacker's ambiguity in finding a unique answer, such as the location or the identity. It includes the level of privacy or the anonymity set size and the entropy. We give below the formulas for each metric:

The anonymity set size (ASS) is the number of neighbor vehicles with a similar state to the subject vehicle V_s that would make this vehicle undistinguishable by the attacker from the rest of the set members. Let V_i, $i \in [1..k]$, be the vehicle with a similar state to V_s, with k being the number of all the neighbor vehicles with a similar state as V_s.

$$ASS = |V_i| = k \qquad\qquad [3.1]$$

The entropy (ETSI 2018) expresses the attacker uncertainty when linking the new pseudonym (after the change) to the subject vehicle; it is defined as follows:

$$Entropy = - \sum_{i=1}^{ASS} p_i \log(p_i) \qquad\qquad [3.2]$$

where P_i is the probability the attacker assigns to each member of ASS being the subject vehicle.

The normalized entropy (ETSI 2018) is calculated as follows:

$$Entropy_n = \frac{Entropy}{Entropy_{max}} \qquad\qquad [3.3]$$

where $Entropy_{max}$ (ETSI 2018) is the maximal value the entropy achieves if the distribution of vehicles is uniform; it is calculated as follows:

$$Entropy_{max} = log_2(ASS) \qquad\qquad [3.4]$$

– The correctness

The correctness metric considers the attacker success rate, which is the probability of successful tracks by the attacker. In trajectory tracking, it is the probability of continuous successful tracks over successive observation slots and areas. It also includes the measurement of error rate in the prediction of positions; this is known as the distance-based metric, which calculates the distance between the real position x and the predicted one $\hat{x}$, and multiplies it by the probability of estimating $\hat{x}$ based on earlier observations o, as follows:

$$\sum_{\hat{x}} P(\hat{x}|o)d(x,\hat{x}) \qquad\qquad [3.5]$$

– The information gain and loss

These metrics consider the amount of data that the attacker intercepts and collects. The more is the gain of the attacker, the less is the privacy of the user (loss). The less is the attackers gain, the higher is the level of the user's privacy.

– Geo-indistinguishability

This metric evaluates location privacy-preserving solutions that avoid sending the exact position of the user, but an appended one, so that the attacker would think that all vehicles within that area are equally likely to be the subject vehicle (Andrés et al. 2012).

– Time

The time metrics include the maximum tracking time, which is the maximum period of continuous correct tracking by the attacker. Another metric is the confusion time, which is the period of time the attacker is uncertain about the correctness of tracks or confused about the predictions it makes.

3.2.2.3. Comparative study

Comparative studies are necessary to distinguish a given solution's properties from other existing methods, highlight its advantages and what it lacks and compare it to the related literature. In a way, it helps in understanding the solution and convinces the users of its benefits. In another, it also helps to detect its characteristics, strengths and weaknesses. It allows the final user to choose the right solution that fits their requirements and be responsible for this choice. It is considered as a pillar for future improvements for related researches and studies. On a conceptual and design level, the comparison may take as metrics: the purposes, methods and key principles, extra requirements and key assumptions for the compared solutions, and the attacker models studied. On the performance level, the simulation is usually fundamentally needed where all compared solutions are simulated under the same settings and against the same attacker model. The level of privacy is then compared. On the analytical level, the privacy evaluation metrics are used to compare the solutions. Some researchers even consider comparing the impact of the solution on the performance of the network, the complexity of implementation and the overhead added.

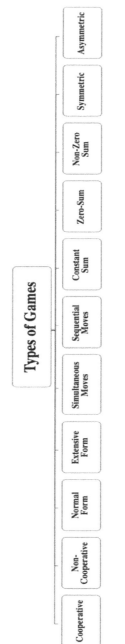

Figure 3.6. *Types of games in game theory*

3.2.2.4. *Game theory*

Game theory is a mathematics-based method to formulate, structure and analyze strategical issues that depends on different factors and decisions impacting its evolution. It was first introduced by John Von Neumann in 1928. It was first applied to economy applications when he released the book entitled "Theory of Games and Economic Behaviour" in 1944, which he co-authored with Oskar Morgenstern. Ever since, game theory has been used for various strategical and predictability applications. Each issue is presented as a game with a set of players and strategies (moves) made by each player, as well as a payoff function, which assigns each player with a payoff depending on their played strategy and the strategies of the other players (Hotz 2006).

Game theory has various types of games depending on the nature of the studied problem. Figure 3.6 illustrates the existing types (EconomicsDiscussion.net n.d.).

In our work, we used game theory to analyze the feasibility of our proposed location privacy schemes, more precisely the identifier change strategy.

3.3. Conclusion

This chapter presented the different proofing and analysis methods used to study the performance, feasibility and strength of both the security and privacy issues in vehicular networks. We focus particularly on the methods used for the evaluation of privacy-preserving authentication protocols and location privacy-preserving schemes, which are our two main research issues and the subjects of this book.

In the next chapter, we explain the various security attacks related to the above-defined problems and we define the attacker model for each.

4

The Attacker Model

4.1. Introduction

In the previous chapter, we explained the various proofing, evaluating and analyzing methods utilized to study the performance of security solutions. These solutions are measured by the resiliency they provide against an attacker or adversary executing different attacks exploiting the system's potential vulnerabilities. In this chapter, we shed more light on the attacker model, also known as the adversary model. We dive more into vehicular network security issues and the known attacks targeting them. We pay more attention to the attacks targeting privacy, mainly in terms of location and identity when the vehicle's user uses location-based services (LBS) and safety applications. The vehicular networks extend the cyber world to the road. Vehicles, which were once a mere means of transportation, are becoming computers on wheels, just as close and reliable as our computers and smartphones. Users spend most of their time, other than being at home or at work, driving their vehicles on roads. Smart vehicles bring together, in an intertwined way, the joy and leisure of being connected to the cyber world and surfing the Internet, with the sorrow of being at risk from cyber attacks and privacy exposure. This may even impact physical safety.

Being an extension of computer and cyber systems on-road is not the unique reason for them being the target of attacks. It is also due to the nature of the vehicular networks that rely on wireless communications, require the real-time exchange of accurate spatiotemporal data, and necessitate the authentication of messages or users depending on the application. In this chapter, we explain how these different requirements, although essential, may threaten the security and privacy of users if used by a malicious attacker. We also explain the various existing security attacks and the preciseness of our attacker model.

This chapter defines the six main types of security objectives: availability, integrity, non-repudiation, confidentiality, authenticity and accountability. The seventh property is particularly important in vehicular networks, which is the revocation of the misbehaving node. It also highlights the prominent security challenges that occupy the vehicular network security researcher's attention. These challenges may also be seen as the major security research axis. Then, it explains the security attacker, their aims and means, their different types and their executed attacks. Lastly, it gives the specification of the used attacker model.

4.2. Security objectives

In this section, we explain the six fundamental security objectives that are the reason that security solutions are developed, those that are the main target of attacks. We define them in general and then in vehicular networks. We added the seventh property for its special importance in vehicular networks.

– Availability

This means that the system can always provide its services to its authorized requesters. For resources, it means that this resource can always be accessed and used by its authorized users. In vehicular networks, the availability of the authority providing certificates must be guaranteed. Similarly, the availability of the vehicles, road side units (RSUs) and service providers must be ensured. By the availability of the vehicles and roadside units, we mean their cyber availability. No obligation should be imposed on the user to be present at a certain location. However, we mean the cooperation of the vehicle and its presence in cyber activities such as re-routing and forwarding. The most dangerous attack targeting the availability is the denial of service (DoS) and distributed denial of service (DDoS), which isolate the targets and make them inaccessible (Geers 2011).

– Integrity

This ensures that the data is not altered by an unauthorized third party. In vehicular networks, the integrity of messages is important either when exchanged between the vehicles themselves, the vehicle and road-side unit, authorities or service providers (Pfleeger et al. 2015; Benarous et al. 2017).

– Non-repudiation

This ensures that the sender of a message cannot deny having sent it. It is particularly useful to hold the sender legally responsible and prosecutable for their emitted messages and/or committed behavior. In vehicular networks, it is used to hold the owner of the vehicle responsible for their on-road cyber activity, especially if misbehavior is detected, such as injecting false data, being selfish, being uncooperative or spreading malware (Benarous et al. 2017). Implicitly, it also means that the user cannot deny their identity, being at a location, or participating in a cyber activity (Pfleeger et al. 2015).

– *Accountability and auditability*

This refers to traceability. In other terms, keeping track of all of the actions that occur in a system. In vehicular networks, it is the result of ensuring the non-repudiation. The user is held responsible for misbehavior initiated on their on-road cyber activity. The authorities cooperate with other vehicles and RSUs to trace the vehicle's activity, for evidence collection and/or revocation (Pfleeger et al. 2015; Benarous et al. 2017).

– *Authentication and authorization*

Authentication means identifying the user of a system. It is followed by authorization, which involves granting or denying the user access to the system and with what rights. These operations are preceded by the subscription of the users to the system where the authentication data are first saved and the access rights are defined. In vehicular networks, we have two types of authentications, which are the authentication of messages and the authentication of a user. The first one is executed to check that a received message comes from a trusted valid user without identifying them. This is done by the verification of the certificate of the key used to sign the message. If it is valid (not expired), not revoked and generated by a trusted authority, then the message integrity is checked. Upon confirmation that it has not been altered, the message is accepted. These messages are often state messages (beacons). The second type is the authentication and authorization of the users to the authorities, service providers or RSUs. This type is just like the conventional authentication. It needs a subscription phase, authentication and authorization (Pfleeger et al. 2015; Benarous et al. 2017).

– *Confidentiality and privacy*

It is mainly threatened by the leakage and exposure of data. Confidentiality and privacy are two fundamental requirements in vehicular networks as they are directly related to the safety of users. Confidentiality is related to the content of exchanged messages. It means that only the intended authorized parties can access, read and/or alter this content. The privacy is more related to the identity of the vehicle's owner, their current location and past parsed trajectories (Lord and Sharp 2011; Pfleeger et al. 2015; Benarous et al. 2017).

– *The revocation*

The revocation is particularly important in vehicular networks. It maintains the correct functionality of the network by preventing misbehavior from committing further abuse. It also prohibits other vehicles from interacting with it in the future. It is usually done upon confirming the vehicle's reports of detecting a malicious misbehaving node. The vehicle is blacklisted by adding its public key certificate to the Certificate Revocation List (CRL) and distributing this list to the network nodes.

4.3. Security challenges

Various security challenges arise which are derived from the above-explained objectives. They attract the attention of researchers. Therefore, the literature is rich with a variety of security schemes which can be classified into the following:

– *Authentication*: one of the most important issues to guarantee the correct functionality of the network, serve the authorized vehicles and hold the vehicles responsible for their cyber activity (tracing who is doing what). The authentication usually requires the provision of identity, permanent certificate or credentials to the other serving entity, which may be the authority, the vehicle or the service provider. Therefore, it contradicts the user's requirement of privacy. The works related to the authentication issue in vehicular networks include adapting the biometric authentication solutions, the design of privacy-preserving authentication methods such as zero-knowledge authentication and the development of lightweight authentication schemes.

– *Privacy*: another key issue: various researchers focused on resolving the identity privacy issue by using the pseudonyms. These pseudonyms are temporal keys which may be considered as temporal cyber identities of the vehicles. To preserve location privacy, various pseudonym change strategies were developed to thwart linking and prevent tracking. Another set of researchers concentrated on developing obfuscation methods to achieve the same aim. Data privacy, also known as the confidentiality, is preserved by the use of encryption algorithms, such as the elliptic curve cryptography.

– *Revocation*: the researchers are searching for a fast and efficient revocation process, especially now that the CRL is continuously growing larger with each revocation. The search process in the CRL needs to be fast and efficient in terms of used resources (CPU, storage space).

– *Pseudonym generation and/or refilling*: a large number of researchers assume that the vehicle has enough certified pseudonyms within it. Other researchers focus on the pseudonym generation and certification issue. We find three groups of research, those who suggest that the pseudonyms and/or their certificates are issued by a trusted authority (Vehicular Public Key Infrastructure or VPKI). The other question left is how they request their refilling upon the pool's expiry. Some suggest regular visits to the authority facility for updates. Others suggest on-road on demand refilling. The second group suggests that the vehicle should self-generate its keys and either self-sign them or form groups where the group leader handles the certification of these keys. This method is authority-independent which means more privacy, but no revocation nor accountability is ensured. The third group includes solutions that combine the VPKI with the group concept. The group leader uses a certified key to sign the vehicle's keys. It keeps local records to ensure non-repudiation and revocation in case of misbehavior.

– *Firewalls, antimalware, intrusion detection and prevention*: another aspect of security is how to protect the vehicle's on-board system from intrusion attacks and malware. This includes the development of tamper-proof devices that save the keys and security algorithms, and the design of antiviruses and firewalls.

– *Digital signatures*: used in vehicular networks to first ensure message integrity and second authenticate that they come from a trusted vehicle. The researchers focus on designing lightweight digital signing algorithms and efficient signature-based message authentication methods.

– *Data alteration and injection*: data alteration may be prevented using digital signature techniques. As for the injection, various researchers work on the early detection mechanisms, the reporting and revocation of the malicious node injecting bogus data, noting that sometimes the data injection is caused by faulty hardware or deliberately added to reduce the attacker's prediction accuracy. The proposed solutions shall distinguish between these cases.

– *Trust and reputation*: this is another set of solutions that take the vehicle's behavior into account to evaluate its reputation and decide whether or not to trust the sender of a message. The interactions between vehicles are not authenticated using conventional methods, but are based on the reputation value. Hybrid methods exist which combines the conventional message authentication with the reputation as an extra level of security. It relies on past interactions to trust or stop interacting with a vehicle. It can also be used with revocation methods, where the node is revoked if its reputation is lower than a threshold value for a period of time.

4.4. Security attacker

In this section, we explain the security attacker's aims, types, means and executed attacks. We also refine our used attacker model with the purpose to deepen the understanding of security issues on vehicular networks, facilitate the understanding of security model used to evaluate our proposed schemes (contributions) and clarify some key security concepts.

4.4.1. *Aims*

The security attacker is also known as an adversary in vehicular networks and a hacker in the cyber world, where they usually aim to damage security systems by targeting one of the above seven security objectives with a set of attacks defined later in section 4.4.4. Note that the attacker may be an individual, or an organization. In the case of privacy, the attacker may even be the government (Big Brother, BB). The BB may not necessarily target the users to pressure them, abusing its use of power, but to maintain order and ensure security.

We mention some of the attacker's potential aims from attacking the vehicular network:

– taking advantage of the road by rearranging the vehicle's distribution via message injecting;

– disrupting the correct functionality of the network by selectively forwarding the packets, isolating nodes or controlling routed packets;

– eavesdropping on messages, violating the privacy of users;

– tracking users, learning their habits, frequented places and routines;

– blackmailing users with learnt secrets;

– encrypting and decrypting, the first is to ask for money (ransom-ware). The second is to read the user's encrypted messages and violate their confidentiality;

– professional attackers do not target users for fun or pleasure, especially as they need to use special equipment and develop their own hacking tools. They do it for the profit they can make. Therefore, they may even target the user's safety for money by planning road traps, or causing the vehicle to malfunction.

4.4.2. *Types*

Raya and Hubaux (2007) classified the attacker into eight types depending on the type of activity, scope coverage and intentions. We explain each type below:

– The *insider* attacker is an authenticated internal member of the system of the network that possesses a certified public key. In our case, it is an authenticated vehicle with a valid and certified long-term public key and short-term public key (pseudonyms).

– The *outsider* attacker is not a member of the system or the network and is considered as an external intruder. The external attacker is less disastrous to the system because they may be detected and they do not know the specification of the security system. Moreover, they are generally limited in terms of access and may execute general attacks. However, this does not make them any safer, innocent or less dangerous. External hackers may devastate the security system and cause undeniable threat to organizations, depriving them of huge fortunes.

– The *active* attacker generates packets and signals. They actively participate in the networks and influence its functionality; they may generate/alter or drop the messages.

– The *passive* attacker is an implicit attacker who limits their activity to eavesdropping and intercepting messages or signals. This attacker is hard to detect because it leaves no trace behind and does not impact the functionality of the network. It highly threatens the privacy of the users and the confidentiality of organization secrets.

– The *local* attacker has a local coverage zone. In other words, they have a local influence, compromise a limited number of entities or cover a small region of the network. In our case, we denote the attacker as local if they have a limited coverage area from a large observation zone.

– The *global* attacker has a wider coverage range than the local attacker. In our case, a global attacker has full coverage of the observation area. This is a very strong theoretical assumption which is hard to achieve in the real world by an individual attacker, unless it is the government. We use this assumption to test our privacy-preserving solution against this strong model.

– The *malicious* attacker is usually aiming for the destruction of the security system, more likely because of a personal grudge than for profit. They may use any means and target any component, entity or user.

– The *rational* attacker is a target-oriented attacker, more predictable and aims to profit from their attacks.

4.4.3. *Means*

We are interested in our research into privacy-related issues when beaconing, using services or providing them. Therefore, we focus on the means used to violate identity and location privacy. We concentrate on the tracking issue. It is one of the biggest threats facing vehicle network users. The vehicle may easily be tracked using road surveillance cameras and dashboard cameras in vehicles. It is further facilitated by the use of an automatic plate number reader which reads the vehicle's license plate automatically, making it easy to search for a vehicle on the roads (Petit et al. 2015). Although the use of this method is famous, it is not easily done by the attacker unless all roads are covered by cameras, they have full access to all of the road cameras, and they can hack the vehicle's on-board cameras to use them. This method is generally used by the police and authorities where vehicles may provide the access to their cameras to cooperate with them or may rent their camera usage as a service. Both the high cost and the difficulty of this method prevent the attacker from using it.

The attacker may also physically follow their targeted vehicles. This is also known as stalking. We do not consider this type of threat although it is a high risk in terms of privacy. But stalking has nothing to do with the user's cyber activity on-road. This issue is handled legally by the intervention of the police and it is out of the scope of our research.

The attacker may use a cheaper method to track the vehicle by its cyber activity on-road; we previously explained that vehicle networks require each vehicle to send periodic messages containing accurate real-time location, speed, direction and identity data. These state messages are fundamental in ensuring the functionality of the network and the safety of the user. However, being sent wirelessly in clear is inviting enough for the attacker, who would install their receivers across the road to intercept these messages and track the vehicle's movements on road. This motivates both active and passive attackers to use this cheaper, more efficient and more accurate method to track the vehicles.

In the rest of the book, we continue to consider this type of method to intercept communication, which is to rely solely on the wireless activity tracking and not any other means such as tracking by cameras.

4.4.4. Attacks

In this section, we list the famous security attacks on vehicular networks, with deeper focus on privacy-related attacks. Then, in the next section, we define a general attacker model for our proposed solutions. Figure 4.1 illustrates the cyber-security threats, which may be hardware- or software-related, also known as physical and logical issues, respectively. It classifies the logical security threats based on what they target: the information, network and system. The right part of the figure lists the prominently used solutions. The figure is followed by the explanation of the security attacks.

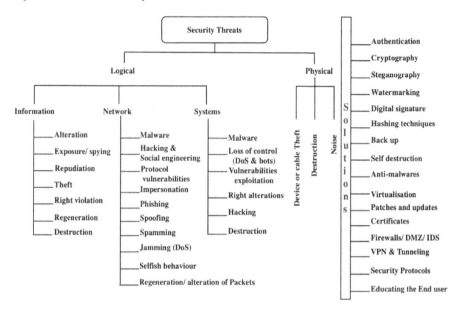

Figure 4.1. *Cyber-security threats and solutions (Benarous et al. 2017)*

The vehicular network security attacks are (Warren and Brandeis 1890; Benarous et al. 2017):

– *Session hijacking*: the attacker forges unprotected sessions after its initiation (authentication, sequence number generation) by replacing the legitimate node and carrying-on the session (Fadlullah et al. 2010).

– *Denial of service (DoS)*: one of the most dangerous attacks on availability. It targets the network or a system to prevent it from providing services. The attacker may use one (DoS) or multiple machines (DDoS) to generate targeted traffic towards the victim node or system to congest it and paralyze it (Gu and Liu 2007).

– *Sink-hole attack*: in this attack, the malicious node attracts the network traffic to pass through it. However, it does not forward all the messages. Instead, it selects which packet to forward and which to drop. This is also known as selective forwarding (Raazi et al. 2011).

– *Black-hole attack*: unlike the sink-hole attack, the malicious node executing this attack does not forward a packet. Instead, it drops them all (Laurendeau and Barbeau 2006).

– *Malware*: are code portions written to cause harm to systems and networks. It includes the viruses, adware, spywares and worms, etc.

– *Replay attack*: where the attacker records exchanged messages for later usage (Fadlullah et al. 2010).

GPS spoofing: the attacker impersonates the GPS (Global Positioning System), trying to replace it by generating a stronger signal with fake positions to the vehicle, which accepts it assuming it came from the legitimate GPS (Mejri et al. 2014).

– *Masquerading or impersonation*: is an attack where the attacker pretends to be (pose as) a legitimate node to execute other attacks, such as data alteration or injection (Laurendeau and Barbeau 2006).

– *Sybil attack*: in this attack, a node obtains and uses multiple identities at the same time to get extra advantages or avoid tracing (Sen 2010; Mejri et al. 2014).

– *Tunneling or worm-hole*: in this attack, the malicious node intercepts the packet from a location and selectively tunnels them to another location. Then, it retransmits them to the network from that location (Hu et al. 2006).

– *Eavesdropping*: is a passive attack where the attacker intercepts, records and analyzes the exchanged packets within its coverage (Sen et al. 2010).

– *Man-in-the-middle*: can be considered as active eavesdropping. The attacker first eavesdrops on the traffic to learn about the nature of exchanged messages. Then, breaks the chain by impersonating the endpoint (the user) and continuing the communication. The legitimate node is usually isolated to prevent it from resuming the communication or re-initiating it (Valency Networks 2008).

– *Isolation attack*: in this attack, the attacker prevents a node or a set of nodes from interacting with the rest of the network nodes (Sen et al. 2010).

– *Social engineering, or human hacking*: the attacker uses their psychological tricks and social skills to conduct background research about their target. In the vehicular network context, it may be preceded by eavesdropping and tracking attacks. For example, the attacker tracking vehicle "A" may link the frequented places to identify the target and collect more information about them. They may use this information to threaten and blackmail the victim (Mitnick and Simon 2011).

– *Linking and tracking attacks*: are privacy targeting attacks. They mainly focus on linking the used pseudonyms and the locations of the vehicle to continue tracking it.

– *Cheating attacks*: are privacy targeting attacks that aim to reduce the anonymity set size of the vehicle by using compromised vehicles (internal attackers). This attack aims to facilitate the linking of the pseudonyms, even when executing a cooperative change strategy. Thus, it enables vehicle tracking. The attacker deludes the vehicle, changing its pseudonym with its cooperation in the change, when in fact it does not, making the vehicle linkable (Guo et al. 2018). Huang et al. (2012) defined the cheating attack to be executed by an attacker with selfish behavior, aiming to take advantage of roads by injecting false data (messages with fake locations, events, identifiers and road conditions) or spreading false routes and mimicking congested routes.

4.4.5. *Our attacker model*

The attacker model targeting identity privacy in the authentication phase uses wireless communications to eavesdrop and actively execute the following attacks: replay attack, man-in-the-middle, impersonation, which were explained above.

As for the attacker model targeting location privacy on roads, it is the external global passive attacker (GPA). They spread their receivers across the observation to fully cover it, as illustrated in Figure 4.2. They are passive because they do not inject, alter or drop the message. This gives them the secrecy and implicit traits, which harden detection by the victim vehicle. In other words, the vehicle may be tracked for a long time before it detects the attacker's presence. It may also continue being tracked without discovering that it is being tracked, unless the attacker uses the collected data in other attacks or for other purposes, such as blackmailing. The attacker is external, which means that they cannot compromise and use other vehicles to execute the eavesdropping, because:

– The cost of using vehicles is highly expensive. The attacker needs to possess (buy and use) a large number of vehicles. They need to cover the road and they are in a static state or run at all times on the observed road. This assumption is not acceptable for various reasons, such as the high cost of fuel the running vehicles would consume daily. The vehicles may not be allowed to park in the attacker's desired spots. Even if the attacker can afford to deploy this number of vehicles, this method of tracking draws attention. It may not only be discovered easily, but also be reported to the police by the tracked vehicles as being physically stalked.

– If the attacker cannot purchase the vehicles, another hypothesis for the internal attacker is either that they use their vehicle to stalk the victim vehicle which is out of the scope of our research, or, they may hack the vehicle's system to control them. This assumption is not only extremely difficult, but even if it was possible to hack a vehicle system, it is smarter for the attacker to directly hack the victim's vehicle system, rather than choosing the hard, costly, unsure way of hacking all or at least a few of the target's neighbors. Furthermore, the vehicle's systems, although of different constructors, are expected to have at least the same level of security, which must be high and unbreakable within the vehicle's lifetime, using the recent technology.

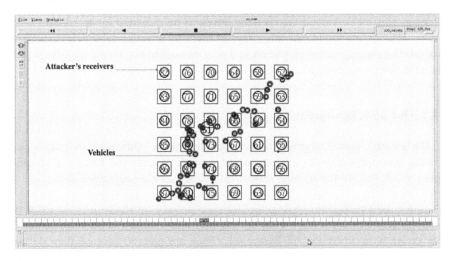

Figure 4.2. *Attacker's receivers' dispositions to cover the observed area. For a color version of this figure, see www.iste.co.uk/benarous/vehicular.zip*

Although the internal attacker is favored in studying the robustness of the security solution requiring active attacks, they are rarely used in the case of passive tracking, because of their cost, difficulty and easy detection. If the attacker is ready to pour that much cost on tracking, it would have been smarter, wiser and more economic to just install a small GPS tracker on the target vehicle. This method is out of our scope of research which aims to reduce and prevent the traceability of the vehicle by its cyber activity. Therefore, in the rest of the book, we continue our discussion about the external GPA which executes one or more of the following attacks.

– *Semantic linking attack* (Boualouache 2016)

In this attack, the external GPA uses the intercepted beacons to form a knowledge-base about the road, the parsed vehicles, their disposition and their speed. The GPA uses the acquired knowledge to predict the vehicle's future positions. When the vehicle updates its identifier, also known as pseudonym, the GPA matches the predicted position with the real emitted positions to link the old pseudonym with the new one. This linking allows it to continue tracking the vehicle, even when it is using a new freshly updated pseudonym. Figure 4.3 illustrates this attack, where A, B, C and D are neighbor vehicles having V_A, V_B, V_C and V_D as their pseudonyms respectively. P_A, P_B, P_C and P_D are their current positions respectively. Each vehicle sends beacons containing their position and pseudonyms. To facilitate the reading, we consider P as a vector containing the position coordinates, the speed and direction. After the vehicles update their pseudonyms, they continue to send beacons with these new pseudonyms. We denote below the emitted beacon before and after the change of pseudonyms:

– **Before** the **change**: Beacon (V_A, P_A), Beacon (V_B, P_B), Beacon (V_C, P_C), Beacon (V_D, P_D).

– **After** the **change**: Beacon ($V_{A'}$, $P_{A'}$), Beacon ($V_{B'}$, $P_{B'}$), Beacon ($V_{C'}$, $P_{C'}$), Beacon ($V_{D'}$, $P_{D'}$).

The GPA matches the real locations $P_{A'}$, $P_{B'}$, $P_{C'}$ and $P_{D'}$ with the predicted location from P_A, P_B, P_C, and P_D to conclude that: V_A and $V_{A'}$ belong to the same vehicle "A". Similarly, V_B, $V_{B'}$ belong to "B", V_C and $V_{C'}$ belong to "C", V_D and $V_{D'}$ belong to vehicle "D".

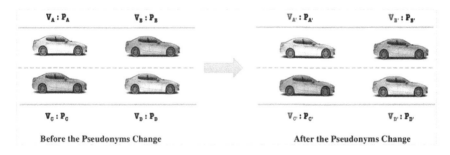

Figure 4.3. *Semantic linking attack. For a color version of this figure, see www.iste.co.uk/benarous/vehicular.zip*

– **Syntactic linking attack** (Boualouache 2016)

We continue to use the same notions. In this attack, the attacker who is external global passive uses the knowledge they accumulated about the road and the vehicle's dispositions to learn which vehicles changed their pseudonyms and which vehicles did not. This is an effective linking attack against non-cooperative-based change strategies. Figure 4.4 illustrates the syntactic attack, wherein only vehicle A changes its pseudonym from V_A to $V_{A'}$, while vehicles B, C and D did not. Therefore, the attacker compares the beacons before and after the change to conclude that A is the only vehicle that did the change and continues tracking it, noting that the possibility that $V_{A'}$ belongs to a new vehicle is neglected because it is impossible for a vehicle to appear at that position in tenth seconds between the beacons.

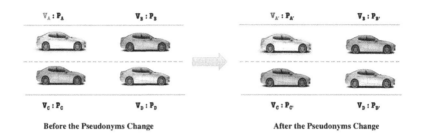

Figure 4.4. *Syntactic linking attack. For a color version of this figure, see www.iste.co.uk/benarous/vehicular.zip*

– *Observation mapping attack* (Kang et al. 2016)

The previously explained attacks rely on the beacon's interception because these heartbeat messages are periodical, accurate and contain sensitive clear data. In this attack and the next one, we consider linking the vehicle by both its safety messages and cloud-based service messages. We used these attacks to evaluate privacy-preserving schemes in the Internet of vehicles and vehicular clouds, etc. Besides its pseudonyms, the vehicle has another unique identifier that it uses in the cloud, which is the virtual machine identifier (VMID). It is the identifier of the customized space to serve the vehicle's queries in the cloud, which is also changed to avoid linking. The attacker in this attack and the next one intercepts both the beacons and the service messages. We are interested in location-based service messages as these are used to track the vehicle. In this attack, the GPA links the pseudonym in the beacon with the VMID in the service message by matching the location information in the beacon with the location in the service message. Figure 4.5 illustrates this attack, where V_A is the pseudonym of vehicle "A", VM_A is its VMID and P_A is its position. The attacker observes the vehicle activity in three time slots where it continuously changes its pseudonym but keeps using the same VMID:

– At t1, the vehicle sends these messages, BCN (V_A, P_A) and LBS (VM_A, P_A) where BCN is the beacon and LBS is the location-based service message.

– At t2, the vehicle sends BCN ($V_{A'}$, $P_{A'}$) and LBS (VM_A, $P_{A'}$).

– At t3, BCN ($V_{A''}$, $P_{A''}$) and LBS (VM_A, $P_{A''}$).

The attacker then concludes that V_A, $V_{A'}$, $V_{A''}$ and VMA belong to the same vehicle "A". This means that regardless of how many times the vehicle changes its pseudonym, they are linked as long as it continues using LBS with the same VMID. The same is correct if the vehicle changes its VMIDs while using the same pseudonym. The VMIDs are linked causing continuous tracking of the vehicle.

Figure 4.5. *Observation mapping linking attack. For a color version of this figure, see www.iste.co.uk/benarous/vehicular.zip*

– *Linking mapping attack* (Kang et al. 2016)

We follow the same notation as before. However, this attack links the VMID and pseudonym, even when they are both changed, as illustrated in Figure 4.6. The attacker who is always eavesdropping exchanged messages, intercepts the messages at each slot and builds their knowledge accumulatively.

– At t_1, the vehicle sends messages BCN (V_A, P_A) and LBS (VM_A, P_A). The attacker intercepting these messages matches the location from both messages and concludes that V_A and VM_A belong to the same vehicle.

– At t_2, the vehicle sends BCN ($V_{A'}$, $P_{A'}$) and LBS (VM_A, $P_{A'}$). Similarly, they conclude that $V_{A'}$ and VM_A belong to the same vehicle.

– At t_3, upon the reception of BCN ($V_{A'}$, $P_{A''}$) and LBS ($VM_{A'}$, $P_{A''}$), the attacker concludes that $V_{A'}$ and $VM_{A'}$ belong to the same vehicle. The attacker's global knowledge is that V_A, $V_{A'}$, VM_A, $VM_{A'}$ belong to the same vehicle. Thus, during the three observation periods, and even though the vehicle changes both of its identifiers (pseudonym, VMID), it was still vulnerable to this attack due to the fact that this change was asynchronous.

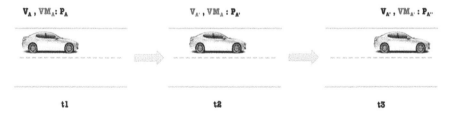

Figure 4.6. *Linking mapping attack. For a color version of this figure, see www.iste.co.uk/benarous/vehicular.zip*

4.5. Conclusion

In this chapter, we explained the security objectives and properties in vehicular networks, listed the major security issues, and defined the attacker, their aims and means. We specified our attacker models and justified our choice. We also highlighted why other models are inappropriate for our research problem, which is to reduce and eliminate vehicle tracking by its cyber activity. Tracking is possible if the attacker can first intercept its exchanged messages like beacons, which contain its public key (identity) and real-time position, heading and velocity. If the vehicle uses the same public key all the time, it can be tracked and eventually its identity is exposed if the attack is followed by social engineering. For example, if the vehicle is always parked at point A, which is a house, at 6 pm, it is highly possible that the owner of the house is the owner of the vehicle. The researcher proposed using temporal public keys known as pseudonyms to reduce tracking. However, if the update of these pseudonyms upon their expiry is within unfavorable context, the attacker may still be able to link the old expired pseudonym with the new freshly updated one. Therefore, they can continue tracking the vehicle. Thus, the change must be done in a way that reduces tracking by eliminating linking attacks. This gave birth to pseudonym change strategies. To study the robustness of these schemes, we used the attacker model defined in this chapter, which executes one or more of previously mentioned linking attacks.

In the next chapter, we explain our contributions in preserving both location and identity privacy when actively using vehicular network services and authenticating the vehicle to authorities, third party service provider or other vehicles. We also illustrate how our proposed solutions thwart linking attacks (for location privacy), and are resilient to security attacks and privacy violation attacks (for identity privacy).

5

Privacy-preserving Authentication in Cloud-enabled Vehicle Data Named Networks (CVDNN) for Resources Sharing

5.1. Introduction

The vehicular networks were exploited to extend the cloud to the roads. The users explore the unused capacities of their vehicles to form dynamic local clouds and provide each other with services such as computation, storage, sensing, video streaming, etc. There are many architectures and classifications proposed in the literature, such as central and local clouds, infrastructure and infrastructure-less cloud, hybrid clouds, vehicles as clouds, vehicles using clouds and vehicles with clouds. The cloud concept relies on virtualization. Due to the mobility of the vehicle, the virtual machine follows it by using the process of live migration (Yu et al. 2013) between nodes. In this chapter, we design a dynamic formation of infrastructure-less vehicular clouds (VC). It is created and maintained solely by road vehicles which join, use and/or provide services to each other without fearing their privacy being risked or leaked. It also ensures accountability and legal responsibility in case of abuse. We denote these networks as Cloud-enabled Vehicle Data Named Networks or CVDNN.

Being the evolution of the vehicular networks, the CVDNN inherits its characteristics and issues. Among them is privacy. It has been the subject of research for many researchers in the last 15 years. In the literature, there was a consensus on the use of pseudonyms to protect identity privacy and to change them using effective strategies to prevent tracking and violation of location privacy. The pseudonyms are used to authenticate safety messages, and ensure the non-repudiation and revocability of misbehaving nodes to assure the correct functionality of the network. They are also used to encrypt messages. We already explained the various pseudonym changing strategies and authentication techniques in vehicular networks in Chapter 2.

In CVDNN, privacy is ensured by mutual authentication using anonymous certificates between the vehicle managing the cloud and the joining members, and also when providing and/or using services which are addressed by their name and geo-location. We explain how the temporal identities of the vehicle members of the cloud are changed securely and synchronously to preserve privacy, alongside the use of location obfuscation to protect location privacy. The emitted location is not the coordinates of the exact position, but an area coordinate where the vehicle is situated.

With the proposed solution, linkability is avoided (linkability of pseudonyms, linkability by location, by identity, by credentials, by IP and MAC addresses). Although our main focus of the chapter is the authentication phase, which highly risks the vehicle's owner's privacy if not done anonymously, we also hint at the identifier change strategy, how they are updated and the impact of the use of this strategy. The same change strategy is further explained with simulation in Chapter 8, on cloud-enabled Internet of vehicles.

This chapter explains background concepts, such as VC and vehicular named data networks. It also describes the Cloud-enabled Vehicle Data Named system. Moreover, it explains the anonymous authentication process and privacy preservation scheme along with its analysis.

5.2. Background

In this section, we explain the key background concepts behind Cloud-enabled Vehicle Data Named Networks, starting by explaining the VC concept. Then, we move on to the description of our system model.

5.2.1. *Vehicular clouds*

We already explained the VC concept and that it is the extension of conventional clouds to road edges in Chapter 1. In this chapter, we dig deeper into the details of its different types and models. Then, we propose new paradigm that combines the VC with data named networks, what we denoted as Cloud-enabled Vehicle Data Named Networks or CVDNN. Vehicular clouds (VC) are the combination of two paradigms, which are the Vehicular Ad hoc Network (VANET) and cloud computing. In the literature, many VC architectures were proposed; we classify them as follows:

– *RSU-based clouds*: also known as infrastructure-based clouds. They are formed by RSUs connected to data servers; they are accessed and used by vehicles (see Figure 5.1(A)).

– *Vehicular cloud with infrastructure*: this type of cloud relies on infrastructure usage, which connects the road-side units, cloud server and cloud manager. The vehicles may use or provide collected data and also put their resources into the cloud. It could also be connected to the central cloud via the Internet. (see Figure 5.1(B)).

– *Vehicle using clouds*: these are conventional clouds which are accessed via Internet cellular service providers, such as: 3G, 4G, 5G, etc. (see Figure 5.1(C)).

– *Vehicles as clouds*: herein, the vehicles form the cloud by sharing and using each other's resources without the need of infrastructure. The vehicles may either be static, when they are parked or in a service station, or they can be moving on roads. Therefore, the vehicles may consecutively form static clouds, which are steadier as the vehicles are static and the communication is more stable. They can also form dynamic on-road clouds with mobile vehicles. The vehicles as clouds are local clouds because shared resources and data have local relevance unless combined by one of the above clouds (see Figure 5.1(D)).

– *Hybrid vehicular clouds*: this one combines the above types. The vehicle uses the central cloud through the Internet via cellular networks such as 3G, 4G, 5G or via the infrastructure (RSU) connected to Internet servers. Furthermore, a vehicle may create or join both local infrastructure-based and infrastructure-less clouds when it is static or mobile on roads (see Figure 5.1(E)).

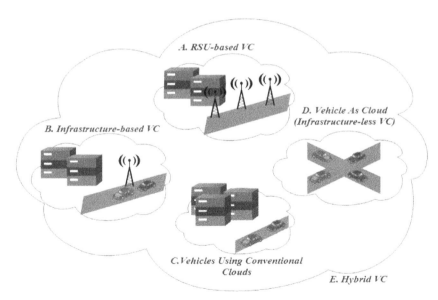

Figure 5.1. *Vehicular cloud types. For a color version of this figure, see www.iste.co.uk/benarous/vehicular.zip*

5.2.2. *Vehicular data named networks*

In this type of network, the packet routing is data-related and not address-based, i.e. the focus is more on its content than on its provider. Therefore, there are two types of nodes, the content provider and the content requester who is interested in that content.

5.3. System description

In the proposed CVDNN, the vehicles unify their resources while on roads to handle difficult computations, sense wider regions, store data or obtain a stable service. This is known as "vehicle as cloud". Note that the road vehicles in the same geographical space are potentially interested in the road data and services of that area. Thus, they have a similar interest because the data has a local relevance, for example, within a radius r and time span t; a user is more likely interested in road information related to geographical zone they are in, the services provided, the road conditions, etc. Moreover, since the services are known by their names or identifiers, it would be easier to search it, and faster to provide it. Due to the fact that the providing vehicles are various, the probability of finding a service providing vehicle in the requester vicinity is higher. Therefore, in CVDNN, the service name and geographical location are used to route packets within the local VC instead of conventional IP addresses, because the data and service are likely to have a local relevance and validity time, and are then discarded after their expiry. If the on-demand services have global relevance, the user does not discard the data. Instead, they would save it by uploading it to their central cloud via Internet using cellular networks (3G, 4G or 5G), when they cross an infrastructure (RSU) connected to the Internet, or use another vehicle's Internet as service. Since the migration of the local cloud vehicle's virtual machine and its state to the central cloud is done via the Internet, the IP-based routing and addressing is used instead of content-based addressing. We emphasize that this migration is done through secure communication to preserve the confidentiality of the data and protect privacy. The authentication to the central cloud managed by the trusted authority or its subsidiaries is done anonymously, as explained in section 5.5.

5.4. Forming cloud-enabled vehicle data named networks

In this section, we explain how the infrastructure-less VC is formed and how the data is routed (see Figures 5.3 and 5.4). The description of the privacy preservation authentication method is discussed in the next section.

The vehicle that wishes to participate in a VC, either by providing its services or resources, waits to receive VC advertisements for the already existing clouds. Upon the reception of an announcement, the vehicle first checks the announcer authenticity. Then, it sends a request to join to the vehicle managing the cloud V_{MC}. When the V_{MC} receives such a request, it authenticates the requester. If this vehicle is willing to provide its resources and/or services, the V_{MC} sorts, manages and registers this data to costume the vehicle's resources and/or service to serve future requesters. If the vehicle requesting to join the VC is a service requester, the V_{MC} costumes a virtual machine (VM) to serve its queries. The VM may exist in the vehicle, providing the service at a specific location, or in various provider vehicles in adjacent locations. The communication between the provider and the requester is secure. The V_{MC} plays the role of a proxy at the beginning to establish a secure session between the vehicles. Note that the data/service with this cloud is routed based on its name and time–location relevance.

If no in-vicinity cloud exists and the vehicle receives no announcement, it announces itself as a V_{MC} and advertises its offered and needed resources and services to its neighbors. Vehicles interested in the received offers check the authenticity of the announcing vehicle. Then, they send their joining replies containing their offers, as well as their needs of resources and/or services. Upon successful authentication, the vehicles form the cloud and securely provide/use its services.

The V_{MC} quits the cloud if the vehicle's service ends; when it goes out of range of the rest of the members or when the cloud has no active members. Before it does, it forwards the cloud state and sessions to a newly elected V_{MC}. If the cloud services are no longer used or no members exist, the cloud is deleted. Note that users interested in saving their used services/data may migrate their local virtual machine to the central cloud.

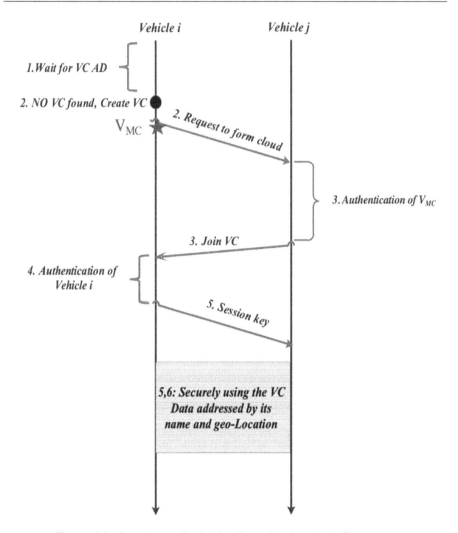

Figure 5.2. *Creating and/or joining the vehicular cloud. For a color version of this figure, see www.iste.co.uk/benarous/vehicular.zip*

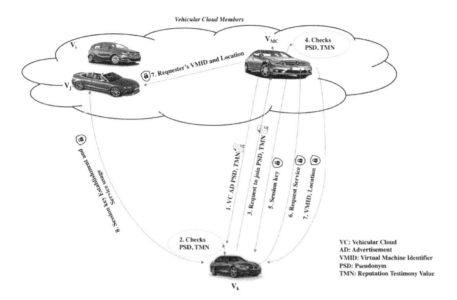

Figure 5.3. *Illustration of cloud-enabled vehicular data named network joining and service usage process. For a color version of this figure, see www.iste.co.uk/benarous/vehicular.zip*

5.5. Migrating the local cloud virtual machine to the central cloud

To migrate the local virtual machine to the central cloud, the vehicle user should authenticate the central cloud by themselves first. The user may use their credentials to log into the cloud account; then, the vehicle updates the central cloud with the local cloud data and service status. Note that all of these communications are secured with encryption to ensure confidentiality and data privacy. Once the update is done, the VM is liberated. Note that the local VM may either be used to update the central VM, merge with it or directly import it (as a new VM or overwriting the existing one) depending on the user's choices and needs.

5.6. Privacy and authentication when using/providing CVDNN services

We previously explained how the vehicle may create or join the VC where both the requester and provider need to check the authenticity of each other implicitly and indirectly. The authentication is mutually done between the vehicle managing the clouds (V_{MC}) and the joining members. Once the V_{MC} authenticates and trusts the joining vehicles either as providers or requesters, the trust is implicitly established by transitivity between the vehicles. As a matter of fact, the authentication is one of the essential and initial steps in creating, maintaining and using secure clouds. However, since it usually requires the use of credentials, it threatens the privacy of VC users in general and the CVDNN in particular. This is due to two reasons: the first is that the credentials may be linked with the pseudonyms and location. Thus, their repetitive usage may lead to the vehicle's tracking. The second is that the authentication is preceded by the registration phase, where the vehicle provides its user's identity or long-term certified public key to the V_{MC}. Therefore, the vehicle exposes itself to the risk of privacy in case this V_{MC} decides to secretly and undetectably trade this data with other interested parties. To avoid risking privacy while achieving the authentication, we propose the use of anonymous certificates signed by the trusted authority (TA). Also, a reputation testimony that is generated by the TA and continuously updated by the vehicle's testimonies about each other's behaviors while using the on-road VC can be used.

As highlighted above, the authentication should be mutual between the vehicle managing the cloud and the vehicles providing/requesting services. The V_{MC} would not accept requests from a revoked (blacklisted) vehicle with a bad reputation or tagged as malicious. Similarly, the vehicles would not join a cloud created or maintained by a malicious blacklisted node with a bad reputation.

NOTE.– The vehicle managing the cloud may be a service provider or user, or both.

5.6.1. *The authentication process*

Before explaining the authentication process, we first clarify the notations used and their indications. V_{MC} is the vehicle managing the cloud. V_j is a vehicle providing or using the cloud's service. **M** represents the messages exchanged, while "→" is the sending operator; on its left is the source and on its right is the destination. The authentication phase starts from checking the authenticity of the V_{MC} announcing the existence of the VC and its provided/needed services and resources. The V_{MC} first sends **M1** as denoted below, containing the list of services, an invitation to join, the certified pseudonym of the vehicle and its reputation. These last two fields are essential to anonymously authenticate the V_{MC} and ensure accountability. The message also contains the location of the vehicle, which is used along with the service name in data routing within the CVDNN:

$- V_{MC} \rightarrow V_j;$

M1: {Broadcasts the list of provided services, an invitation to join, pseudonym, location, anonymous certificate (of the pseudonym) and the reputation testimony}

When V_j receives **M1**, it checks the pseudonym certificate validity. Then, it verifies that the pseudonym is not revoked, i.e. not found in freshly updated CRL (Certificate Revocation List). Lastly, it examines if the reputation testimony value is higher than the threshold required. If all of the above-mentioned tests end positively, this means that the V_{MC} is not revoked, its in-use pseudonym is still fresh and its reputation is good. Then, the user of vehicle V_j, if interested to use/provide this cloud services, requests to join it by sending the message **M2** to V_{MC}; **M2** content is denoted below. It mainly contains the reputation value of the vehicle along with the certified pseudonym which is used to authenticate this vehicle:

$- V_j \rightarrow V_{MC}$;

M2: {Request to join, pseudonym, location, anonymous certificate (of the pseudonym) and the reputation testimony (signed by the TA and encrypted by the vehicle's private key corresponding to the pseudonym in-use)}

When V_{MC} receives **M2**, it checks that the pseudonym certificate is valid, then that the pseudonym is not in the CRL (not revoked). Lastly, it confirms that the reputation value surpasses the minimum acceptable threshold. If all of these conditions are satisfied, then the vehicle's request to join the VC is accepted. V_{MC} generates the message **M3** including a session key and sends it to V_j. The session key is generated from: the location of V_{MC} and V_j, pseudonyms and a random value to ensure its uniqueness. Moreover, **M3** is encrypted using the private key of V_{MC} and the public key of V_j (pseudonym). **M3** is denoted below:

$- V_{MC} \rightarrow V_j$;

M3: {session key KS}

Upon receiving **M3**, V_j starts the secure communication with V_{MC}. It specifies in message **M4** the requested service, the provided service or the resources that it is willing to share. We emphasize that these communications are secured by symmetric encryption using the secretly shared session key KS. **M4** is denoted below:

$- V_j \rightarrow V_{MC}$;

M4: {Service-name-requested and/or available-resources-shared, location} KS

After receiving **M4**, V_{MC} virtualizes the resources contained in **M4**. If V_j is a service provider, it customizes a virtual machine to handle the requested service. If V_j is a service requester, the identifier of this virtual machine or VMID and its location is then securely forwarded to V_j in message **M5** denoted below:

$- V_{MC} \rightarrow V_j$

M5: {VMID, Location} KS.

It is noteworthy that the location field never points to an exact location where the vehicle is, but to a slightly larger location covered by the vehicle's receiver's range, to ensure that the vehicle gets the message, but location privacy is preserved, in case the attacker tries to track the vehicle by its cloud activity and by matching it with its safety beaconing. Also, when the vehicle requested service or resource is satisfied by multiple adjacent vehicles, the location field points to a larger area containing all of these vehicles. Similarly, the location in the V_{MC} messages is not the exact coordinates of the vehicle's position, but of an area it is within and can cover. This way, the location privacy of the service provider, user and the vehicle managing the cloud is preserved.

The V_{MC} sends the requesting vehicle, its VMID and the location of the service provider; the requester and the provider denoted as V_j and V_k respectively generate a session key to continue a secure communication while using the VC services. This measure protects the user's confidentiality from an external eavesdropper, neighbor vehicles and even the vehicle managing the cloud. If the user is requesting a temporal storage service or Internet access from the providing vehicle, they may even want to encrypt their data using their pseudonym (public key) to prevent the vehicle providing the serving from preying on it.

5.6.2. *The reputation testimony*

In the previous section, we mentioned the vehicle's reputation as an essential metric in mutually authenticating the vehicles creating and joining the cloud. However, we did not mention how it is calculated or what it means. In this section, we shed more light on it and explain how it is calculated.

The reputation and trust-based solutions in VANET have been used to complement the cryptography solutions questing security and resiliency against the insider attacker model, especially when the attacker is a dishonest vehicle injecting malicious or falsified data (Kerrache et al. 2016).

In the proposed CVDNN, the reputation is a value initially assigned by the trusted authority to the vehicles; it is signed by its private key to reassure other vehicles of its integrity and authenticity. This value is updated either by increasing it or decreasing it depending on the vehicle's behavior while using the VC services. This behavior is reported by other adjacent vehicles playing the role of witnesses, testifying about the behavior of other vehicles and rating the quality of the provided service. Each vehicle uploads its testimonies about other vehicles it has interacted with, to provide them with or use their services when it crosses an RSU or connects to the Internet.

Upon the reception of testimonies, the TA calculates a fresh new reputation value and forwards it back to the corresponding vehicles. The vehicle uses the freshly received reputation which has a validity time span.

Note that the vehicle testifying about other vehicles must send their pseudonyms from the interaction and their testimony value at the time. The reporting vehicle must sign the reputation testimony using its valid pseudonym. This is to ensure the integrity of the report, and to hold the vehicle accountable for its testimonies and prevent it from falsifying testimonies.

By default, we initialize the state vehicles (police, ambulance, gendarmerie and military) reputation value to one. For other vehicles, we choose the average between 0 and 1 (0.5). Note that 0 indicates that the vehicle is not trusted and malicious and 1 means that it is fully trusted because it is authoritarian. Assigning an average value to vehicles means we are not biased and do not hold any prejudice about the vehicles being on either side (good or bad). This value is changed with the vehicle's continuous feedback. It varies from 0 to 1. It is increased if good testimonies are sent and decreased otherwise. The vehicle is blacklisted (revoked) if its reputation reaches 0. The reputation value update is done by using the formulas below:

$$Reputation = \varphi(ORV) + (1 - \varphi)(NRV). 0 \leq \varphi \leq 1$$

where ORV is the old reputation value and NRV is the new reputation value, and φ can be configured depending on the importance we give to the old value (history).

NRV is calculated based on the received testimonies (let TMN be the testimony). NRV is the mean of testimonies of vehicles i, $\forall$ i.

$$NRV = \frac{\sum_{\forall i} TMN_i}{\sum i}$$

Note that TNM_i is calculated by vehicle$_i$ based on service continuity (SC), data reliability (DRL), selfishness (SF), cooperation in the VC (COO) and the use of certified pseudonyms (CPS):

$$TMN_i = ORV_i*(\alpha*SC + \beta*DRL + \gamma*SF + \delta*COO + \theta*CPS)$$

Where: $\alpha + \beta + \gamma + \delta + \theta = 1;$ $SC = \{0,1\};$ $DRL = \{0,1\};$
$SF = \{0,1\}, COO = \{0,1\}; CPS = \{0,1\}$

And $\{0 \le \alpha \le 1; 0 \le \beta \le 1; 0 \le \gamma \le 1; 0 \le \delta \le 1; 0 \le \theta \le 1\}$

Further parameters may be added in the future, if the cloud services are fee-charged, or the resources are rented. Then, the metrics about the payment/rental are added as well.

5.7. The privacy in CVDNN

Our main focus is on how to ensure the privacy of the vehicle while creating, using and providing the CVDNN services by proposing an anonymous mutual authentication scheme protecting identity privacy. Nevertheless, since we proposed our own CVDNN, and continue to discuss how to avoid linkability caused by the use of the same pseudonym for a long period, or if it is changed inappropriately.

The linkability exposes the user's location and allows their on-road tracking. If linked with their activity on CVDNN, it becomes even more threatening, because not only is their location at risk, but also their shared data. This leads to the leakage of their preferences, liking, routines, etc.

We have explained that the VC is formed by cooperative vehicles and that the V_{MC} shares a session key with each member. Thus, the V_{MC} is able to securely synchronize with the members to update their pseudonyms and VMID at the same time. This confuses the attacker as the change happens simultaneously. Upon the reception of the V_{MC} message, each vehicle replies to this message to V_{MC} by providing its current and predictable future locations (for the next T period of time) in an encrypted message. The V_{MC} updates the vehicles of the cloud about the future location of their VMs, as well as the VMID names. When the V_{MC} finishes the synchronization task, every vehicle is made aware of where its corresponding VM will be and its new name (new VMID). Every vehicle ceases broadcasting beacons and halts service messages for T period of time (messages are cached at each node). After T period of time, every vehicle starts broadcasting beacons with new pseudonyms for safety beacons, and continues to use the cloud service with new VMIDs, without redoing the authentication, interrupting or delaying the service.

We remind the reader that the locations in cloud service messages are not accurate like in safety beacons. This is deliberately done to prevent matching by location and increase the robustness of the above-explained scheme. The cloud service messages reach the area the vehicle is in. Even if the eavesdropper in that area intercepts the message, they are unable to read it. Only the session key holders which are the vehicles originating and expecting the message may read it.

5.8. Discussion and analysis

We have explained the privacy-preserving authentication when joining the cloud, and the privacy preservation scheme when using the cloud. In this section, we analyze our proposal using the BAN logic and then discuss how the security measure token prevents security and privacy attacks.

5.8.1. *The privacy when joining the VC*

The authentication is fundamental when forming the cloud to guarantee the correct functionality and ensure liability and accountability. It also allows the TA to revoke misbehaving nodes. However, it may disclose certain required information about the user, potentially threatening their privacy.

To preserve privacy while joining the CVDNN (providing/using a service), we suggested the use of anonymous certificates instead of permanent certificates or credentials. The proposed method preserves identity privacy. In this section, we prove that the proposed anonymous authentication achieves the aims served by conventional authentication methods. To do so, we use Burrows, Abadi and Needham logic, which is commonly used to analyze the correctness of authentication protocols (Liu et al. 2017). Below, we first explain the notation used and its meaning. Then, we give the idealized version of the authentication messages explained in section 5.6.1 using BAN idealization rules. Note that only the first three messages are used since the fourth one is sent once a successful authentication is done. We continue by underlying the mutual authentication objectives. In our case, the mutual authentication is between the vehicle requesting to join and the vehicle managing the cloud, where they are required to both trust each other. Lastly, the demonstration is explained. It uses the assumption of the system and BAN postulates to check that the underline objectives are reached and achieved from the sequence of exchanged messages.

Notation

– P_{MC}, P_J and P_{TA} are the public keys of vehicles MC, J and trusted authority, and P_{MC}^{-1}, P_J^{-1}, P_{TA}^{-1} are their corresponding private keys

– $SIG_{P_{TA}^{-1}}(x)$ *is the signing message x using P_{TA}^{-1}*

– KS *is the Session Key*

– RPT *is the Reputation Value*

Messages (simplified and idealized following the BAN logic)

– M1. $V_{MC} \rightarrow V_J$: P_{MC}, $SIG_{P_{TA}^{-1}}(P_{MC})$, $\{RPT_{MC}, SIG_{P_{TA}^{-1}}(RPT_{MC})\}$ P_{MC}^{-1}.

– M2. $V_J \rightarrow V_{MC}$: P_J, $SIG_{P_{TA}^{-1}}(P_J)$, $\{RPT_J, SIG_{P_{TA}^{-1}}(RPT_J)\}$ P_J^{-1}.

– M3. $V_{MC} \rightarrow V_J$: $\{\{KS\}_{P_{MC}^{-1}}\}$ P_J.

Assumptions

– J believes TA   ... (1)

– MC believes TA   ... (2)

– MC believes (TA controls $MC \overset{P_J^{-1}}{\leftrightarrow} J$)   ... (3)

– MC believes (TA controls $MC \overset{P_J}{\leftrightarrow} J$)   ... (4)

– J believes (TA controls $MC \overset{P_{MC}^{-1}}{\longleftrightarrow} J$)   ... (5)

– J believes (TA controls $MC \overset{P_{MC}}{\longleftrightarrow} J$)   ... (6)

– MC believes ($\overset{P_{TA}}{\longrightarrow} TA$)   ... (7)

– J believes ($\overset{P_{TA}}{\longrightarrow} TA$)   ... (8)

Objectives

– MC believes ($\overset{P_j}{\rightarrow} J$)

– J believes ($\overset{P_{MC}}{\longrightarrow} MC$)

– MC believes J believes $MC \overset{KS}{\leftrightarrow} J$

– J believes MC believes $MC \overset{KS}{\leftrightarrow} J$

Demonstration

Upon receiving M1, Vehicle J deducts the following:

1) J sees P_{MC}, $SIG_{P_{TA}^{-1}}(P_{MC})$, $\{RPT_{MC}, SIG_{P_{TA}^{-1}}(RPT_{MC})\}$ P_{MC}^{-1} .... *(Principal 4 of BAN Logic Postulates)*

2) J sees P_{MC} .... *(Principal 4 of BAN Logic Postulates)*

3) J believes (TA said $\xrightarrow{P_{MC}} MC$) .... *(from the assumptions 1, 5, 6 and 8, Principal 1 and 3 of BAN Logic Postulates)*

4) J sees RPT_{MC} ... *(Principal 4 of BAN Logic Postulates, assumption 8 and first deduction)*

5) J believes (TA said $\xrightarrow{P_{MC}} RPT_{MC}$) .... *(using assumption 8 and 3 of BAN Logic Postulates)*

6) J believes ($\xrightarrow{P_{MC}} MC$) ... *(using the assumptions, above deductions and Principal 3: 'jurisdiction' of BAN Logic)*

Upon receiving M2, Vehicle MC deducts the following: (demonstrated using the same method as above)

1) MC sees P_J, $SIG_{P_{TA}^{-1}}(P_J)$, $\{RPT_J, SIG_{P_{TA}^{-1}}(RPT_J)\}$ P_J^{-1}.

2) MC sees P_J

3) MC believes (TA said $\xrightarrow{P_J} J$) .... *(from the assumptions 2, 3, 4 and 7)*

4) MC sees RPT_J

5) MC believes (TA said $\xrightarrow{P_J} RPT_J$)

6) MC believes ($\xrightarrow{P_J} J$)

Upon receiving M3, Vehicle J deducts the following:

1) J sees $\{KS\}$ P_{MC}^{-1} .... *(from assumption 6)*

2) J sees $\{KS\}$ ... *(from assumption 8)*

3) J believes (MC said $MC \xleftrightarrow{KS} J$) ... *(using the assumptions, above deductions and Principal 3: 'jurisdiction' of BAN Logic)*

4) J believes $MC \overset{KS}{\leftrightarrow} J$ *(using the assumptions, above deductions and Principal 3: 'jurisdiction' of BAN Logic)*

5) J believes MC believes $MC \overset{KS}{\leftrightarrow} J$ *(using the assumptions, above deductions and Principal 3: 'jurisdiction' of BAN Logic)*

6) MC believes J believes $MC \overset{KS}{\leftrightarrow} J$ *(using the assumptions, above deductions and Principal 3: 'jurisdiction' of BAN Logic)*

5.8.2. *Privacy while using the VC*

The synchronous and simultaneous update of pseudonyms and VMIDs within the group of VC members, the additional usage of the silent period T and the extended location instead of exact coordinates create an infrastructure-less robust mix-zone. The initial communication within this zone is encrypted and then it is followed by the silence. The combination of taken measures makes the update successfully undetected and the service continued without re-authentication or packet loss. Consecutively, both the identity and location privacy are preserved.

Moreover, the CVDNN inherits the named data network (NDN) data forwarding and requesting policy. It relies on service name and geo-location to demand and obtain packets and services. This further increases privacy as the same service name in a geo-location may be requested by multiple interested vehicles, especially if it is related to a popular content or event. The popularity of content further confuses the attacker, reducing the linkability by service and content. Even distinguishing and tracking the requester or provider becomes harder because anyone who has the content can provide it, and also because we are not using IP and MAC addresses, except when the VM is migrated to the central cloud via the Internet. We prevent tracking by IP and MAC in local clouds.

5.9. Conclusion

In this chapter, we presented Cloud-enabled Vehicular Data Named Networks (CVDNN). They are dynamically formed on roads by vehicles willing to unify their resources to provide each other with various services. We explained the anonymous reputation-based privacy-preserving authentication method used to preserve privacy, while ensuring the correct functionality and accountability. The formed VC are distributed and infrastructure-less, allowing the vehicles to use cloud services that are beyond their own singular capability, such as: sensing, calculating, storage, or

Internet access, etc., even in rural areas where the infrastructure coverage may not be available and access to the conventional cloud becomes hard, if not impossible.

The solution preserves both the identity in the authentication phase and the location of the vehicles by using extended location instead of accurate coordinates. Furthermore, the linkability of the identifier used while exploring cloud services is avoided by their synchronized simultaneous update with vehicle cloud members after applying silence. The attacker cannot track the vehicles that create infrastructure-less mixes when updating their identifiers. They also cannot read the service messages exchanged between the cloud vehicles because they are secured with the session key.

6

Privacy-preserving Authentication Scheme for On-road On-demand Refilling of Pseudonym in VANET

6.1. Introduction

In Chapter 2, we highlighted the importance of authentication, which is fundamental for distinguishing authorized users of a system or a network. Most of these authentication systems rely on credentials, identity, certified keys, tokens or biometric prints to identify their users. The authentication ensures the security from external attackers and the traceability of internal users. However, it risks the user's privacy, either deliberately when the system owner exchanges personal data for profit, or unintentionally when the system is hacked externally.

Privacy has been topping the priority of users and the legislation system. The annual scandals related to privacy violation in the cyber world alone are enough to turn the public opinion against the violators and pressure the legislative system to make privacy laws stricter. The impact of privacy violation in vehicular networks is more dangerous due to its direct relation to the safety of drivers. Nevertheless, it is at higher risk in these networks because the vehicles communicate with each other through Vehicle-to-Vehicle (V2V) and with infrastructure through Vehicle-to-Infrastructure (V2I) via wireless Dedicated Short-Range Communications (DSRC) (Bitam et al. 2015; Benaissa et al. 2017) to exchange sensed data and ensure safety applications (Dressler et al. 2018), for which, the users need to continuously and timely broadcast their identity, location, speed and direction.

The identities in vehicular networks are often called pseudonyms, which are pairs of life timed geo-limited public and private keys. Their usage and frequent update strategies have two aims: the first is to protect identity privacy (anonymity), and the second is to preserve location privacy (untraceability) from tracking. Anonymity and untraceability are two of the most desired characteristics from the vehicular network.

Concerning pseudonym usage, which is the key element in protecting the privacy in the vehicular networks, the majority of research works in the literature concentrated on its change and revoke strategies. They initially assume that the vehicles are preloaded with them (Emara 2016). However, even though that is the case, due to storage limits, the preloaded pool of pseudonyms will be consumed and expire sooner or later. This leads to the axial problem of how the pseudonyms are refilled in that case. Two hypothesizes are possible, either the periodical physical presence of the vehicle at the authority's facilities to flash it with a new pool, or, to save the time, effort and the cost of repetitive trips, refilling the pseudonyms pool on-road on-demand (Ma et al. 2008). Eckhoff et al. (2011) proposed that vehicles with a similar state should exchange their pseudonyms with each other. This method does avoid the repetitive refilling of pseudonyms and their related storage issues. However, it violates the non-repudiation requirement allowing multiple pseudonym usage, potentially causing a Sybil attack. Moreover, it risks message confidentiality as the vehicles may read each other's encrypted messages when exchanging keys.

In this chapter, we introduce a privacy-preserving on-road on-demand pseudonym refilling method. To obtain pseudonyms from an authority, the vehicle first needs to authenticate itself successfully to it. This is to help the authority record the pseudonyms and/or certificates to their requester, ensuring accountability and non-repudiation. Unlike the conventional authentication that requires either the use of real identity, public key or credentials, our authentication is anonymous. While developing it, we studied the existing authentication and its impact on privacy. We noted that the requests using the credentials/identity repetitively can be linkable by an interested eavesdropper even though it is encrypted. Moreover, the authorities are often assumed as trusted and intrusion-resilient. However, although we use the same assumption, we would like to develop a privacy-preserving solution that can be used even with a semi-trusted authority or service provider. In fact, if a user provides their identity to the regional authorities, they cross to request pseudonyms (/certificates). The case of authorities' employees using this data to track the user or issue a speeding ticket out of greed, for gain or personal vengeance cannot be completely ruled out. Therefore, to prevent the risk of authorities' abuse of power, anonymous authentication methods are an optimistic suitable choice, emphasizing that the solution should balance the anonymity with the non-repudiation, while being secure and resilient to security attacks.

In fact, anonymous authentication methods are trending due to the awareness of the public about the privacy issue and its impact. Various methods were developed for diverse types of systems. Healthcare probably tops the list of interest for the researcher as a sensitive area where the privacy of the patients ought to be confidential.

Mehmood et al. (2018) proposed a scheme to authenticate patients to the cloud-based healthcare application using the group rotating signature concept. Initially, the patient is registered and provided with a group key to be used in the first phase of authentication, which is then followed by the zero-knowledge protocol. Another example is that of Gope et al. (2018), where they developed a lightweight anonymous authentication protocol for Radio Frequency Identification (RFID) systems using Physically Unclonable Functions (PUF). Also, Wang et al. (2018) and Yue et al. (2018) proposed an anonymous authentication scheme in VANET. Wang et al. (2018) used aliases instead of the real vehicle identity, and instead of saving a copy of these aliases at the Certifying Authority (CA), they are encrypted and saved in the subliminal channel of certificate signature. Yue et al. (2018) used the zero-knowledge protocol to authenticate the vehicle to the tracing manager before joining a group. The group signature concept is used for message authentication between vehicles. Gao and Deng (2018) used the ring signature to anonymously authenticate the exchanged messages, while Liu et al. (2018b) proposed a certificateless short signature anonymous mutual authentication scheme in the Internet of vehicles. These are but a few examples to illustrate the interest of researchers in the anonymous authentication schemes in different areas and system types.

Here, we aim to protect privacy while achieving authentication in vehicular networks, by using the anonymous tickets followed by an anonymous challenge-based authentication. In the rest of this chapter, we use the terms anonymous certificate or tickets to refer to the same concepts.

This chapter describes the network model, and its functionalities, components and purpose. It explains the proposed anonymous authentication scheme. It also examines the solution in terms of its satisfaction to the security properties and its resiliency to famous attacks. Moreover, its logical correctness is checked using the BAN logic and its automated verification is done using SPAN and AVISPA tools.

6.2. Network model and system functionality

This section introduces the network model and describes the system functionality.

6.2.1. *Network model*

In Chapter 1 we explained the vehicular network components. This section is added to remind the reader and elaborate further on the network model which is illustrated in Figure 6.1, where:

– **TA** refers to the ***Trusted Authority***, which registers every VANET vehicle upon its purchase. It issues two types of certificates which are: the permanent certificate containing the identity of the user and their long-term public key and the anonymous ticket containing only a reference number and digital signature. It is the sole authority saving the vehicle's and owner's private and sensitive data that are used exclusively when needed if the vehicle misbehaves and the cooperation with the juridical system is mandatory.

– **RA** refers to the ***Regional Authorities***, which are subsidiaries of the TA dispersed over diverse regions. They are responsible for issuing the temporal certified pseudonyms and/or their certificates (for self-generated pseudonyms). The RA keeps track of the used pseudonyms within its region without identifying their owners. Therefore, when misbehavior occurs, the collaboration of TA and RAs is needed in order to revoke the malicious misbehaving vehicle.

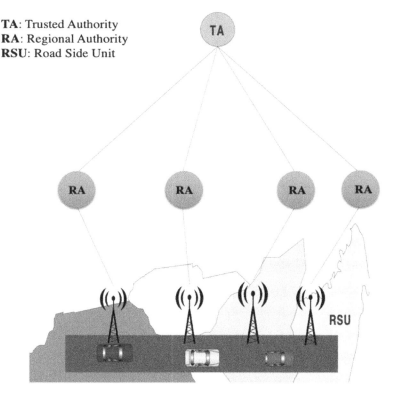

Figure 6.1. *Network model (Benarous and Kadri 2018). For a color version of this figure, see www.iste.co.uk/benarous/vehicular.zip*

We assume that these authorities (TA and RA) can be trusted and are resilient to attacks and intrusions. We also assume that all of the communication between them is secured by encryption and cannot be deciphered by a hacker.

– **RSUs** refer to *Road Side Units*, which are static infrastructure with a wide coverage range for both emission and reception of messages. We used them for packets retransmission.

– **OBUs** refer to **On-Board Units** or the vehicles, which are mobile nodes with tamper resilient devices saving security parameters, keys and algorithms.

6.2.2. *The system functionality*

Having defined the network model, we now continue to describe the functionality of the system. When a vehicle registers to the TA, it obtains its unique set of parameters, settings and security algorithms, which are stored in its tamper-proof device (TPD). It also receives set of anonymous tickets and a certified long-term pair of public and private keys. We remind the reader that in our model, only the TA saves the vehicle and its owner's information. Moreover, the registration phase happens at the TA's facilities and it requires the provision of proof of vehicle ownership. Also, since it involves no wireless communication, it is assumed to be safe and secure. Other assumptions about the network are that:

– the TA is trusted and secured against intrusions and attacks;

– the user's data is encrypted and saved in tamper resilient devices of the TA;

– the tickets are anonymous which means that it is identity-less. It only contains reference numbers and TA digital signatures.

After the registration is done, the TA securely forwards the vehicle's issued tickets references and unique secret parameters to the RA where the owner of the vehicle lives. When the vehicle enters this region, it authenticates itself to the RA by providing one of its tickets to request a pool of pseudonyms and/or certificates for its self-generated pseudonyms. Note that the ticket usage is followed by a challenge phase to prove that the vehicle is the real owner of the anonymous ticket. The details about the authentication phases are explained in the next section. We emphasize that the communication between the RA and the vehicle is secured with encryption.

Regardless of whom generates the pseudonyms (RA or vehicle), it is the RA who issues their corresponding certificates, which include a reference number, temporal public key (pseudonyms), geographical space, validity start and expiry time, and the RA's digital signature. Figure 6.2 illustrates the message sequence chart of the authentication and pseudonyms/certificate requests.

Note that the vehicle may travel and cross various regions where it needs to request pseudonym refilling from their corresponding RAs. In this case, the RA may forward the received ticket to the TA to obtain its related secret parameters, which it uses to challenge the vehicle and authenticate it.

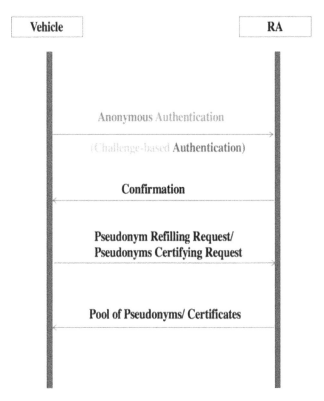

Figure 6.2. *Message sequence chart of the pseudonym/certificate refilling request. For a color version of this figure, see www.iste.co.uk/benarous/vehicular.zip*

6.3. Proposed scheme

In the previous section, the network model components and the overall system functionality description were briefed. Also, we indicated that an anonymous authentication method is used to preserve identity privacy. In this section, we explain this method in detail along with its phases.

The vehicle in a region to request pseudonym/certificate refilling has to first send its ticket to the RA. The RA then quizzes the vehicle to check that it is the real owner of the received ticket. The vehicle responses to the challenge by anonymously authenticating itself without exposing its identity. Once this phase is successfully finished, the RA provides the vehicle with the pseudonyms and/or certificates. If the vehicle has already self-generated its private keys and completed the authentication just to request their certificates, then at this phase the certificates of the public keys are delivered to the vehicle. If the vehicle has requested certified pseudonyms, then at this phase the authority securely supplies them along with their corresponding private keys to the requesting vehicle.

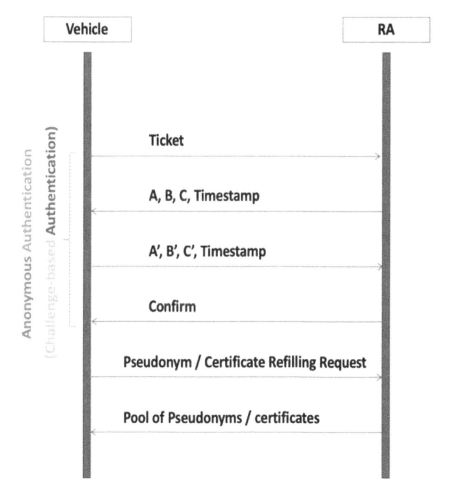

Figure 6.3. *Message sequence chart of the anonymous authentication scheme. For a color version of this figure, see www.iste.co.uk/benarous/vehicular.zip*

In Figure 6.3, we illustrated how the RA challenges the vehicles to prove its ownership of the ticket used in the pseudonym refilling request. We remind the readers that each registered vehicle has unique algorithms and parameters saved in their tamper resilient devices flashed by the TA, and also that the RA has a copy of the parameters that are used in anonymous authentication challenge phase. Equation [6.1] (EQ1) represents the challenge algorithm used by the vehicles. This phase is also referred to as zero-knowledge based authentication because it preserves both the vehicles' and owner's real identity.

$$EQ1 = R^P \, mod \, Q \hspace{4cm} [6.1]$$

P and Q are the secret parameters unique to each vehicle, and R is a large prime random number.

To challenge the vehicle, the RA first checks that the ticket is not revoked and is still valid, then it sends the vehicle an encrypted message containing three freshly generated large random prime numbers (nonces). Upon receiving this message, the vehicle needs to calculate and send its results within the underlined time span of response otherwise the authentication fails. The results are calculated by applying the algorithm in EQ1 on the received numbers generated by the RA. EQ1 has unique secret parameters for each vehicle and all communications are encrypted to prevent the attacker from guessing or calculating the results. When the RA receives the results within the authentication time span, it examines the results correctness for the vehicle to be authenticated as the real owner of this anonymous certificate. The RA then checks that the vehicle has already consumed all its pseudonyms requested using an earlier ticket without being revoked for misbehaving before it satisfies its request. This is to ensure that the vehicle does not abuse its anonymity right persevered by the use of tickets to selfishly acquire multiple valid pseudonyms for the same time slots. This is done to prevent the pseudonym overlapping and the Sybil attack from occurring. Once this is done, the vehicle may request its pseudonyms to be certified or request certified pseudonyms (pseudonym + certificate) from the RA.

Note that the possibility of the attacker responding correctly to the three results within the given short time span without knowing neither the random numbers nor the secret values of P and Q is infinitesimal. Also, the parameters extraction from results within the short span of authentication with today's technology is difficult (if not impossible) because it necessitates resolving a discrete logarithm problem.

The pseudonym acquisition scheme is illustrated in Algorithm 1. We first explain the notations we used to facilitate the understanding of the algorithm.

– "**V** →**RA: m**" means that V sends RA the message m.

– "**V:**" precedes the vehicle executed code.

– **Encrypt (m, P)** encrypts m using the public key *P*. The result is the encrypted message.

– **Decrypt (m, p)** decrypts **m** using the private key *p*.

– **Generate ()** is the function that generates large prime numbers.

– **EQ1(X)** is the implementation of equation EQ1 on the random prime number X.

– **Current_Time ()** returns the system's current time.

– **AUTH_SPAN** is the authentication response maximal threshold.

– The symbol:

- ": =" means assignment;

- "=" means equality;

- "[ ]" delimits the message fields.

– P_{RA}, P_V are the public keys of the RA and the vehicle respectively.

– P_{RA}^{-1}, P_V^{-1} are the private keys of the RA and the vehicle respectively.

– **PSD$_i$** is a certified pseudonym.

– **PSD_Validity** is the validity time of the pseudonym.

– **Generate_PSD_Cert (PSD_Validity)** generates a non-overlapping pseudonym and/or certificate by assigning it a validity time that is higher than that of the last one generated.

– **Online (ticket)** checks if the vehicle using the current ticket is currently connected using another ticket, i.e., double simultaneous sessions.

– Get-PSD-Validity () gets the last certified pseudonym validity time.

– A, B and C are random large prime numbers.

– A', B' and C' are calculated by the vehicle using EQ1 on A, B and C. They are of integer type.

– A", B" and C" are calculated by the RA using EQ1 on A, B and C. They are of integer type.

The algorithm is role based. Thus, the vehicle and RA codes are separately written. In the algorithm, there are three types of events which are:

– local processing;

– message emission;

– message reception preceded by the keyword "*Reception of*".

Algorithm 1: Pseudonym Acquisition Scheme

V:

> *If* (Check (Certificate$_{RA}$))
> > Timestamp$_V$:= Current_Time()
> > **V→RA:** Encrypt ([Ticket, P$_V$, Certificate$_V$] P$_{RA}$)
>
> *Endfi.*
> *Reception of* **RA→V:** Encrypt ([A, B, C, Timestamp$_{RA}$], P$_V$)
> Decrypt ([A, B, C, Timestamp$_{RA}$], P_V^{-1})
> *If* (Timestamp$_{RA}$> Timestamp$_V$) *AND* (Current_Time()< (Timestamp$_V$ + AUTH_SPAN))
> > A':=EQ1(A)
> > B':=EQ1(B)
> > C':=EQ1(C)
> > Timestamp$_V$:= Current_Time()
> > **V→ RA:** Encrypt ([A', B', C', Timestamp$_V$], P$_{RA}$)
>
> *Else*
> > Authentication *fails*
>
> *Endfi.*

RA:

> **Reception of V→RA:** Encrypt ([Ticket, P$_V$, Certificate$_V$] P$_{RA}$)
> Decrypt ([Ticket, P$_V$, Certificate$_V$], P_{RA}^{-1})
> *If* (Check (Certificate$_V$) *AND* **Not** Online (Ticket))
> > A:=Generate()
> > B:=Generate()
> > C:=Generate()
> > Timestamp$_{RA}$:= Current_Time()
> > A":= EQ1(A)
> > B":= EQ1(B)
> > C":= EQ1(C)
> > **RA→V:** Encrypt ([A, B, C, Timestamp$_{RA}$], P$_V$)
>
> *Else*
> > Authentication *fails*
>
> *Endfi.*
> **Reception of V→ RA:** Encrypt ([A', B', C', Timestamp$_V$], P$_{RA}$)
>
> Decrypt ([A', B', C', Timestamp$_V$], P_{RA}^{-1})
> *If* (Timestamp$_V$> Timestamp$_{RA}$) *AND* (Current_Time()< (Timestamp$_{RA}$ + AUTH_SPAN))
> > *If* ((A'=A") *AND* (B'= B") *AND* (C'= C"))
> > > Authentication *Successful*
> > > Timestamp$_{RA}$:= Current_Time()
> > > *For* (i=1,i<=n, i:=i+1)
> > > > PSD_Validity:=Get-PSD-Validity()
> > > > PSD$_i$:=Generate_PSD_Cert(PSD_Validity)
> > >
> > > *Endfor*
> > > **RA→ V:** Encrypt ([PSD$_1$, PSD$_2$,…PSD$_n$, Timestamp$_{RA}$], P$_V$)
> >
> > *Else*
> > > Authentication *fails*.
> >
> > *Endfi.*
>
> *Else*
> > Authentication *fails*.
>
> *Endfi*

6.4. Analysis and discussion

In this section, the performance of the proposed scheme is analyzed, starting with the illustration that it fulfils security and privacy objectives expected from an authentication protocol. This is followed by a discussion about its resiliency to prominent security attacks, then, proving that it is logically correct using the BAN logic. Finally, its verification is done using SPAN and AVISPA.

6.4.1. *Security analysis*

In this section, the proposed solution is analyzed in terms of its satisfaction to security and privacy properties and its resiliency to well-known attacks.

– *The privacy (anonymity and unlinkability)*

For the privacy, we study the robustness of solution against the Global Passive Attacker (GPA) aiming to identify the vehicle's owner and track their locations and parsed trajectories. We have already explained the characteristics of this attacker in Chapter 4. In the following, we justify and clarify how our protocol protects against GPA and the measures taken to prevent identification and linkability.

First, our scheme does not disclose the personal information of the user, especially their real identity while driving on-road; neither when authenticating to the RA nor when authenticating to vehicles because pseudonym certificates are identity-less. The user provides their information solely to the trusted authority when doing the initial registration. This operation happens when they first purchase their vehicle. In other words, when they are physically present at the TA's service facility. Since this registration does not rely on wireless communication, it does not risk the user's privacy and is considered secure.

Second, the anonymous certificates (tickets) are used to request pseudonyms and/or certificates. Therefore, the user's identity is preserved.

Third, the linkability by ticket is prevented as the vehicle has multiple tickets to use. For each pseudonym/certificate refilling request, a new ticket is used in a round robin way to prevent the same ticket from being used for two consecutive demands. Therefore, two sequential requests will not be linked to the same user. These precautions are made to hinder the linkability by patterns in encrypted communication.

Finally, the privacy is conditionally preserved using our authentication method. This is an essential requirement to ensure the non-repudiation and correct functionality of the network. It is important to keep privacy a priority for honest users. However, it is also fundamental to trace the misbehaving nodes and hold them responsible, in order to preserve the correctness of the network. We explain more about it when we discuss the non-repudiation and accountability traits.

– Message integrity

The integrity of messages is important. However, it is known that the altered messages are detected at the lower layers where they are dropped and a retransmission is needed in that case. However, the integrity of clear messages containing the tickets, pseudonyms and certificates is further preserved by being digitally signed, while the encrypted messages containing the random number or their corresponding results are ensured implicitly, since only the intended parties can encrypt and decrypt the messages and alter their content (asymmetric cryptography).

– Short-term linkability and long-term linkability

Short linkability is needed for the network's functionality. Thus, it must be guaranteed. Contrarily, the long-term linkability is undesirable, as it risks both the location and identity privacy. The multiple anonymous ticket usage for pseudonym requests prevents this type of linkability from happening when using our scheme, since two successive requests with two different anonymous tickets are not linked by the GPA.

– Non-repudiation and accountability

In our scheme, the RA does not know nor store the vehicle's (or its owner's) identity. However, the RA maps the pseudonym/certificate requests with the used ticket in the authentication phase. This enables it to ensure the non-repudiation of the vehicle on its cyber activity while using these pseudonyms. Suppose that a vehicle misbehaves on-road, disrupting the correct functionality of the network. As soon as the misbehavior is reported to the RA by the vehicles, the RA confirms the reports. Then, it retrieves the ticket's reference used to obtain the pseudonym of the reported vehicle. The vehicle's valid non-used pseudonyms are revoked and the ticket is blacklisted to prohibit its future usage. If needed, the identity may be resolved in cooperation with the TA. The ticket is sent by the RA to the TA, which checks its issued tickets to identify the subject ticket's owner. The TA also blacklists all of the issued tickets of the misbehaving user and informs the RAs. The RAs update the vehicles with the revoked pseudonyms. Note that the identity may not necessarily be resolved upon each revocation; it depends on the severity of the misbehavior and the RA's policy of punishment.

– *Forward security*

Forward security means that if the keys or sensitive encrypted data is exposed, much of past and future communication is at risk. In our scheme, forward security is ensured because even though the attacker may somehow know the encryption key of the vehicle, or may read A', B' and C' sent in the challenge phase, they cannot extract the parameters P and Q or the nonces A, B and C from the sole knowledge of A', B' and C'. Moreover, the pseudonym is a short-lived public key (temporal). If the corresponding private key is exposed, then only the messages encrypted with this key are read by the attacker and no other older messages or parameters. Therefore, the forward security property is satisfied. Note that the knowledge of the private key is not possible as they are stored in the vehicle's tamper-proof device, which is highly protected.

– *Replay attack*

Our proposed authentication method is resilient to replay attacks thanks to the challenge phase following the use of anonymous tickets. Without its addition, the attacker would be able to intercept any ticket and use it later to request their pseudonyms without them being linked to their real identity. In this case, the attacker would follow the replay attack with more severe active attacks such as the Sybil attack. Suppose that an Attacker A_{tk} is to reuse intercepted messages from an earlier session sent by a vehicle containing the ticket $Ticket_V$ of vehicle V and the results it calculated noted as A', B' and C'. Then, A_{tk} sends $Ticket_V$ to RA, which would start the challenge phase by generating three random numbers a, b, c and timestamps the message. The RA waits for a specific time before dropping the authentication session if it receives no valid response within it. A_{tk} uses the intercepted message containing A', B' and C' *and a timestamp* as its response to the challenge. RA rejects the received response and closes the authentication session as the timestamp from the received message is older than the current and the received values A', B' and C' are different from the expected results. Thus, the replay attacker fails to authenticate themselves successfully.

– *Session hijacking attack*

To protect against session hijacking, the communications were secured by encryption. Let us suppose that the attacker could interfere after the emission of the ticket. They have to resolve the challenge successfully to continue the communication. This is not possible because they are unable to read the encrypted message containing the nonces. Therefore, it cannot provide the expected results (see Table 6.1). If the attacker is to interfere after the authentication phase to either certify the pseudonyms or request for their refilling, they need to send messages encrypted with the authority's public key. In response, the authority sends the requested certificates/pseudonyms encrypted with the vehicle's public key that has initiated this session. Hence, the attacker cannot read its content because they are not the owner of the (vehicle's) private key that may be used to decrypt the message.

Note that in what has preceded, we started by supposing that the attacker "*could successfully interfere*". This means that they correctly guess the sequence numbers of the exchanged messages and are faster in generating their messages before the legitimate vehicle does. This is a difficult task to fulfill in the short time of authentication and refilling.

– *Man-in-the-middle attack*

Our solution also protects against man-in-the-middle (MITM) attacks because of the use of certified keys. Let us suppose that vehicle V is authenticating itself to the RA and Attacker A_{tk} is an internal attacker with a legitimate certificate executing an MITM attack. A_{tk} cannot proceed as they are not the authority and the authentication fails after the examination of key certificate. Therefore, our solution is resilient to the MITM attack. The results obtained by AVISPA in Figures 6.4 and 6.7 indicate that the protocol is safe against such an attack.

– *Impersonation attacks*

Similarly, the certificate usage prevents the attacker from impersonating both the vehicle and the RA. If we hypothetically suppose that they succeed in surpassing the certificate verification, they will fail to provide the correct responses in the challenge phase on the sent nonces and thus fail to carry on with the authentication while impersonating nodes. This attack is a sub-phase of the MITM attack. Since the solution was proved with AVISPA to be resilient to the MITM attack, then it is also resilient to the impersonation attack.

– *Guessing and brute-force attacks*

In the challenge phase of our proposed solution, the RA freshly generates three random numbers for one-time usage (nonces), encrypts them with its public key and sends them to the vehicle. The attacker desiring to break the authentication scheme without the knowledge of the vehicle's secret parameters has to correctly guess A, B, C, P and Q to calculate A', B' and C' or use brute-force to determine all of the possibilities to find A', B' and C'. They must provide a correct response for all three results within the authentication time span. With the random numbers being large, the attacker's chances to successfully guess/use brute-force to determine the results accurately and quickly using current technology is infinitesimal given that the modulus operator is not reversible. It also means resolving a discrete logarithm problem (Da Cunha et al. 2014), which means finding the P in EQ1 using S and R ($P=Log_R(S)$), where S is the result and R is the random number ($S=R^P$ mod Q).

In Table 6.1, we illustrate, using an example, the time required by the attacker to use brute-force to find the values of A', B' and C' without knowing the parameters. We estimated the time needed to try all possibilities without knowing any parameters to find the values using (Mandylionlabs) brute-force calculator. We also used (PrimePages n.d.) to estimate the combinations (possibilities) needed to get to A', B' and C'. Note that the random prime numbers used were obtained from (Sunshine). In addition, decillion=10^{33} and duodecillion=10^{39} (Benarous and Kadri 2017) were used.

Random prime numbers	Challenge (EQ1) response	EQ1 parameters		Execution time	Brute-force attack	
A, B and C	A', B' and C'	P	Q		Time estimation (Mandylionlabs)	Number of tries (Mandylionlabs)
10 digits					2,376 Duodecillion Year	
20 digits					2,376 Duodecillion Year	
30 digits					950 Duodecillion Year	
40 digits	60 digits	9 digits	60 digits	5 milli-seconds	950 Duodecillion Year	72 decillion combinations
50 digits					950 Duodecillion Year	
100 digits					2,376 Duodecillion Year	

Table 6.1. *Illustration of brute-force estimated time of execution and number of combinations*

– *Sybil attack*

Our solution prevents pseudonym overlapping by prohibiting the use of anonymous tickets to request multiple pseudonyms with the same validity time. Thus, it thwarts the use of multiple identities to execute a Sybil attack, owing to the fact that the RA rejects the vehicle's requests using multiple tickets for pseudonyms with the same validity period to ensure that no two pseudonyms are used simultaneously.

Let us suppose that the vehicle V_a uses both Ticket$_1$ and Ticket$_2$ to request its pseudonyms. Let p_1, p_2 and p_3 be the pseudonyms obtained using Ticket$_1$ and p_4, p_5

and p_6 be the pseudonyms obtained using Ticket$_2$. Vl$_1$, Vl$_2$, Vl$_3$, Vl$_4$, Vl$_5$ and Vl$_6$ are their validity times respectively. Presuming that V_a can execute the Sybil attack, then it must be in possession of multiple pseudonyms that are valid during the same lifetime. If we assume that it can use two pseudonyms at the same time, then this would mean that Vl$_1$=Vl$_4$, Vl$_2$=Vl$_5$ and Vl$_3$= Vl$_6$ for the V_a to use p$_1$ and p$_4$ at the same time, p$_2$ and p$_5$ simultaneously, finally, p$_3$ and p$_6$ at the same time each during its validity period. This cannot happen, as our algorithm prohibits two simultaneous connections using two different tickets and increases the validity between each generated pseudonym. This means that Vl$_1$<Vl$_2$<Vl$_3$ and Vl$_4$<Vl$_5$<Vl$_6$. Therefore, even though the requests are made using these tickets in a consecutive way, the Sybil attack cannot happen because Vl$_1$<Vl$_2$<Vl$_3$<Vl$_4$<Vl$_5$<Vl$_6$.

6.4.2. *Burrows, Abadi and Needham (BAN) logic*

After studying the measures taken to satisfy security properties to protect against well-known attacks, we continue to prove that our anonymous scheme fulfils the authentication objectives using the Burrows et al. (1989) logic. To do so, we first write the scheme formally, and then use the postulates to demonstrate that the goals are achieved. This logic is used to prove the correctness of authentication schemes, such as the works of (Irisa 2006; Hussain et al. 2015; Gao and Deng 2018).

Before starting the correctness demonstration, we first explain the notations used. Then, BAN logic postulates, followed by the formal idealization of the scheme's messages, assumptions of the solution and the underlined objectives.

– Notations:

- Let **A, B, Q, P, RA, TA** and **V$_J$** be the entities where A, B, P and Q are the abstract users; RA and TA are the regional and central trusted authorities respectively; V$_J$ is the vehicle.

- **P$_{TA}$, P$_{RA}$** and **P$_J$** are the public keys of the trusted authority TA, the regional authority RA and the vehicle J. P_{TA}^{-1}, P_{RA}^{-1}, and P_J^{-1} are the private keys of the TA, RA and vehicle J respectively.

- $SIG_{P_{TA}^{-1}}(x)$ is the digital signing function that encrypts the hash of message x with the private keyP_{TA}^{-1},.

- **C** corresponds to the three large prime random numbers, also known as nonces.

- **Par** is unique to each vehicle and it stands for secret parameters.

- $<C> Par$ is the outcome of the challenge algorithm that takes the random numbers (C) and the parameters Par as input.

- $A \overset{x}{\rightleftharpoons} B$: this notation signifies that only A and B know the secret x.

- $(\overset{P_A}{\rightarrow} A)$: P_A is entity A's public key.

- $(A \overset{K}{\leftrightarrow} B)$: only A and B know the secret Key K.

– **Messages (simplified and formally idealized using Logic of BAN)**:

- M1. $V_J \rightarrow RA$: $P_J, SIG_{P_{RA}^{-1}}(P_J), \{NUM, SIG_{P_{TA}^{-1}}(NUM)\}P_{RA}$.

- M2. $RA \rightarrow V_J$: $P_{RA}, SIG_{P_{TA}^{-1}}(P_{RA}), (C)P_J$.

- M3. $V_J \rightarrow RA$: $(RA \overset{<C> Par}{\rightleftharpoons} V_J)P_{RA}$.

- M4. $RA \rightarrow V_J$: (Pseudonyms, Certificates)P_{RA}^{-1} .... *(M4 is not necessary for the demonstration)*.

– **Assumptions**:

- V_J believes TA ... (1)

- RA believes TA ... (2)

- RA believes $(\overset{P_{TA}}{\rightarrow} TA)$ ... (3)

- V_J believes $(\overset{P_{TA}}{\rightarrow} TA)$ ... (4)

- $TA \overset{Par}{\rightleftharpoons} RA$... (5)

- $TA \overset{Par}{\rightleftharpoons} V_J$... (6)

- RA believes (TA controls $RA \overset{P_J^{-1}}{\leftrightarrow} V_J$) ...(7)

- RA believes (TA controls $RA \overset{P_J}{\leftrightarrow} V_J$) ...(8)

- V_J believes (TA controls $RA \overset{P_{RA}^{-1}}{\leftrightarrow} V_J$) ...(9)

- V_J believes (TA controls $RA \overset{P_{RA}}{\leftrightarrow} V_J$) ...(10)

– **Objectives**:

- V_J believes RA

- RA believes V_J

– *Demonstration*:

RA deduces the following when it receives M1:

1) RA sees P_J , $SIG_{P_{RA}^{-1}}(P_J)$, $\{NUM, SIG_{P_{TA}^{-1}}(NUM)\ \}P_{RA}$.... (BAN logic postulates, Principal 4)

2) RA sees P_J.... (Principal 4 of BAN logic postulates)

3) RA sees NUM .... (Principal 4 of BAN logic postulates)

4) RA believes (TA said NUM).... (BAN logic postulates 1 and 4, Assumptions 2 and 3)

When Vehicle V_J receives M2, it concludes the following:

1) V_J sees P_{RA} , $SIG_{P_{TA}^{-1}}(P_{RA})$, $(C)P_J$. .... (BAN logic postulates, Principal 4)

2) V_J sees C.... (BAN logic postulates, Principal 4)

3) V_J sees P_{RA} .... (BAN logic postulates, Principal 4, Assumption 1)

After the reception of M3, RA deducts as follows:

1) RA sees $RA \overset{<\,C\,>\,Par}{\rightleftharpoons} V_J$.... (BAN logic postulates, Principal 4)

2) RA believes V_J said $< C > Par$.... (BAN logic postulates, Principal 4, Assumptions 5 and 6)

From the above deductions (M1.4, M2.2, M3.2), the assumptions, and BAN logic Principal 3: "jurisdiction":

1) V_J believes RA

2) RA believes V_J

6.4.3. *SPAN and AVISPA tools*

The BAN logic demonstrated logic correctness of the scheme. Yet, this proof is not automated and an additional automated robustness analysis is needed. Therefore, we specified the proposed anonymous authentication using HLPSL and verified it with the tools SPAN (Security Protocol ANimator) (AVISPA 2002) and AVISPA (Automated Validation of Internet Security Protocols and Applications) (T.A. Team 2006). In our specification, we alleviated the algorithm defined by (EQ1) to a simpler algorithm, which is the Xor operation. Departing from the fact that if the scheme is deemed robust with XOR algorithm, then it is so with the more complex algorithm given in EQ1.

Both the vehicle and the regional authority specifications of the authentication protocol are presented in Figure 6.4.

Vehicle code

---

role **vehicle** (A, B: agent, Ka, Kb: public key, SND, RCV: channel (dy))
played by A def=
 local State: nat,
 Na, Nb, Nc, Nd, Ne, Nf, P0: text,
 init State: = 0
 transition
    0.   State = 0 ∧ RCV (start) =|>
          State': = 2 ∧ Na': = new () ∧ Nb': = new ()
                 ∧ Nc': = new () ∧ P0': = new ()
                 ∧ SND ({Na'. Nb'. Nc'. P0'. A}   Kb)
                 ∧ **secret (P0', p0, {A,B})**
∧**witness (A, B, authority_vehicle_nabc, Na'. Nb'. Nc')**
    2. State = 2 ∧ RCV ({Na.Nb.Nc. Nd'. Ne'. Nf}   Ka) =|>
       State': = 4 ∧ SND ({Nd'. Ne'.Nf}   Kb)
∧ **request (A, B, vehicle_authority_ndef, Nd'.Ne'.Nf')**
end role

Regional Authority Code

---

role **authority** (A, B: agent, Ka, Kb: public key, SND, RCV: channel (dy))
played by B def=
local State: nat,
Na, Nb, Nc, Nd, Ne, Nf, P0: text,
 init State: = 1
 transition
    1. State = 1 ∧ RCV({Na'.Nb'.Nc'.P0'.A}   Kb) =|>
       State': = 3 ∧ Nd': = xor(Na',P0')
                  ∧ Ne': = xor(Nb',P0')
                  ∧ Nf': = xor(Nc',P0')
              ∧ SND({Na'.Nb'.Nc'.Nd'.Ne'.Nf}   Ka)
∧ **witness (B, A, vehicle_authority_ndef, Nd'.Ne'.Nf')**
    3. State = 3 ∧ RCV({Nd.Ne.Nf}   Kb) =|>
       State': = 5
∧ **request (B, A, authority_vehicle_nabc, Na.Nb.Nc)**
end role

Figure 6.4. *Vehicle's and RA's HLPSL specification code*

The security objectives are:

– secrecy_of p0;

– authentication_on vehicle_authority_ndef.

In the specification, "secret" instruction is used to ensure the secrecy of P0 from entities other than the regional authority and the vehicle. P0 refers to the ticket's reference number. The events "request" and "witness" are used to verify that the authenticating node is correct in trusting that its intended peer is participating in this session, is at a certain state, and agrees on a given fresh value[1]. In our specification, they were used to ensure the authenticity of the generated random numbers and the calculated outcomes. Note that the numbers (**d, e, f**) are the Xors of (**a, b, c**) (where Xor is the alleviated challenge defined in EQ1).

Figure 6.5 illustrates the OFMC verification output, which illustrates that the protocol is safe. An OFMC verifier is an On the Fly Model Checker that analyzes security protocols, which is used by the SPAN and AVISPA tools.

```
% OFMC
% Version of 2006/02/13
SUMMARY
  SAFE
DETAILS
  BOUNDED_NUMBER_OF_SESSIONS
PROTOCOL
  /home/span/span/testsuite/results/sample.if
GOAL
  as_specified
```

Figure 6.5. *Result of the specified protocol using SPAN and AVISPA*

Figure 6.6 shows the specified authentication protocol Message Sequence Chart (MSC). Figure 6.7 illustrates exchanged messages in the presence of a passive intruder who intercepts the messages but cannot read them, and who tries to execute the replay attack but fails. This indicates that by using our scheme, the vehicle authenticates to the regional authority securely and anonymously, even with the presence of an intruder.

---

1 See: https://www.isi.edu/nsnam/ns/.

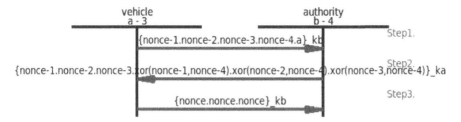

Figure 6.6. *Message sequence chart of the specified authentication method. For a color version of this figure, see www.iste.co.uk/benarous/vehicular.zip*

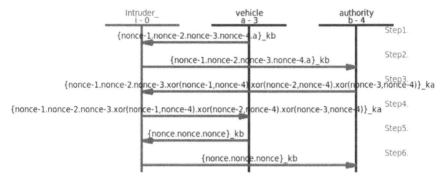

Figure 6.7. *Message sequence chart of the authentication method in the presence of an intruder. For a color version of this figure, see www.iste.co.uk/benarous/vehicular.zip*

6.5. Conclusion

In this chapter, we presented a secure privacy-preserving scheme for pseudonym refilling on-demand and on-road. The solution is distinguishable for ensuring anonymity and being identityless. The anonymous tickets usage and the authentication without the exchange of the vehicle's identity or its permanent certificate ensured both the privacy and authentication. The RA securely issues the vehicle with the requested pseudonyms and/or certificates once the authentication is done successfully and no overlapping is detected. This authentication and verification processes ensure the accountability (non-repudiation), the revocation of misbehaving nodes and the prevention of a Sybil attack.

To demonstrate that the proposed scheme achieves the authentication objectives, BAN logic was used. Moreover, to prove that it is safe and resilient to replay attacks, the tools SPAN and AVISPA were used. They required the scheme to be specified using the HLPSL. In addition, as we illustrated, our scheme satisfies the security properties of privacy, integrity, non-repudiation and forward security. It was also designed to be resilient to the following attacks: man-in-the-middle, Sybil, impersonation, replay, session hijacking, guessing and brute-force attacks.

Our authentication method was specifically applied to pseudonym refilling requests in vehicular networks, as it is repetitive and may not only threaten identity privacy, but also cause linkability and tracking. However, this is not the sole application it may be used in. Our future perspectives include applying it to other applications, such as service requests from third-party service providers, or even in other systems and networks that are privacy sensitive, like e-health or the Internet of Things.

This chapter, as well as Chapter 5, both proposed authentication methods that preserve identity privacy in the authentication phase, either when forming and joining the CVDNN, requesting pseudonym refilling or using any third-party service. In the next chapters, we concentrate on preserving the location privacy of vehicular network users on-road to prevent tracking, by proposing various solutions aiming to reduce and thwart linkability.

7

Preserving the Location Privacy of Vehicular Ad hoc Network Users

7.1. Introduction

In Chapter 1, we explained the different types of vehicular networks, and in Chapter 2, the privacy issue in these networks. Then, in the two previous chapters, we proposed two anonymous authentication methods that preserved identity. Identity preservation helps in preventing tracking. However, location privacy may be threatened by the vehicle's cyber activity, more precisely, when it is periodically broadcasting state messages containing its locations. In this chapter, we propose two schemes that protect location privacy on-road. Before we explain the solution, we first remind the reader about the type of vehicular network we are interested in. We already explained in Chapter 1 that the privacy issue differs in the self-contained autonomous vehicles from interdependent autonomous vehicles. In the first, the vehicle is self-dependent; the decisions are made based on its sensed data that are processed locally. Since the concept of a network does not really exist, the privacy in this type is not threatened unless the vehicle system is compromised. On the contrary, since these vehicles are equipped with cameras sensing roads, the privacy of other road users, such as pedestrians, cyclists and other vehicle drivers, is at risk. In the second type, the vehicles exchange road data and state messages with each other. Thus, the concept of a network exists. Yet, these messages are what risks the location privacy in the vehicular ad hoc networks (VANET). The risk comes from the fact that state messages are sent wirelessly in clear for fast processing. They are sent with high frequency, and they contain the vehicle's location, speed, headings and public key (pseudonym), which is used to check the message signature to ensure authenticity and integrity. The pseudonyms have a validity period during which they can be used, and all messages signed with it are linked, leading to the short linkability and tracking. Short linkability is a desired trait as it ensures the stability of the network, the stable service usage and a correct routing. On the contrary, the long linkability and trajectory tracking are undesirable because they violate the location privacy of road users. The long linkability means that the vehicle is tracked by all its used pseudonyms. That is, even though the vehicle updates its pseudonyms, a linkability between the old and newly updated pseudonyms leads to continuous tracking. Figure 7.1 illustrates how the attacker uses their installed receivers on roads to track vehicles from afar. In the figure, the VANET is formed by Road Side Units (RSU) and vehicles, or On-Board Units (OBU) broadcasting beacons.

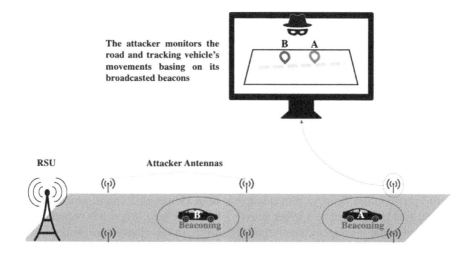

Figure 7.1. *Vehicle Ad hoc Network illustration under attacker's observations. For a color version of this figure, see www.iste.co.uk/benarous/vehicular.zip*

To preserve location privacy and prevent trajectory tracking, the linkability of pseudonyms should be prevented during the update. In Chapter 2 we resumed the existing solutions in the literature that were developed for this aim. We developed our solutions to be road, crowd and infrastructure independent, as none of the above conditions may be continuously available during the update phase. Existing solutions using them showed optimistic results, but they were context dependent. The proposed solutions rely on obfuscation of location prior to the change. The first proposal uses a camouflage technique before changing the pseudonym. The results obtained by simulation using an NS2 simulator against a global passive attacker executing a semantic attack and a syntactic attack are optimistic. The average tracking ratio was 27%, with the overall tracking ratio varying from 17% to 40% at worst in a low-dense scenario. This demonstrates the robustness of the proposed solution in preserving location privacy.

In the second proposal, we take advantage of the crowd if within dense roads and execute the obfuscation technique elsewhere. The solution gave a better performance against the modeled attacker executing semantic and syntactic attacks when simulated. It reduced the tracking ratio to an average of 10.4%, varying from 6.3% to 17% at worst.

The chapter describes the attacker model. It explains the first proposed solution that is camouflage-based along with its analysis. It also illustrates the second proposed solution that is neighbor-aware and executes obfuscation when in low-density roads.

7.2. Adversary model

We already explained in Chapter 4 how the attacker may intercept the vehicle's wirelessly broadcasted beacons and use them to track its past and current location. We defined various types of linking attacks that are executed by the attacker to achieve their aim. In this chapter, our attacker is a global passive attacker (GPA) who implicitly installs their receivers to fully cover the road (observation area). The GPA executes two linking attacks that are the semantic and the syntactic attacks. We remind the readers that these attacks were already explained in Chapter 4. The attacker model was simulated using an NS2 simulator with a grid of 100 receivers, with the range of each (500 m) fully covering the road. This model was used to evaluate the performance of both of our proposals explained in this chapter. Table 7.1 resumes the parameters settings of the attacker.

Tools	NS2
Simulation time	900 seconds
Map	1,000 x 1,000, Manhattan grid
Number of attacker's receivers	100
Attacker coverage range	500 m

Table 7.1. *Simulation parameters of the attacker*

7.3. Proposed camouflage-based location privacy-preserving scheme

To preserve location privacy, we use a camouflage mechanism prior to the update of the pseudonym to thwart the linkability, even within roads with low density. Before the vehicle pseudonym's minimum lifetime T_e is reached, the vehicle starts executing the camouflage technique. Let this time be denoted as T_s, where $(T_s < T_e)$. For time $\Delta t = T_e - T_s$, the vehicle is executing the camouflage technique, and at T_e, it implements the change. The change strategy is illustrated in Algorithm 1, and the camouflage technique is illustrated in Algorithm 2.

Algorithm 1: Pseudonym Change Scheme

Input: T_s, T_e: time; k-fake: integer.
While (true)
    Current_Time:= getCurrentTime()
    If (Current_Time=T_s)
            While (Current_Time $\leq T_e$)
            Camouflage_Technique(k-fake)
            Current_Time:= getCurrentTime()
            EndWhile
        Pseudonym:= new Pseudonym ()
        Position:= CurrentPosition()
        Speed:= CurrentSpeed()
        Send Beacon (Pseudonym, Position, Speed)
        EndIf
EndWhile

The camouflage technique generates a virtual crowd before implementing the change by creating fake messages to confuse the attacker. Hence, our solution is crowd independent and protects privacy, even within low-density roads. The fake messages contain fake pseudonyms, locations and speeds. The locations follow the road restrictions and are not random, to prevent the attacker that is aware of the road map from detecting the fake. The fake messages are sent along with the real ones. This gives the attacker the illusion that there are k vehicles on-road that are broadcasting k beacons with k pseudonyms during Δt and slightly after the change. We remind the readers that the tracking is done by message interception. No cameras nor signal tracking tools are used. The fake pseudonyms are either self-generated, not certified, signed by the vehicle's expired pseudonyms, not signed at all or a set of expired pseudonyms.

Algorithm 2: Camouflage_Technique (integer k)

Psd:= CurrentPseudonym()
Pos:= CurrentPosition()
Speed:= CurrentSpeed()
Send Beacon (Psd, Pos, Speed)
For (i=1; i≤k; i+1)
   Psd$_i$:= FakePseudonym()
   Pos$_i$:= FakePosition()
   Speed$_i$:= FakeSpeed()
   Send Beacon (Psd$_i$, Pos$_i$, Speed$_i$)
End-for

7.3.1. Analytical model

We already defined the analytical metrics in Chapter 3. In this chapter, we use the anonymity set size ASS, and the entropy as our evaluation metrics. The ASS is calculated as follows.

Let V be a vehicle implementing the change, and k be the number of fake messages sent before the change with k fake pseudonym. Therefore, it can be considered as k virtual fake vehicles. m is the number of cooperative neighbor vehicles changing their pseudonyms simultaneously with V. l is the number of non-cooperative neighbor vehicles which do not implement the change, or implement it asynchronously with V.

The following cases are distinguished:

1) V is alone when it changes its pseudonym:

$ASS = k$

2) V is within m vehicles when it changes its pseudonym:

$ASS = k (m + 1)$

3) V is within l vehicles when it changes its pseudonym:

$ASS = k+l$

4) V is within $l + m$ vehicles when it changes its pseudonym:

$ASS = k(m+1) + l$

The entropy H is calculated as follows:

$$H = -\sum_{i=1}^{ASS} p_i log_2(p_i)$$

where p_i is calculated as follows:

$$p_i = \frac{1}{k(m + 1) + l}$$

The tracking time **T** is divided on n time interval t_i, which is the lifetime of the pseudonym. Tracking the vehicle for **T** means tracking its trajectory parsed during

T. Therefore, the probability of tracking the vehicle in n consecutive observation interval t_i is the probability to track its parsed trajectory noted as $P_{trajectory}$, where the probability of tracking it in t_i is p_i.

$$P_{trajectory} = p_1 * p_2 * \ldots * p_i * \ldots * p_n$$

We now analytically compare the probability of tracking the vehicle's parsed trajectory, if it is alone on-road during all the observation period T. Without using our camouflage technique, the vehicle can certainly be tracked whether it changes its pseudonym or not i.e., $p_i=1$, $i \in [1, n]$ and $P_{trajectory}=1$.

In our case, if V is alone on-road:

$$p_i = 1/k, \; k > 1$$

and p_i is identical in all intervals.

Therefore, $P_{trajectory} = (P_i)^n < 1$.

This further proves that our solution reduces the tracking as the observation period increases, and the vehicle continues its pseudonym change using our camouflage technique.

7.3.2. *Simulation*

7.3.2.1. *Settings*

In this section, we explain the simulation settings and scenarios, and the process used to sort the results. The simulation was done using an NS2 simulator. Both the attacker's and the vehicle's code were written in C++ language. The scenarios were written in TCL files, where we specified the simulation settings given in Table 7.2. The mobility models of the vehicle were generated using the MobiSim tool on a Manhattan grid map, where the vehicles number varied from low to high density.

Before explaining the results treatment process, we first explain how we fixed the number of vehicles in the created virtual crowd denoted as *k-fake* or shortly *k*, and the duration for which the camouflage technique is used Δt or dt. To decide their values, we investigated their impact on the level of privacy provided by trying various values. We also considered their impact on the resulting over-head by evaluating the number of sent and received messages. We conducted the investigation on a scenario with 25 vehicles with the same map specified in Table 7.2. Figure 7.2 resumes the investigation results. We found that the tracking ratio was the lowest with almost full resiliency to syntactic attack when Δt = 2 and k-fake = 3. Also, the over-head and message dropping interpreted by the number of sent and received messages were acceptable. Therefore, we chose to use these values for *k*, Δ*t* in the rest of the simulation.

Tools	NS2, MobiSim
Mac layer	802.11p
Simulation time	900 seconds
Map	1,000 x 1,000, Manhattan grid
Pseudonym minimum lifetime	30 seconds
Vehicle range	300 m
Number of vehicles	10–200

Table 7.2. *Simulation parameters*

Note that because we are concentrating on the safety applications requiring the periodic broadcast of state messages known as beacons, it is difficult to calculate the dropping ratio as the destination is not unique, and also because these messages are sent even though the vehicle is alone on road. Instead, we compared the exchanged messages to investigate the impact of increasing the number of generated fake beacons during Δt interval. We found that it increased overall.

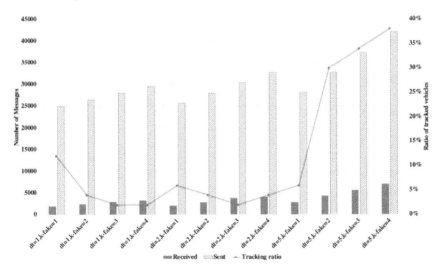

Figure 7.2. *Investigating the impact of varying Δt and k-fake on the privacy, number of sent and received messages. For a color version of this figure, see www.iste.co.uk/benarous/vehicular.zip*

7.3.2.2. *Results and analysis*

Now, the Δt and k values are fixed to give the lowest tracking ratio with the minimum impact on the overhead and dropping ratio. We continue to explain how the simulation results were processed and the tracking ratio was calculated. Then, we illustrate the results in the coming figures, comment and analyze them.

Our simulation generates trace files for the vehicle's activity and the attacker's tracks. The vehicle's trace file is sorted and organized to enable the extraction of the number of the pseudonym change, as well as the verification of the attacker's tracking accuracy, while the attacker's trace file is processed to separate the tracking by attack and calculate the tracking ratio and the pseudonym linking ratio.

Let R_{track} be the tracking ratio of the attacker, R_{Sem} is the tracking ratio of the Semantic attack and R_{Syn} is for the Syntactic attack. T_{psd} is the total number of pseudonym changes. T_v is the total number of vehicles. L_{psd} is the total ratio of linked pseudonyms; L_{psd1} is the ratio of linked pseudonyms by semantic attack and L_{psd2} by the syntactic attack. l_{psd1} is the number of linked pseudonyms by semantic attack and l_{psd2} by syntactic attack. V_{sem} is the number of tracked vehicles by semantic attack and V_{syn} by syntactic attack.

The ratios are calculated as follows:

$$R_{sem} = \frac{V_{sem}}{T_v} \tag{7.1}$$

$$R_{syn} = \frac{V_{syn}}{T_v} \tag{7.2}$$

$$R_{track} = (R_{sem} + R_{syn})/2 \tag{7.3}$$

$$L_{psd1} = \frac{l_{psd1}}{T_{psd}} \tag{7.4}$$

$$L_{psd2} = \frac{l_{psd2}}{T_{psd}} \tag{7.5}$$

$$L_{psd} = (l_{psd1} + l_{psd2})/2 \tag{7.6}$$

Figure 7.3 illustrates the number of used pseudonyms by each vehicle for each scenario. The number of used pseudonyms is presented in the vertical axis, while the number of vehicles is given in the horizontal axis. The number of pseudonyms increases as the number of vehicles does, where the vehicles should change their pseudonyms upon expiry, independently, using our strategy.

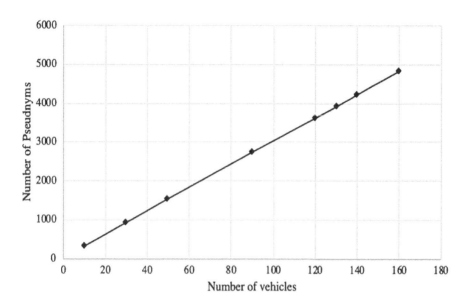

Figure 7.3. *Number of pseudonyms used per vehicle*

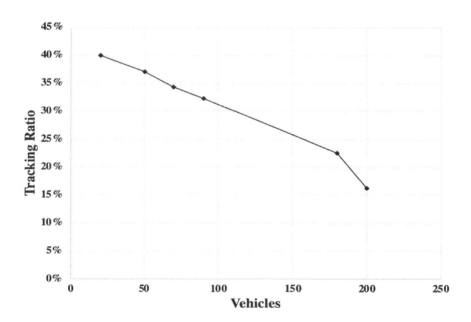

Figure 7.4. *Ratio of tracked vehicles*

Figure 7.4 shows the attacker's tracking ratio (R_{track}). This ratio was between 17% for a high-density scenario and 40% for a low-density scenario. Thus, the privacy is preserved with at least 60%, which is the ratio obtained in the worst-case scenario when the update happens in low-density roads. This is considered as a high ratio for such a scenario.

Figure 7.5 resumes the linked pseudonyms ratio L_{psd} that varied from 0.9 to 4.8% and did not exceed 5%. This further proves the robustness of the solution in achieving the pseudonyms unlinkability upon their update, thus preventing the trajectory tracking and preserving the location privacy.

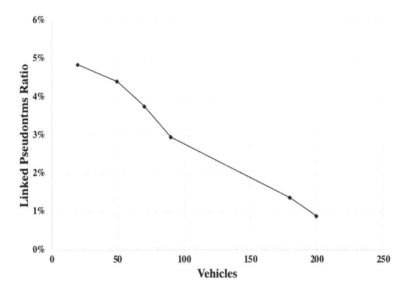

Figure 7.5. *Ratio of linked pseudonyms*

We compared our solution to the periodical pseudonym change scheme where the vehicles update their pseudonyms upon their expiry independently without taking any extra measure. We found that our solution has a lower ratio than that of the periodic change, especially in low-density roads where the tracking ratio difference is huge. It was 70% when using periodic change and 15% when using our solution against an attacker executing a syntactic attack. Therefore, our solution reduces the tracking ratio considerably, especially in the case of low-density roads, out-performing the standard periodic change solution in preserving location privacy. Figure 7.6 illustrates the obtained tracking ratio for both solutions.

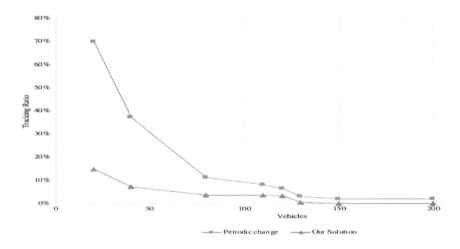

Figure 7.6. *Ratio of tracked vehicle. For a color version of this figure, see www.iste.co.uk/benarous/vehicular.zip*

7.4. Proposed hybrid pseudonym change strategy

In this section, we explain the second proposal. We first begin by describing the assumptions used and then illustrate the proposed scheme, followed by the simulation results.

7.4.1. *Hypothesis and assumptions*

We follow the IEEE 1609.2 standard indicating that the public key certificate has a validity time and space. This means that the pseudonyms are time and space slotted. For example: let vehicle V1 have three pseudonyms (A, B, C), and V2 have three pseudonyms (D, E, F).

– "A" is valid within region R1 and has the lifetime of 60 seconds starting from t1= 11 h 30 min.

– "B" is valid within region R1 and has the lifetime of 60 seconds starting from t2= 11 h 31 min.

– "C" is valid within region R1 and has the lifetime of 60 seconds starting from t2= 11 h 32 min.

– "D" is valid within region R1 and has the lifetime of 60 seconds starting from t1= 11 h 30 min.

– "E" is valid within region R1 and has the lifetime of 60 seconds starting from t2= 11 h 31 min.

– "F" is valid within region R1 and has the lifetime of 60 seconds starting from t3= 11 h 32 min.

Therefore, both vehicles V1 and V2 change their pseudonyms at the same time and within the same region. If these vehicles happen to be in the same vicinity (neighbors), then, this change is implicitly cooperative without the explicit synchronization between the vehicles. The privacy level achieved is the same as that of the schemes where the change happens within a cooperative crowd.

7.4.2. Changing the pseudonyms

Figure 7.7 illustrates the change scenarios, which are either triggered by:

– reaching the limits of authorized geographical space (see Figure 7.7 I.A, II.A);

– the expiry of the validity time (see Figure 7.7 I.B, II.B).

Part "I" of Figure 7.7 is the illustration of the example explained above. The vehicle is within a crowd when it updates its pseudonym either because it reaches the geographical limits (A) or the expiry of its lifetime (B). Therefore, it explains the case of implicit cooperative change.

In Part "II", the vehicle senses its neighborhood prior to the update. If it finds that it is within less dense roads with a number of neighbors less than the expected threshold k, it starts executing an obfuscation method by altering the beacon's location and speed fields before the pseudonym update, in order to confuse the attacker. For Δt period of time, the vehicle sends beacons with the speed field set to 0, and the position set to the one before the change. After the update, the vehicle sends beacons with its real position and speed and freshly changed pseudonym. By doing so, the attacker is deluded into thinking that the vehicle has stopped on-road while it is running, and therefore cannot link the new pseudonym used from a new far location from that announced by the vehicle using the old pseudonym. The vehicle with the new pseudonym is detected as the new one instead of linking the freshly used pseudonym with the old one (see Figure 7.7 II. A, B).

As we explained before, Δt is the time needed to confuse the attacker through the use of obfuscation to break their accurate predictability. Note that the attacker relies on the vehicle's current and past locations, velocity and headings to predict its next location. Thus, when they receive erroneous or inaccurate spatiotemporal data, their predictions become wrong and fuzzy.

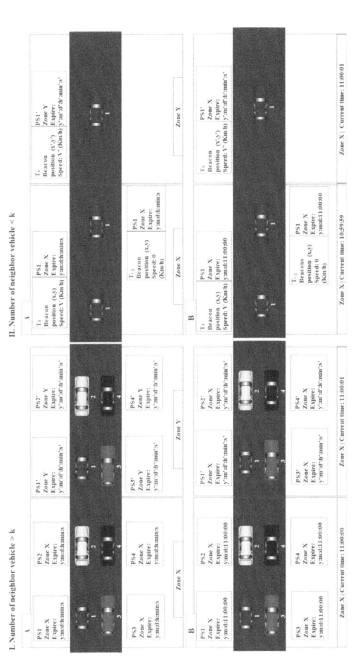

Figure 7.7. *The proposed pseudonym changing scheme. For a color version of this figure, see www.iste.co.uk/benarous/vehicular.zip*

Although we aim to protect privacy, we give the highest priority to safety applications. Thus, if an emergency event occurs requiring the vehicle to send its real location in a report, it ought to do so.

Figure 7.8 gives a flow chart description of the proposed pseudonym changing process when the trigger is the expiry of the pseudonym.

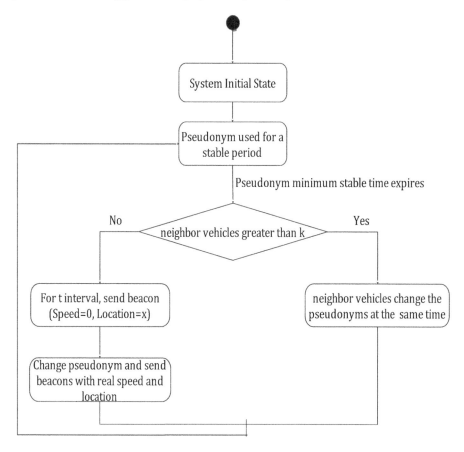

Figure 7.8. *Pseudonym changing process*

Algorithm 3 resumes the pseudonym change algorithm triggered either by the expiry of the pseudonym lifetime or the attainment of geo-space limit.

Algorithm 3: Pseudonym Change Algorithm

Begin

  While (true)

      Current_neighbors = Count-neighbors()

      If (Pseudonym Lifetime expire) *OR*

        (Pseudonym exceeds Geo-space limits) *then*

          If(Current_neighbors>= threshold-neighbors) *then*

            Pseudonym= new pseudonym ()

          Endif

      Else

          Current_position= position()

          Speed=0

          Current_pseudonym= Pseudonym

          While (Time < Tchange)

            Beacon (Current_pseudonym, Current_position, Speed)

            Send (Beacon)

          EndWhile

          Pseudonym= new pseudonym ()

      Endif

    Beacon (Pseudonym, position (), speed())

    Send (Beacon)

    EndWhile

End

7.4.3. *The simulation*

After explaining the proposed solution, we continue to resume the simulation results of our solution against a GPA. The implementation was done using an NS2 simulator (Statista 2016). The process of sorting the results is similar to the one used in the previous solution and so are the simulation settings, which were resumed previously in Table 7.2. We used three simulation scenarios with low, medium and high traffic density (50, 100 and 150 vehicles respectively). The GPA modeled executes two linking attacks, which are semantic and syntactic. Figure 7.9 presents the number of pseudonyms used for each scenario.

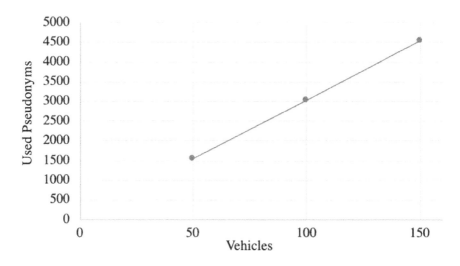

Figure 7.9. *Number of pseudonyms used*

Figure 7.10 resumes the obtained tracking ratio for each scenario. Overall, the tracking ratio decreased as the traffic density increased, which means that there are more chances that the vehicle changes its identifier within a cooperative crowd. Moreover, the solution's robustness and high performance in preserving the location privacy was translated by the low tracking ratios, which did not exceed 17%.

Figure 7.11 illustrates the linked identifiers ratio by both attacks per each scenario. Although the total number of pseudonym changes is large, the ratio of linked pseudonyms is low. It did not exceed 1%. This further proves that the solution is robust.

To further analyze the performance of our solution. We compared it with the periodical pseudonym change strategy. Figure 7.12 illustrates the obtained tracking ratio for both solutions per scenario. Our solution has a lower ratio than the periodical change solution, thus, a higher resiliency to the implemented attacker model executing semantic and syntactic attacks.

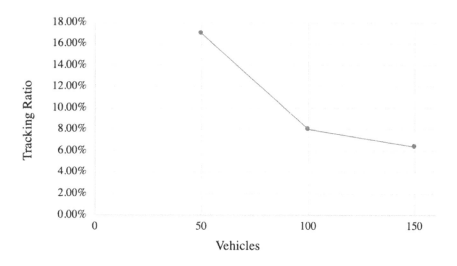

Figure 7.10. *Ratio of tracked vehicles*

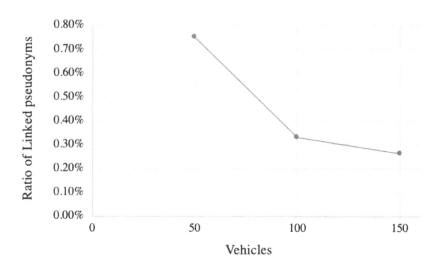

Figure 7.11. *Ratio of linked pseudonyms*

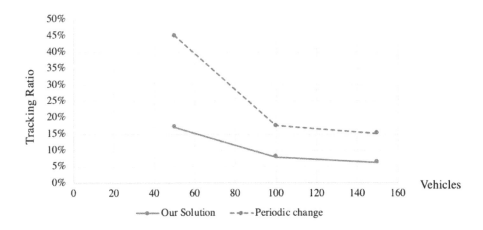

Figure 7.12. *Ratio of tracked vehicle for both solutions. For a color version of this figure, see www.iste.co.uk/benarous/vehicular.zip*

7.5. Conclusion

This chapter illustrated two new obfuscation pseudonym-based change strategies that reduce linkability and tracking to preserve the location privacy of VANET users.

The first solution uses a camouflage technique by creating a virtual crowd to confuse the attacker and reduce linkability. The solution both analytically and through simulations proved to have a good protection level, and it reduced the tracking ratio from 100% (without the use of a change strategy) within low-density roads to only 40%. It gave an average tracking ratio of 27%, which is good as it means that the privacy is protected with over 73%.

To further reduce this tracking ratio, we proposed another obfuscation solution to delude the attacker and reduce their accuracy. This solution is neighbor-aware and pseudonyms slotted. This means that if the vehicle is within a crowd, they all change at the same time as the pseudonyms have the same end validity time. If the vehicle is within less dense roads, it deludes the attacker prior to the change with beacons indicating that it is stopping. Then, when it does the update, it continues broadcasting its accurate position and speed. Since the attacker relies on the accurate beacon content to track the vehicle and predict its locations, erroneous and inaccurate beacons lead to fuzzy prediction and tracking failure. Indeed, the solution gave an average level of protection of 89.6% with an average tracking ratio of 10.4%, varying from 6.3% to 17% at worst. We remind the readers that neighbor vehicles may rely on their cameras, lidars and radars to make up for the one-hop neighbor vehicle inaccurate beacons. Moreover, the vehicle may halt the obfuscation technique to report emergency events if they occur, since the highest priority is always given to safety applications.

8

Preserving the Location Privacy of Internet of Vehicles Users

8.1. Introduction

The Internet of vehicles (IoV) is part of the Internet of Things (IoT). It can be seen as its instantiation with a particular type of moving object, which are the smart vehicles, as its main type of nodes. The IoT is without doubt one of trendiest and widely commercialized technologies with its various real-world applications, such as smart homes, smart cities, e-health and intelligent transportation systems. Figure 8.1 illustrates the number of IoT connected devices since 2015. Its speedy growth is estimated to continue to reach 30 billion by 2020 and surpass 75 billion connected devices by 2025 (Heinze 2016). The number of connected vehicles in the IoT more precisely in the IoV is estimated to reach 380 million vehicles by 2021 (Sun Tzu Said 2022).

Although the IoV concept is often associated with the IoT, the concept of connected vehicles is much older. It has been used since 2004 upon the introduction of VANET. Yet, unlike IoT, which was commercially blooming, the concept of VANET lacked real-world realizations and faced some technical and juridical obstacles that prevented it from prospering. It is now being appended and is taking advantage of the commercially accepted concept of the IoT and is currently known more commonly in the IoV (Yang et al. 2014).

In the IoV, the vehicle may provide or use data and services from other vehicles, objects, infrastructures, sensors and humans. It communicates with other vehicles via vehicle-to-vehicle (V2V), with infrastructures via vehicle-to-infrastructure (V2I), with objects via vehicle-to-everything (V2X), with sensors via vehicle-to-sensors (V2S) and with humans via vehicle-to-human (V2H) communications respectively.

The data are stored in the cloud and can be accessed by vehicles, humans or things. Therefore, the IoV provides a wider range of stable services.

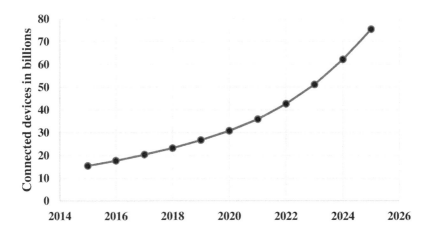

Figure 8.1. *The number of IoT connected devices (based on the statistics of Heinze (2016))*

Although IoV services are captivating, the fact that they may risk both their user's identity and location privacy is too perilous to be ignored. To overcome this issue, several solutions are being elaborated, mainly concentrating on using temporal identifiers for the vehicle's cyber activity to protect its identity privacy. Identifier-based solutions focus on the strategies that render the identifier update unlinkable in order to prevent the vehicle's tracking on-road.

In this chapter, we propose three solutions: the first is crowd-based to thwart identifier linkability and protects against tracking when using cloud enabled-IoV location-based services (LBS) and safety applications. We analyzed its performance against a modeled global passive attacker executing semantic, syntactic, observation mapping and linkage mapping attacks. We also compared it to a state of art solution through simulation by using NS2. The results found are optimistic, the privacy was preserved with more than 70% outperforming the performance of the state-of-the-art solution it was compared to. The second proposal strengthens the previous one with the use of concerted silence to preserve privacy with over 84%. Finally, in the third proposal, we enhanced the second solution by adding the obfuscation method on the location fields to achieve a protection level that exceeded 90%.

This chapter explains the cloud-enabled Internet of vehicles (CE-IoV) network model and functionality. It highlights the privacy particular challenges in the IoV and describes the attacker models targeting it. It also explains the first proposed privacy-preserving scheme, which relies on the cooperation of the crowd to thwart linkability. Furthermore, it includes the simulation settings and results, as well as a comparison study against an existing state-of-the-art solution. Likewise, it proposes the second scheme, which is an amelioration of the previous scheme that strengthens it through the use of silence. Then, the third further strengthens the second proposal by adding the obfuscation method.

8.2. CE-IoV

The literature contains numerous models of the IoV network, as explained in Chapter 1. Kang et al.'s (2016) model is the closest to ours where the CE-IoV is formed by LBS providers, a cloud manager managing the infrastructure-based local cloud, a registration authority managing the central cloud. This authority is responsible for generating the virtual machine identities (VMID), which are delivered to the local clouds that in turn convey them to the registered vehicles.

Similarly, our model has the same basic components, but it is more realistic, flexible and considers the vehicular network constraints. It fulfills the following requirements:

– connectivity that is provided by the vehicle-to-vehicle, vehicle-to-infrastructure and cellular communications;

– continuous stable services regardless of environment (urban, sparse or highway) through the use of connectivity and cloud computing technologies;

– reliability, availability and balanced workload distribution, where we considered that:

- in an urban environment, obstacles may hamper the connectivity, even though infrastructures or RSUs are available,

- in a sparse environment, the infrastructures are less available, affecting the connectivity negatively, leading to service discontinuity,

- in highways, the number of deployed RSUs is sufficient to form local clouds.

Taking the above requirements into account, we amended Kang et al.'s (2016) model as follows:

– The *local cloud* is VWC (Vehicle with Cloud). It is a hybrid cloud combining both infrastructure-based clouds and infrastructure-less distributed dynamic clouds.

– The *central cloud* is managed by a set of distributed registration authorities to balance the load and prevent the single point of failure. We note the registration authorities for ease of explanation as one global authority named trusted authority or TA. Both the local and central clouds customize virtual machines to handle the user's queries. Each machine has a unique identifier known as the VMID.

– The regional intermediary authorities (RA) manage the local clouds managers. The RAs obtain VMID lists from the TA, and they distribute them to local cloud managers. These authorities also maintain an intermediary revocation list.

Figure 8.2 illustrates the organization of the network components in our proposed CE-IoV model.

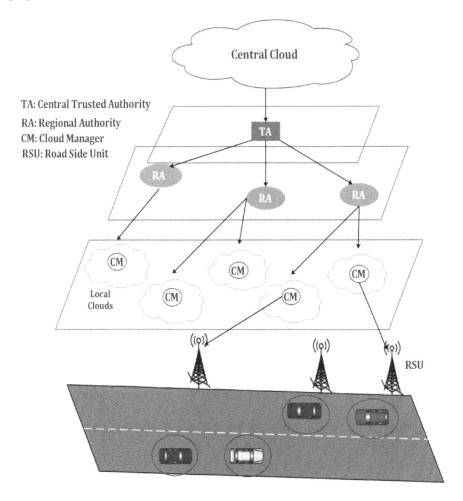

Figure 8.2. *Network model. For a color version of this figure, see www.iste.co.uk/benarous/vehicular.zip*

The proposed model has the following benefits:

– The use of distributed registration authorities, shortened to TA for ease of understanding, equilibrates the workload balance between the authorities and prevents the single point of failure.

– Similarly, the use of RAs reduces the workload on the TA as both the verification and revocation are handled by them (RAs) optimally.

– The hierarchical organization illustrated in Figure 8.2 permits the valid non-blacklisted identifiers re-usage across regions. It also gives the network a flexibility trait.

– Hybrid cloud usage ensures connectivity and the continuity of the service regardless of the environment (sparse, urban or highway).

– The virtual machine live migration following the vehicles' movements between vehicles, infrastructures and clouds ensures service continuity without interruptions or repeating authentications.

Figure 8.3 illustrates the network functionality, starting from the registration and authentication, and ending with the CE-IoV services usage.

The registration at the TA: initially, every IoV vehicle registers to the Trusted Authority (TA). This initial phase allows the vehicle to subscribe to the Regional Authorities (RA) it passes as it moves on-road. The TA delivers its corresponding long-term certified private/public keys that can be used either for digital signature or encryption to the registered vehicle, alongside a virtual machine with a unique identifier, customized specially to handle the vehicle's future service queries (see Figure 8.3, phase 4), and also, the secretly delivered credentials that may be used when authenticating to the cloud services. The TA updates the RAs with the registered members (see Figure 8.3, phase 5). The initial registration is done only once upon purchase and all sensitive security-related data are stored encrypted in the vehicle's tamper-proof device to protect it from being duplicated, altered or deleted.

The registration at the RA: for the vehicle to obtain its pool of certified pseudonyms (see Figure 8.3, phases 1–3). It is done by using the credentials and certified long-term public key delivered by the TA upon the initial registration. If the vehicle is not found in the RA's database, the RA first verifies with the TA that the vehicle is registered, and then it delivers the pseudonyms requested.

The authentication with the Cloud Manager (CM): to use the cloud services advertised by the CM, the vehicle authenticates itself to it (CM) using its credentials and VMID (see Figure 8.3, phase 6). The CM checks with the RA to confirm that the vehicle is registered (see Figure 8.3, phases 7 and 8). Then, it provides it with an organized list of temporal VMIDs (see Figure 8.3, phase 9). The CM maps them with the vehicle's credentials and long-term public key, and stores them in its local database to ensure traceability and accountability.

The request of LBS (see Figure 8.3, phase 10): the vehicle uses the received VMIDs and credentials to securely benefit from the LBS services, while preserving privacy.

Note that the TA provides the RA with a large pool of VMIDs (M), which it distributes on the CMs by giving each a smaller pool of size (m) (see Figure 8.3, phase 0).

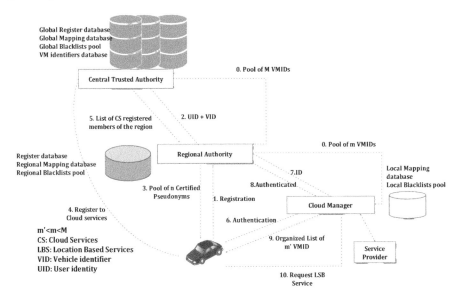

Figure 8.3. *General description of the cloud-enabled Internet of vehicles. For a color version of this figure, see www.iste.co.uk/benarous/vehicular.zip*

8.3. Privacy challenges

We already explained the privacy concept in Chapter 2. In this section, we discuss the particular challenges imposed by the IoV network nature.

1) The vehicle sends periodical messages containing its certified public key, position, speed and direction, which leads to its tracking if intercepted by a malicious attacker.

2) The communications within the network are wireless.

3) The user's desire for anonymity and unlinkability contradicts the non-repudiation required by the juridical system. A solution balancing all of these traits is needed.

4) The attacker is at an advantage as they are passive and undetectable.

5) The privacy-preserving solution should not negatively impact network functionality nor cause service discontinuity.

8.4. Attacker model

We explained in Chapter 4 that the attacker violating the privacy is a Global Passive Attacker (GPA) who aims to track the vehicle by its cyber activity. They may install cheap receivers across the observation region to eavesdrop on the vehicle's beacons that contain its pseudonyms and real-time positions, and LBS messages of CE-IoV containing VMIDs and positions provided by the vehicle in-board GPS. The GPA executes four linking attacks to track the vehicle, which are: the observation mapping attack, the linking mapping attack, semantic linking attack and syntactic linking attack. All of the mentioned attacks were already explained in Chapter 4.

We remind the readers that as the GPA is passive they are difficult to detect. This gives them various advantages, such as the long tracking periods, wider knowledge about the road restrictions, cyber-profiling and the possibility of trading the user's tracking and secrets undetectably. The GPA would know the victim user vehicle's entire past trajectory without the victim user's knowledge. Just as Sun Tzu said in his book, *The Art of War*: "*If you know the enemy and know yourself, you need not fear the result of a hundred battles.*" (Sun Tzu 1910; Pan et al. 2017). Thus, the GPA has the upper hand since the targeted victim is unaware that they are being tracked and are acting naturally, allowing the attacker to gather a wide range of real data about them.

In Table 8.1, we gave the simulation setting of the GPA. The simulation was done using an NS2 simulator on the Manhattan grid, with moving vehicles generated using the MobiSim tool (Mobisim; Mousavi et al. 2007). The GPA installs their receivers as a grid across the road to fully cover the map. This assumption may not be plausible in reality due to the cost and the difficulty of installing all of these receivers without being noticed by the police. However, this is the strongest hypotheses in theory and the worst case that may be imagined to happen in reality. If the solution tested under these assumptions proves to work well, then it will be strong against any weaker realistic model.

8.5. CLPPS: cooperative-based location privacy-preserving scheme for Internet of vehicles

Having described the implemented attacker model, in this section, we continue to explain the proposed scheme illustrated in Figure 8.4. The scheme protects the privacy on two levels: the safety beaconing level and the CE-IoV LBS level. The details of each level are given in the following sections.

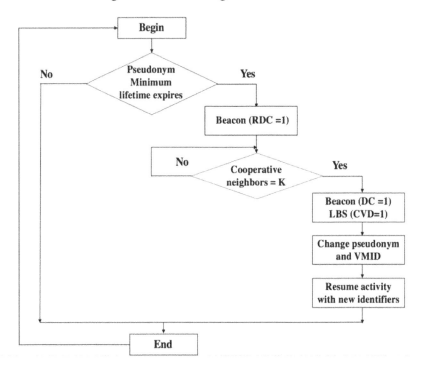

Figure 8.4. *Diagram of the proposed identifier changing scheme*

– Anonymity and location privacy in safety beaconing level

To ensure anonymity, pseudonyms are used and their change with robust strategies is needed to protect the location privacy from linking and tracking. Our change strategy relies on the cooperation of neighbors. The vehicle needs to synchronize its pseudonym change with its neighbors to thwart linking. However, since we mentioned that the privacy solution should not negatively influence the network functionality, the synchronization between vehicles needs to be optimal, without adding extra messages or increasing the over-head on the network. This is especially true as the more vehicles there are in the vicinity, the higher the chances are for collision, and message drop or broadcast storms to occur. Therefore, to implement our scheme with the least over-head possible, we used two bits from the beacon header extra non-used bits, one is RDC (Ready to Do the Change) set to 1 when the vehicle wants to announce its will and readiness to update its pseudonym and to 0 otherwise. The other bit is DC (Do the Change), which is set to 1 when the vehicle has satisfied its pseudonym update context and to 0 otherwise. Note that the expiry of the minimum stable lifetime of the vehicle's pseudonym is the trigger to set RDC to 1. The pseudonym change context is receiving k beacons from k distinct neighbor vehicles willing to do the change, which means their RDC is set to one. When the vehicle sets its DC to 1, it does the change on the next time slot. Hence, its next beacon would be signed with the freshly updated pseudonym. Similarly, vehicles that receive DC flagged beacons also change their pseudonyms in the next time slot and resume their beaconing with their newly updated pseudonyms, achieving a simultaneous change and reducing the attacker's tracking accuracy from 1 to $1/k$ as their target could be any one from the k potential candidates. Naturally, the confusion increases as the number of neighbor vehicles simultaneously doing the change does.

– **Anonymity and location privacy in the CE-IoV LBS level**

As illustrated in Figure 8.3, when the vehicle updates its pseudonym used in the safety beacons, it also simultaneously changes its VMID used in CE-IoV LBS. Similarly, we use a bit as in the service messages header CVD (Change VMID) to inform the CM of the VMID change, which in turn records this change. We remind the readers that the aim of using organized lists of VMID is to help both the CM and vehicle know the next VMID to be used without the need to send extra messages as both have the same copy of the ordered list. Since the vehicle updates its VMIDs sequentially from the list, the CM can map and record that easily.

Therefore, the VMIDs are updated simultaneously with the pseudonyms in a cooperative way, as previously explained. Upon the successful change, the vehicle and its cooperating neighbors update their identifiers and continue their activities with their new VMIDs and pseudonyms without the need to re-do the authentication to the service provider. Furthermore, since the CM records the change, it informs the service provider of the new VMID to tunnel all the pending queries with the old VMID to its destination after the update, which ensures a continuous service.

8.5.1. *Simulation*

In this section, we explain how we simulated our proposal and tested it against the modeled GPA explained in section 4, executing four types of linking attacks. We first begin by resuming the settings, and then analyze the obtained results.

8.5.1.1. *Settings*

We simulated our proposal using an NS2 simulator on the Manhattan map grid, with its mobility model for moving vehicles generated by the MobiSim tool, noted as scenarios. We created five scenarios on the same map with the same simulation span (900 seconds), where the number of vehicles per scenario increased from 10 vehicles for low density, to (50, 100) vehicles for medium density then to (150, 200) vehicles for high density. Each vehicle periodically broadcasts state messages to its neighbors, and sends LBS messages to a service provider and connectivity messages to the CM.

We have already explained how we implemented the global passive attacker in section 8.4. In Table 8.1, both the vehicle's and attacker's simulation settings are explained.

Tools	NS2, MobiSim
Mac layer	802.11 p
Simulation time	900 seconds
Map	1,000 x 1,000, Manhattan grid
Pseudonym minimum lifetime	30 seconds
Vehicle range	300 m
K cooperative neighbors	2
Number of attacker's receivers	100
Attacker coverage range	500 m
Scenario 1 vehicle number	10
Scenario 2 vehicle number	50
Scenario 3 vehicle number	100
Scenario 4 vehicle number	150
Scenario 5 vehicle number	200

Table 8.1. *Simulation parameters for the vehicles*

8.5.1.2. *Results*

After explaining the simulation settings, we continue to clarify how the results are sorted and processed to be meaningful and illustrative in analyzing the solution's performance against the modeled attacker. After sorting them and extracting the needed ratios, we illustrate them in the coming figures. Then, we comment and analyze them.

Our simulation generates two trace files. One is for the vehicle's cyber activity including its beacons and LBS messages. The other is for the attacker's tracks when eavesdropping and intercepting vehicles' messages. The vehicle's trace file is processed to separate its activities, where each activity trace is saved in a separate file. Thus, we obtained a beaconing trace file and LBS messages file. These files are used to confirm that the pseudonym and VMID are changed simultaneously, to obtain the number of updates and also to check the attacker's tracking correctness and accuracy.

The attacker trace file was also processed to separate the tracking by attack resulting in four trace files for each type of attack, which are semantic, syntactic, linking mapping and observation mapping. For each attack, the number of correctly tracked nodes and correctly linked identifier changes were extracted, which were used to calculate the ratios defined in the following formulas and presented in the graphs:

Ratio of tracked vehicles per attack =

$$\frac{Number\ of\ correctly\ tracked\ vehicles\ per\ attack}{Total\ number\ of\ vehicles\ per\ scenario} \qquad [8.1]$$

Ratio of tracked vehicles =

$$AVERAGE\ (ratios\ of\ tracked\ vehicle\ per\ attack) \qquad [8.2]$$

Ratio of linked identifier per attack =

$$\frac{Number\ of\ correctly\ linked\ identifiers}{Total\ number\ of\ changed\ identifiers\ per\ scenario} \qquad [8.3]$$

Figure 8.5 illustrates the calculated tracking ratio of the modeled GPA when the vehicles execute our proposed scheme. In general, the ratio was low, not exceeding 30%, which means that location privacy was preserved with 70%.

Also, except for the second scenario which was less than 27%, all of the other scenarios tracking ratios were less than 15%. We remind the reader that the vehicles distribution on the roads is random. Although we controlled the map, simulation duration and vehicle number for each scenario, we decided not to impose any constraints obliging the vehicles to be close or in the same vicinity with approximate mobility. This was done to ensure the fairness of the conducted simulation and avoid obtaining over-estimated results coming from favorable settings. Therefore, in Scenario 2, where the ratio was higher than the rest, it is most likely due to the vehicle not being in a favorable context at all times.

Another observation on the ratios is that they decreased as the number of vehicles increased. Note that the lower the tracking ratio, the higher the level of privacy, the best the solution is.

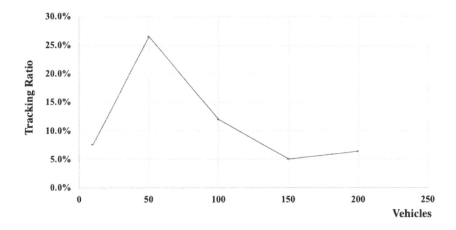

Figure 8.5. *Ratio of tracked vehicles*

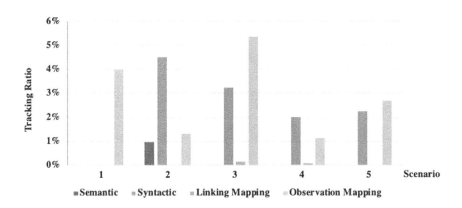

Figure 8.6. *Ratio of tracked vehicles for each attack. For a color version of this figure, see www.iste.co.uk/benarous/vehicular.zip*

In Figure 8.6, the tracking ratios for each attack for each scenario are illustrated, where the numbers 1 to 5 reflect the simulated scenarios, as given in Table 8.1. We note that the tracking ratios for semantic and linking mapping attacks were approximately null for all scenarios. The syntactic attack tracking ratio was less than

5%, while the observation attack tracking ratio was less than 6%. Both ratios were less than 10%. This indicates that we can ensure with more than 94% that the solution is almost resilient to these attacks, and therefore, it preserves privacy.

8.5.2. *Comparative study and performance analysis*

To further illustrate the performance of the proposed solution against the modeled attacker, we decided to compare it with the state-of-the-art solution of Kang et al. (2016). Table 8.2 describes the key differences between our solutions and highlights the advantages and disadvantages of each solution.

Privacy approaches	Non-Cooperative	Cooperative
	Kang et al	Our Strategy
Principle	-The pseudonyms and VMIDs are changed simultaneously. - The vehicle synchronizes with the CM to do this change. The synchronization process implies the request to change, getting approval, checking the time continuously, choosing the VMID, and informing the cloud manager to record it.	The identifiers (pseudonym, VMID) are changed simultaneously using flag-based cooperative change strategy to ensure the unlinkability and anonymity. The cloud manager does not need to be included and synchronized with to do the change. Instead, it is just informed to record it.
Advantage	- The simultaneous change of identifiers protects against observation and mapping linking attacks. - Prevents repetitive authentications.	- Preserves the identity and the location privacy. - Prevents services interruption and repetitive authentication - The use of Flags and organized list of identities (CE-IoV) optimizes the network over-head. - Protects against observation mapping, linking mapping, syntactic and semantic attacks.
Drawback	-The strategy used to change the pseudonym is not mentioned. However, judging by the given details and seeing that there was no cooperation between adjacent vehicles before or after the change, it does not protect against syntactic linking attacks. -The synchronization process causes over-head to the network.	

Table 8.2. *Comparative study between our proposed solution and the proposed solution by Kang et al. (2016)*

To do the comparative performance study, the solution of Kang et al. (2016) was simulated under the same settings, scenarios given in Table 8.1 and against the same modeled attacker. Similarly, the resulting trace files were processed in the same way as ours to extract the tracking ratios, as previously explained. The results are illustrated in Figures 8.7–8.10.

Figure 8.7 presents the ratio of tracked vehicles by the GPA for both solutions. It can be seen that our tracking ratio is lower than that of Kang et al. This means that our proposal outperforms Kang et al., as a lower ratio means a stronger privacy protection.

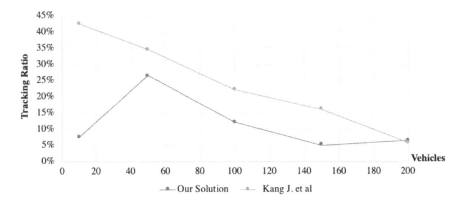

Figure 8.7. *Ratio of tracked vehicles for both solutions. For a color version of this figure, see www.iste.co.uk/benarous/vehicular.zip*

Figures 8.8–8.10 illustrate the tracking ratio obtained by the syntactic, semantic and observation mapping attacks respectively for both solutions. The results obtained by our solution are better for all of the above attacks. Note that both solutions gave a low tracking ratio against the semantic and linking mapping attacks under the simulated scenarios.

Another comparison metric that may also be considered is the number of identifiers changed for each solution, although frequent identifier change alone does not necessarily improve the privacy protection. Contrariwise, it may cause service disruption and identifier over-consumption. Therefore, we designed our solution to enable the identifier change to happen only within a favorable context that would reduce the linkability, which is to change within a cooperative crowd. Our argument is further proved by the obtained results, where our solution gave a higher protection and a lower tracking ratio compared to Kang et al.'s solution, suggesting frequent identifier update independently upon expiry, although the number of identifiers changed in their solution is about three times in average greater ours.

In addition, our solution in comparison with Kang et al. reduces the overhead of synchronization. In their solution, various messages are exchanged with the cloud manager (CM) to implement the VMID change, including the request of the change, getting approval, continuous time synchronization, choosing a VMID and informing the CM about it to record it. On the contrary, our solution relies on the use of flagged messages with two bits at max being used for synchronization purposes. We also optimized the VMID request, approval and record messages by the use of organized VMID lists. Thus, the vehicle only needs to inform the CM about the change in a flagged message and the CM would be aware of the next VMID to be used.

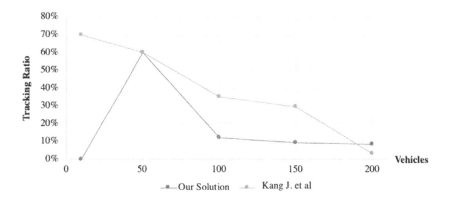

Figure 8.8. *Syntactic attacker's ratio of tracked vehicles for both solutions. For a color version of this figure, see www.iste.co.uk/benarous/vehicular.zip*

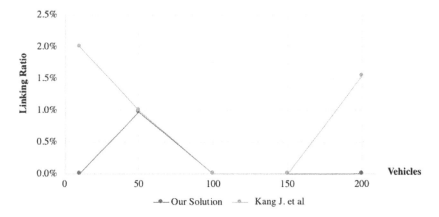

Figure 8.9. *Semantic attacker – ratio of linked identifiers. For a color version of this figure, see www.iste.co.uk/benarous/vehicular.zip*

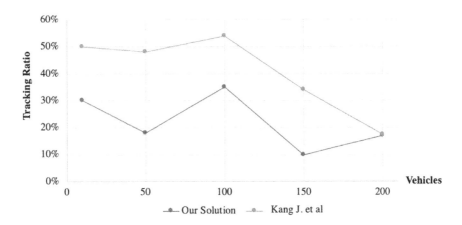

Figure 8.10. *Observation mapping attack – ratio of the tracked vehicle. For a color version of this figure, see www.iste.co.uk/benarous/vehicular.zip*

8.6. CSLPPS: concerted silence-based location privacy-preserving scheme for Internet of vehicles

In the previous section, we presented a cooperative-based solution to preserve location privacy in the CE-IoV. The solution gives optimistic results when tested through simulations against a global passive attacker, which is known to be a strong attacker model, with the overall tracking ratio between 5% and 27% approximately.

In this section, we aim to further reduce this tracking ratio by proposing a solution named the Concerted Silence-based Location Privacy-Preserving Scheme for Internet of vehicles (CSLPPS). CSLPPS is an amelioration of CLPPS proposed earlier. It relies on both the cooperation of the vehicles and their synchronized silence as the identifier change strategy is used to simultaneously update the pseudonym and VMID.

8.6.1. *The proposed solution*

Similarly with the previous proposal, the vehicle participates in safety applications by periodically broadcasting beacons signed with its pseudonym. It also uses the IoV LBS served through the clouds, where a virtual machine is customized to serve its queries with a unique VMID. Both of the VMIDs and pseudonyms are changed simultaneously to avoid linkability and traceability using the CSLPPS.

We use the same principal of flagged messages where the flags (bits) RDC, DC, CVD mean ready to change, do change and change VMID, respectively. The first two are customized un-used bits from the beacon's header and the last is from the service/connectivity message header. The CM is informed of the VMID change to record it through the reception of a flagged message, with CVD set to 1.

We assume that upon the initial registration of the vehicle to the regional authority, the change strategy along with its parameters, that are the threshold of cooperating vehicle K and the silent period T, were flashed in it and that the cloud managers are aware of them.

When the vehicle pseudonym is about to expire, it senses its neighbor vehicles and informs them about the change by setting RDC to 1. Vehicles that have a similar state, i.e. the desire to change their pseudonyms, also send beacons with RDC = 1. When a vehicle receives K beacons from K different neighbors also willing to change their pseudonyms, it sets its DC in beacons to 1 and CVD in service/connectivity message to 1. The first is to inform the neighbor vehicles to enter silence and then implement the change. The second is to inform the CM to record the change and inform the service provider with the new VMID to be used. The vehicle ceases broadcasting although it may still receive messages. The CM cashes the pending queues and responses until the change is done (end of silence) and relays them to the vehicles using its new VMID. When the silent period ends, all vehicles that updated their identifiers may resume their activities using the newly changed identifiers. They can continue beaconing with their fresh pseudonyms and continue exchanging LBS messages via the new VMIDs without the need for re-authentication.

In a nutshell, the vehicles synchronize to cooperatively enter silence (concerted silence) to simultaneously update their identifiers, with the aim of confusing the attacker and reducing their linking and tracking capabilities.

8.6.2. *Simulation results*

To evaluate CSLPPS and study its performance, we simulated it against a global passive attacker using the same tools, parameters, maps and scenarios as previously explained in the cooperative approach. The results were also compared to Kang et al.'s solution.

We first give the simulation results. Then, we give the comparative study details. Figure 8.11 presents the ratio of correctly tracked vehicles when changing their identifiers CSLPPS obtained by the GPA executing four linking attacks. The attacks are semantic, syntactic, observation mapping and linking mapping attacks. The ratio is calculated using the same methods explained in section 8.5.2.1. The overall ratio did not exceed 16% and it decreased to reach approximately 6% as the number of vehicles per scenario increased. On average, the tracking ratio was 10.1%, which is lower than the results obtained by the previous proposal, which was 11.5% on average, and even lower than that of Kang et al., which was 24.2% on average.

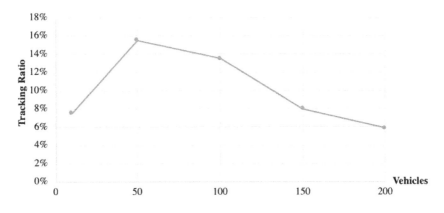

Figure 8.11. *Ratio of tracked vehicles*

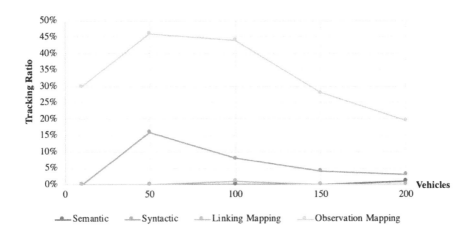

Figure 8.12. *Ratio of tracked vehicles for each attack. For a color version of this figure, see www.iste.co.uk/benarous/vehicular.zip*

Figure 8.12 illustrates the ratio of tracked vehicles for each attack. The solution is almost robust to semantic and linking mapping attacks. The results for the other two attacks decrease as the number of vehicles increases. The tracking ratio for the syntactic attack was between 0 and 16% and for the observation attack it was between 20 and 45%.

8.6.3. *Comparative study performance analysis*

We compared our proposal to Kang et al.'s solution. The results obtained and illustrated in Figure 8.13 demonstrate that our solution is better translated by the lower tracking ratios for all scenarios. Figures 8.14–8.16 show the detailed tracking ratios by attack type for both solutions, which are the syntactic, semantic and observation mapping attacks respectively.

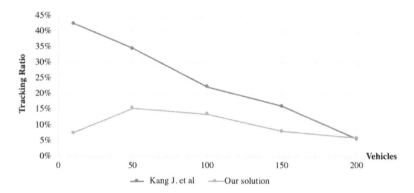

Figure 8.13. *Ratio of tracked vehicles. For a color version of this figure, see www.iste.co.uk/benarous/vehicular.zip*

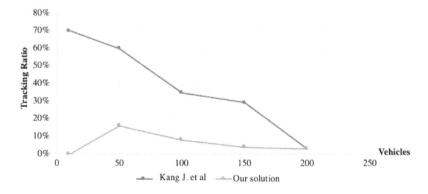

Figure 8.14. *Syntactic attacker's ratio of tracked vehicles. For a color version of this figure, see www.iste.co.uk/benarous/vehicular.zip*

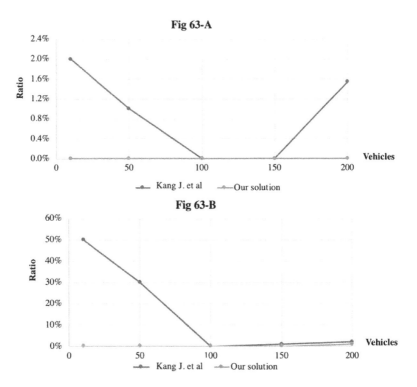

Figure 8.15. Semantic attacker (A. ratio of linked identifiers,
B. ratio of tracked vehicles). For a color version of this
figure, see www.iste.co.uk/benarous/vehicular.zip

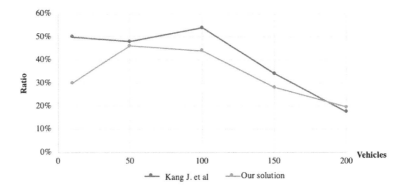

Figure 8.16. Observation mapping attack – ratio of tracked vehicles. For
a color version of this figure, see www.iste.co.uk/benarous/vehicular.zip

8.7. Obfuscation-based location privacy-preserving scheme in cloud-enabled Internet of vehicles

The above-explained proposals protect location privacy by reducing the linkability of identifiers. Both relied on strengthening the update strategy. The first relies on the cooperation of the neighbors and the second additionally uses concerted silence. With the aim of further decreasing the tracking ratio, we polish the proposal by adding the obfuscation method to protect the location of the vehicles. Therefore, in this final solution, we combine the cooperation, silence and obfuscation to develop a robust identifier strategy that showed the best results so far when tested through simulation against a GPA, with an average tracking ratio of 7.15%. The proposed solution and its analysis are explained in the coming sections.

8.7.1. *The proposition*

The solution uses the same logic as the previous two proposals, which are resumed in the use of flagged message to coordinate the change between the vehicles and inform the CM.

When the vehicle wants to update its identifiers, it sets the RDC flag (bit) in the beacon to 1, informing the neighbor vehicles of the change. Vehicles receiving this beacon, with the desire to also update their identifiers, set their RDC flag to 1 and their locations to that of the sending vehicle. Upon the reception of k beacons from k distinct neighbors, the vehicle sets its DC to 1 and CVD to 1 in both its beacon and service/connectivity message and enters silence. Vehicles receiving the DC flagged beacons also set their DC to 1 and enter silence. The CM records the change and informs the service provider about the next VMID to be used. It cashes the coming responses to the vehicle until after the change. Note that vehicles not participating in the change may continue sending messages to the vehicles updating their pseudonyms. The vehicles cease broadcast when in silence, but may continue receiving messages. Since the messages are broadcasted, even though the location is not accurate, as long as it is within the vehicle's range it can reach it. Figure 8.17 illustrates the proposed identifier change strategy organized in five successive steps: step 1 is the vehicle announcing its identifier change; step 2 is the vehicles announcing their cooperation by unifying their positions to that of the sender and informing each other about their willingness to do the update; step 3 is the vehicles confirming the change, informing the CM and entering silence; step 4 illustrates that all vehicles cease their broadcast and are silent for the designated period; and step 5 is the vehicles resuming their activities with their newly updated identifiers.

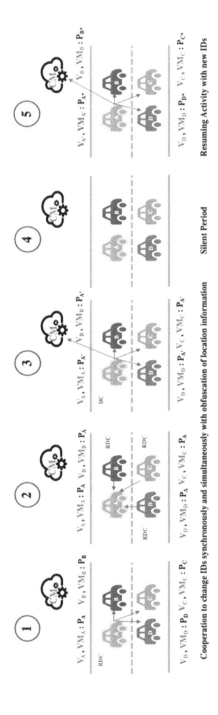

Figure 8.17. *Pseudonym and VMID change strategy*

As we saw in the previous sections, the frequent identifier change within an unfavorable context does not enhance the privacy level. On the contrary, it over-consumes the identifiers uselessly. Therefore, in our solution, the identifiers are not changed unless the vehicle is within a cooperative crowd.

8.7.2. *Study of feasibility using game theoretic approach*

To study the feasibility of the proposed solution, we used the game theory. The change strategy is considered as the game G. As in Al-Momani et al. (2016), we used a dynamic game (G) with complete and perfect information. G is defined as the triplet (P, S, U), where P and S are a set of players and strategies respectively and U are the payoff functions. G has two stages as follows:

– *Stage 1*: more or less related to the announcing vehicle's actions and decisions. This initial stage is the announcement of the change and requesting cooperation from the neighbors. To do so, the vehicle sets its RDC to 1 and waits to have *k* neighbors with RDC equal to 1. Next, based on the other vehicles (players) cooperation, it decides to implement the change when it has at least *k* cooperative neighbors by setting its DC flag to 1 and broadcasting the decision. The DC flag is set to 0 otherwise.

– *Stage 2*: related to the neighbor vehicles cooperation where they decide upon the reception of RDC flagged message representing the cooperative change announcement. The decision is either to implement the change of their pseudonyms and VMID, or not.

Let $P = \{P_i\}_{i=1}^{n}$ consist of the set of players. Let P1 be the announcer in stage 1 and $P_2, \ldots, P_n$ be the neighbors. P_1 has two moves: ready to do the change defined as R and not ready defined as NR. Thus, the set of strategies S_1 for P_1 is equal to {R, NR}. For the rest of the players P_i (i $\in$ [2, n]) and $S_i = \{C, NC\}$, where C means cooperative and NC means not cooperative to do the change.

The location privacy loss denoted by d_i is calculated as follows:

1) $d_i = 0$, if the vehicle is silent;

2) $d_i = \lambda(T_c - T_i)$, otherwise, the vehicle is not silent.

where λ is the tracking power of the attacker, T_c is the current time, and T_i is the time since the last pseudonym VMID successful change.

The cost of change γ is the sum of the cost of acquiring new pseudonym γ_{psd} and VMID γ_{vmid}, the cost of this change affecting the routing of data γ_{rt}, and the cost of this change affecting it safety applications γ_{sa}:

$$\gamma = \gamma_{psd} + \gamma_{vmid} + \gamma_{rt} + \gamma_{sa}$$

The payoff function $U = \{U_i\}_{i=1}^{n}$ is defined for player P_i as U_i, and is calculated using d_i and γ as follows:

1) $U_i = - d_i$, if P_i does not change its pseudonym and VMID;

2) $U_i = -d_i - \gamma$, if P_i implements the change within a non-cooperative crowd;

3) $U_i = \frac{-d_i}{k} - \gamma$, if P_i implements the change within a cooperative crowd (k neighbors);

4) $U_i = -\gamma$, if P_i implements the change within a cooperative crowd (k neighbors), executes the obfuscation method and enters a silent period.

In our solution, we propose that the vehicle either implements the change within a cooperative crowd after applying the silent period, or it does not. Thus, $U_i = -\gamma$ or $- d_i$ respectively. For the rest of the demonstration, we set the threshold of cooperative neighbors k to 3.

We first consider four players P_1, the initiator and P_2, P_3 and P_4 the neighbor vehicles. If P_1 chooses NR, the game is over for all the vehicles and none of them implement the change. Thus, $U_1 = -d_1$, $U_2 = -d_2$, $U_3 = -d_3$ and $U_4 = -d_4$.

If P_1 chooses R and P_2, P_3 and P_4 choose C, then the change happens for all the four vehicles, followed by a silent period, the payoff function would then be $U_1 = -\gamma$, $U_2 = -\gamma$, $U_3 = -\gamma$ and $U_4 = -\gamma$. If P_1 chooses R and one or more neighbor(s) P_2, P_3, P_4 choose NC, the change does not happen and the payoff function would be: $U_1 = -d_1$, $U_2 = -d_2$, $U_3 = -d_3$ and $U_4 = -d_4$. The same conclusion can be drawn if the game had n players (n > k). This proves the feasibility of the solution.

8.7.3. *The simulation*

We simulated both the vehicles and the attacker model using NS2 on MobiSim generated mobility files. Table 8.3 resumes the simulation parameters. The attacker model is a passive global attacker that executes four linkability attacks, which are the semantic, syntactic, observation mapping and linking mapping attacks. The attacker spreads their receivers as a grid to fully cover the map.

Tools	NS2, MobiSim
Mac layer	802.11 p
Simulation time	300 seconds
Map	700 x 700, 5 lane freeway
Pseudonym minimum lifetime	30 seconds
Vehicle range	300 m
K	3
Silent period	2 seconds
Number of attackers	36
Attacker coverage range	500 m
Scenario 1: number of vehicles	50
Scenario 2: number of vehicles	100
Scenario 3: number of vehicles	200
Scenario 4: number of vehicles	250

Table 8.3. *Simulation parameters*

Figure 8.18 presents the tracking ratio per attack for each scenario. It can be noted that the solution is almost resilient to semantic, syntactic and linking mapping attacks. The tracking ratio using observation attack varied from 23% to 32%. The vehicle may be tracked during the lifetime of its identifier. However, as long as the identifier update is not linked, long-term linkability is avoided and trajectory tracking is prevented and so is the identification through the profiling. This is ensured with our solution, as in more than 90% of the cases, the vehicle is perceived as a new one by the attacker after it updates its identifiers, without its old and new identifiers being linked.

Figure 8.19 illustrates the overall tracking ratio obtained by the GPA, the four linking attacks (semantic, syntactic, linkage and observation). The ratio was between 6% and 9%. It decreased as the number of vehicles per scenario increased. This is because the more vehicles, the higher the chances of having close vehicles, the higher the chances of cooperation and the larger is the size of the anonymity set (cooperative crowd). Note that the larger anonymity set increases the confusion of the attacker and decreases the accuracy of their tracking.

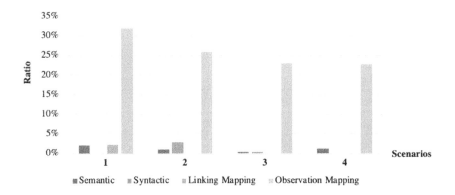

Figure 8.18. *Attacker's tracking ratio for each attack. For a color version of this figure, see www.iste.co.uk/benarous/vehicular.zip*

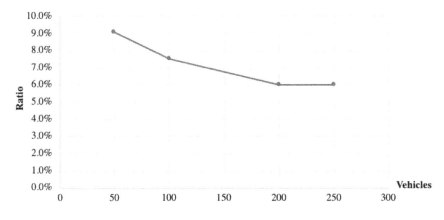

Figure 8.19. *Average ratio of detected vehicles*

In Figures 8.18 and 8.19 we illustrated the tracking ratio that did not exceed 10% overall, with almost full resiliency to semantic, syntactic and linking mapping attacks. For the observation linking attack, we added another metric known as the entropy or the quality of privacy. It is calculated by $H = -\sum p_i \log_2 p_i$, where p_i denotes the probability that an observed vehicle i is the target vehicle. The authors stated that the higher the H, the higher the location privacy level. When we applied this metric to our results, we obtained high entropy values between 6.43 and 26. This means that location privacy was preserved, and it was difficult for the attacker to link the pseudonym changes.

8.7.4. *Analytical model*

As explained in Chapter 3, location privacy is measured by various metrics. In this section, we use three metrics to analytically analyze the robustness of our proposed solution, which are the average anonymity set size, entropy and normalized entropy.

The average anonymity set size or AASS is defined as follows:

$$\mathrm{AASS} = \frac{\sum Anonymity\ set\ per\ change}{Total\ number\ of\ changes},$$

The entropy: $H = -\sum p_i \log_2 p_i$

The normalized entropy: $H_n = \dfrac{H}{\log 2 (AASS)}$

Figure 8.20 illustrates the results obtained when applying these metrics on the simulation results. We note that the average anonymity set, entropy and normalized entropy increase as the number of the vehicles per scenario does. The anonymity set size augmentation with the increase in vehicles is related to the rise of possibilities of having crowded and dense roads during the identifier update phase. Moreover, the high values obtained for the entropy indicate the robustness of the solution in preserving location privacy.

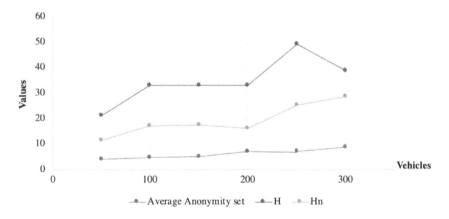

Figure 8.20. *Average anonymity set, entropy and normalized entropy. For a color version of this figure, see www.iste.co.uk/benarous/vehicular.zip*

8.7.5. *Comparative study*

Just like the two previous proposals, we conducted a comparative study between our solution and that of Contreras-Castillo et al. (2018). Both solutions were simulated under the same settings defined in Table 8.3, against the same attacker model, using the same scenarios.

Figure 8.21 illustrates the overall tracking ratio for both solutions. Our solution gave lower ratios reducing the tracking ratio of Kang et al. by approximately half.

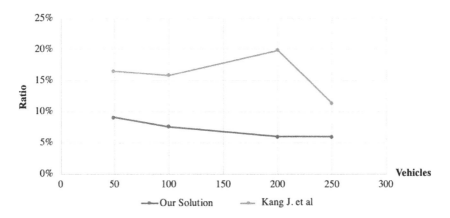

Figure 8.21. *Average ratio of detected vehicles. For a color version of this figure, see www.iste.co.uk/benarous/vehicular.zip*

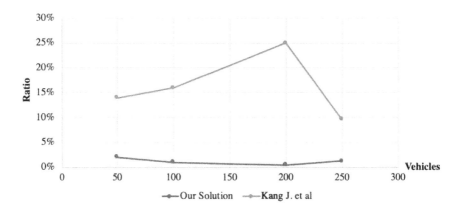

Figure 8.22. *Ratio of tracked vehicles – semantic attack. For a color version of this figure, see www.iste.co.uk/benarous/vehicular.zip*

Figures 8.22–8.24 present the tracking ratios for both solutions by attack, which are the semantic, syntactic and observation mapping respectively. We can see that our solution is almost resilient to both the semantic and syntactic attacks, outperforming the solution of Kang et al., which gave a tracking ratio between 10–25% for the semantic attack and 2–16% for the syntactic attack. Both solutions were almost resilient to the linking mapping attack. Our solution out-bested that of Kang et al., with a lower tracking ratio for the observation mapping attack.

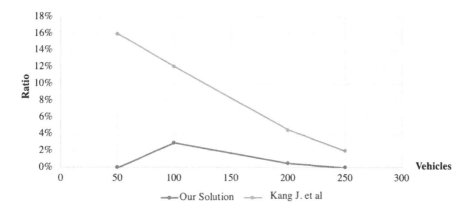

Figure 8.23. *Ratio of tracked vehicles – syntactic attack. For a color version of this figure, see www.iste.co.uk/benarous/vehicular.zip*

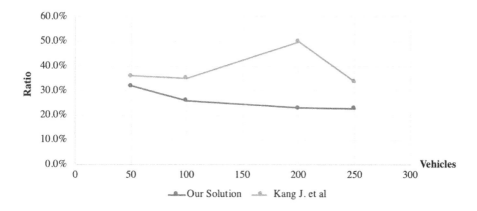

Figure 8.24. *Ratio of detected vehicles – observation mapping. For a color version of this figure, see www.iste.co.uk/benarous/vehicular.zip*

8.8. Conclusion

In this chapter, we proposed three location privacy-preserving solutions that prevent linking and tracking. The solutions achieved a high level of privacy protection and each amelioration increased the protection level, starting from 70% to 90%. These ratios are considered in the worst case against the strongest attacker covering the road completely. The proposals rely on the use of temporal identifiers in both the LBS queries and beaconing known as the VMID, and pseudonyms, respectively, both of which are changed simultaneously. In the first proposal, the change occurs within a cooperative crowd. In the second proposal, we strengthened the first scheme by using silence (concerted silence). In the third proposal, we further enhanced the solution by adding the obfuscation measure to thwart linkability.

9

Blockchain-based Privacy-aware Pseudonym Management Framework for Vehicular Networks

9.1. Introduction

In the previous chapters, we concentrated on the privacy issue in vehicular networks where the security system is centered around the public key infrastructure (PKI). The central PKI has a certifying authority (CA) to certify the long-term and short-term public keys (pseudonyms). To obtain a certificate for a self-generated keys or to request the keys (pseudonyms) in vehicular networks, each vehicle has to be registered to the CA. This registration requires the provision of authentic data about the user, such as their identity and the vehicle identification number (VIN). The certified pseudonyms are used to encrypt the communications, and their paired private keys are used to digitally sign the messages. Thus, it can be seen that they are fundamental security concepts in vehicular networks. The Vehicular Public Key Infrastructure (VPKI) system is strong and powerful both in terms of security and the privacy level it provides. Its strength originated from it being centralized and private. Only the CA can register the vehicles and their owners, and issue the certificates. The provided data is accessed only by the CA and is kept private from outsiders. The vehicle may either check the validity of a key or a certificate offline if it already has the CA public key to check the certificate digital signature, or, it may query the CA for the public key in case it does not have it and then do the verification. If the vehicle uses a certified pseudonym, its activities are traced by the CA. In case of misbehavior, it may be revoked and held accountable (conditional privacy). In other words, the CA has complete control over the user's registration, key generation/certifying, update and revocation process. This is also known as the pseudonym life cycle. Note that the centralization and confidentiality of the VPKI may be considered as its weaknesses, and are common to all centralized systems. These vulnerabilities expose it to targeted attacks, leading to it being a single point of failure.

Before explaining our potential replacement to the VPKI that resolves the single point of failure issue, we first briefly explain the role of pseudonyms in vehicular networks and how the VPKI handle them. This helps to extract the main traits that a potential replacement solution must have and the tasks it must handle.

Like we hinted at before, pseudonyms are either utilized to encrypt data/service messages or sign beacons, which are sent on a periodical basis to exchange state data. The signature in the beacon serves to authenticate the message and check its integrity before accepting it (Lozupone 2018). The message authentication prevents the injection of random bogus data from an outsider attacker. Although it does not protect against an internal attacker nor does it prevent them from injecting fake messages, it ensures that the internal attacker is held accountable, cannot deny their behavior and is revoked from the network to limit their influence. The revocation mechanism is executed by the CA after it receives reports from vehicles about a detected misbehavior. The revoked pseudonyms are then added to the certificate revocation list (CRL) that is timestamped and signed by the CA, and distributed to the vehicles to alert them and prohibit them from interacting or trusting the revoked node. One more unique trait to the VPKI is that the certificates of the pseudonyms are anonymous to preserve the identity of the vehicle users.

In a nutshell, a potential replacement framework of the centralized VPKI should ensure these requirements:

– *Security*: the key/certificate delivery is through secured communication channels. The integrity, authenticity and non-repudiation should be ensured. The keys and security algorithms should be encrypted, confidential and stored securely against intrusions.

– *Privacy*: the certificates are anonymous and identity-less to protect privacy. They are signed by the CA key and are traced back to this issuing authority. The two main traits to respect are the anonymity and unlinkability. The pseudonyms of the same user should not be linked to each nor to their identity. This is highly important as the linkability leads to both identification and tracking due to the correlation between the pseudonym and location broadcasted in the signed beacons.

– *Revocation*: which has to be fast and efficient, is essential to maintain the correct functionality of the network. In VPKI, the revocation is ensured by the CA that would revoke all the pseudonyms of a misbehaving user and may even disclose their identity to a juridical system if needed.

In this chapter, we design a secure decentralized pseudonym management framework as a potential replacement of the VPKI. The solution resolves the single point of failure issue, satisfies the above requirements and provides the same role and even a higher security level. The framework utilizes the public and distributed blockchain technology. It is a blockchain of blockchains formed by the pseudonym blockchain maintained by the vehicles and a revocation blockchain managed by road-side units. The framework takes advantage of the vehicular network components, which are the vehicles and RSU dispersed on roads to create secured distributed public replacements of VPKI that preserve privacy and ensure revocation. Thus, it reduces the cost of deploying and maintaining a CA and its subsidiaries.

This chapter explains the fundamental perquisites, such as the public key infrastructure (PKI), vehicular PKI, blockchain technology and the blockchain of blockchains. It also resumes the related works. Furthermore, it clarifies the key security concepts related to our proposed solution that are needed. It explains the proposed framework. Moreover, it analyzes the security and privacy properties of the framework. Lastly, it summarizes a comparative study between the vehicular PKI and our proposed framework.

9.2. Background

This section explains the key background-related concepts that facilitate the understanding of the proposed solution, which are as follows.

9.2.1. Public key infrastructure (PKI)

The public key infrastructure is also referred to as the two-key cryptography system, where the key used in the encryption is different from the one used in the decryption. In the digital signature, the encryption key, which is kept private or secret, is used to encrypt a hash value, which is the digest of the message and the decryption key which is publicly known to be used to decrypt the message and obtain the hash. The public key encryption is the inverse, the public key is used to encrypt and the private key is used to decrypt the messages. This way, only the intended party is allowed to read the encrypted content, which is the party that holds the pairwise of the public key used in the encryption. Note that although the pair keys are mathematically related, it is difficult to derive the private key from the public key. The conventional PKI by digitally certifying the public keys resolves the impersonation issue which occurs when a user pretends to be the owner of a public key that is not theirs. A digital certificate not only maps the public key to its owner, but also timestamps it and specifies its lifetime. It may be updated by prolonging its lifetime and revoked if misused. In what follows, we explain the key certifying process, certificate verification and revocation processes. We also describe the private key recovery process.

– The certifying process

The pair of public and private keys is generated by the user, and the public key is sent to the CA to be certified. The CA generates a certificate containing the user's name, public key and a validity period. The certificate is signed using the CA's private key.

The certificate X.509 contains the following fields: version, serial number, signature algorithm identifier, issuer distinguished name, validity interval, subject distinguished name, subject public key information, issuer unique identifier, subject unique identifier, extensions, signature.

– The certificate verification process

The verification of a certified public key starts by checking the CA's public key. It then proceeds by using this key to extract the hash value from the digital signature. This value is compared with the calculated one to ensure the received certificate integrity. Lastly, the validity of the public key is verified, which means that it is not expired yet and not revoked (blacklisted). The public key is accepted once all of the above conditions are satisfied, i.e. it is valid, non-revoked and integral.

– The certificate revocation process

The certificate is revoked if the private key is disclosed, if its holder is expelled or if they misuse it for unintended aims. The CA saves the revoked certificates in a list called the Certificate Revocation List (CRL). The CRL records the serial number of the certificate, the revocation date and reason. The list is timestamped and signed by the CA.

– The recovery of private key

The private key is fundamental for both the decryption and the signing process. Therefore, it is necessary to have a back-up copy that can be used if the original key is lost or ruined. The user may choose to either make local back-ups to preserve their privacy, or to save a copy at the CA, which may risk the privacy. If the user chooses to store a copy at a third-party company, not only may their privacy be at risk, but the confidentiality of their data may be violated if the private key is used to expose the encrypted content of messages, because the key owner becomes the data owner.

The private key may also be split into parts, where each is saved separately on different servers, entities or cards to prevent the risk of exposing the data confidentiality. When needed, the key is reconstructed by reassembling its parts (Khodaei 2012; Dini 2018).

9.2.2. Vehicular PKI

The vehicular networks public key infrastructure VPKI has a Root Certifying Authority (RCA), a Pseudonym Certificate Authority (PCA), a Long-Term Certificate Authority (LTCA) and a Pseudonym Resolution Authority (PRA). Upon registration, each vehicle obtains a long-term certified pair of public and private keys and a set of pseudonyms, also known as short-term pairs of public and private keys. The RCA signs the other authority (PCA, LTCA and PRA) certificates. The long-term certificates are used to request pseudonyms from PCA that are issued by the LTCA. The identity resolving of the pseudonym revocation is handled by the PRA. The VPKI guarantees the security properties ensured by the conventional PKI, which are authenticity, non-repudiation and integrity, and also ensures identity privacy, as the pseudonym certificate does not include the owner's identity. It only includes the serial number, the short-termed public key, the validity period and the PCA signature. In the VPKI, the revocation of a node is caused by its cyber misbehavior on-road. The PRA receives the misbehavior reports and includes the misbehaving node pseudonyms in the revocation list CRL, which is forwarded to the vehicles to alert them about the malicious nodes. The collaboration of RCA, PCA and LTCA is needed to resolve the identity of the misbehaving user (Crosby et al. 2015).

9.2.3. Blockchain technology

The interest in blockchain (BC) technology has increased ever since the introduction of Bitcoin in a paper by Nakamoto Satoshi a decade ago. Recently, the attention of various researchers and professionals is directed towards developing blockchain-based distributed applications. They are trying to shift application orientation from being centralized suffering from the single point of failure problem, to being distributed and decentralized build over the blockchains. The blockchain or the public ledgers are distributed immutable databases of transactions about physical or digital assets, where each transaction is validated by the network peer's consensus (Dib et al. 2018).

Figure 9.1 illustrates the blockchain architecture, which is organized on six layers (Nakamoto 2008) to facilitate its understanding: the application, data ledger, consensus, P2P exchange, network and hardware layer. In the following, we briefly explain each layer:

– The *application layer*: crypto-currencies such as Bitcoin (Buterin 2014), Ethereum (Alonso 2018) and Monero (Yaga et al. 2018) are famous, but are not the exclusive type of blockchain applications. In fact, this layer defines the blockchain role. In this chapter, our defined application is a pseudonym management framework that may replace the vehicular networks PKI.

– The *data ledger layer*: this layer identifies the transactions, blocks and the blockchain structure which depends on the nature of the recorded assets.

– The *consensus layer*: the transaction/block validation procedures and consensus protocol are specified in this layer depending on the blockchain type permissioned or permissionless.

– The *P2P exchange layer*: the blockchain is formed by connected peers forming the peer-2-peer (p2p) network competing on the transaction's validation and the block's creation. They also interchange the validated blocks to keep the blockchain up to date.

– The *network layer*: the p2p networks used by the blockchain are overlaid over the Internet, where the users download and register to the blockchain.

– The *hardware layer*: this layer is related to the servers and machines utilized by the blockchain peers for the blocks and transaction validation.

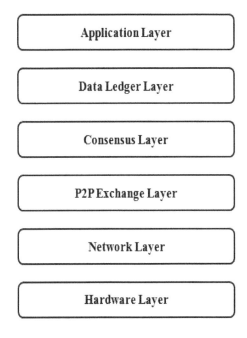

Figure 9.1. *Blockchain architecture layers*

– *The transaction content*

A transaction (Tx) archives physical or a digital asset ownership change. Its content depends on the blockchain implementations and purpose. In general, it has: the sender's address, sender's public key, a digital signature, transaction inputs and outputs.

The input of the transaction lists the assets to be transferred and its source.

The output of the transaction defines the amount of transferred assets, the identifier of the new owner(s) and the spending conditions of these assets or values. The identifier of the sender/receiver is either a public key or its cryptographic hash, known as the one time address.

The transaction validation depends on the implemented protocol requirements, such as ensuring that the owner possesses enough assets, that they satisfy its spending conditions and that no double spending occurred simultaneously, etc.

The transaction authenticity proves that the sender of an asset has owned it. It is ensured by signing the transaction's input with the sender's private key. To check the authenticity, the blockchain peers use the sender's public key found in the asset source transaction's output to check the hash (Zheng et al. 2017). Figure 9.2 illustrates the transaction structure.

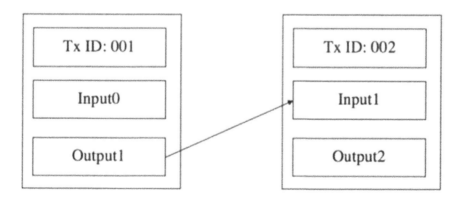

Figure 9.2. *Transaction illustration*

– *The block structure*

When the user creates a transaction, it is in a pending state until it is validated by the blockchain peers. The validation of a transaction is affirmed by creating and successfully publishing a block containing it. The block has two parts, the header, known as the metadata, and the data, which are the valid transactions (Zheng et al. 2017), as illustrated in Figure 9.3.

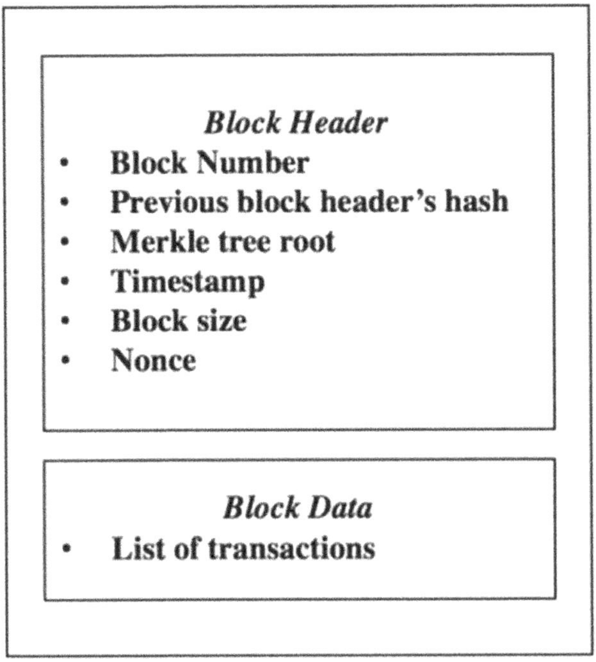

Block Header
- **Block Number**
- **Previous block header's hash**
- **Merkle tree root**
- **Timestamp**
- **Block size**
- **Nonce**

Block Data
- **List of transactions**

Figure 9.3. *Block structure*

– *Chaining the blocks*

We previously mentioned that the transaction validation is confirmed by being published in a block. The blocks are not orphan and not independent. For the block to be accepted, it must be correctly chained to the blockchain. To do so, the nodes compete to resolve a challenge. The first peer to resolve it adds the block. The chaining is by the hash usage, as illustrated in Figure 9.4, where each block contains a hash of the previous one. This prevents the alteration and injection of blocks Zheng et al. (2017).

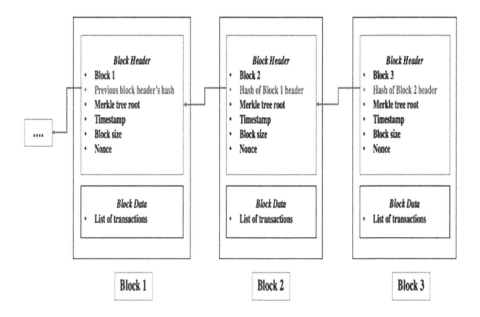

Figure 9.4. *Chains of blocks (blockchain). For a color version of this figure, see www.iste.co.uk/benarous/vehicular.zip*

– *Consensus models*

The consensus process differs based on the blockchain type and implementation. In the permissioned blockchains, only permitted nodes create and publish valid blocks, contrary to the permissionless blockchains where all peers are able to create blocks following a consensus model. In the following, a few existing consensus models are briefly explained (Zheng et al. 2017):

- **Proof of work (PoW)**

The addition of the block is done by the node that first resolves the puzzle, such as the one that finds a hash of block header that is less than the threshold value, i.e. looking for a nonce to add to the block header, so that by hashing it, we get the desired threshold.

- **Proof of stake (PoS)**

Unlike PoW, PoS does not need intensive calculations. Instead, it relies on the invested stakes in the blockchain, assuming that users who have more stakes are less likely to abuse the blockchain. Therefore, the user that has the highest stakes is likely to be the one to add the next block. Instead of being rewarded for the block creation like in PoW, the user receives transaction insertion fees.

- Round robin

This method is used in permissioned blockchains, where each node waits for its turn to come for it to add a block to the blockchain. Thus, all permitted nodes eventually participate in the block's creation.

- Proof of authority

The proof of authority or identity is another model that is used in permissioned blockchains where only the blockchain authorized nodes are permitted to create blocks.

- Proof of elapsed time

In this model, nodes are assigned with random wait timers, within which they stay idle. The node whose timer expires first, creates and publishes the block. This process is repeated for every block to be published.

– Blockchain types

We mentioned earlier that there are two types of blockchains, which are the permissioned and permissionless blockchains. Here, we explain each of these types.

In the public, also known as the permissionless blockchain, all nodes have writing access and they compete by resolving the PoW to create and publish blocks.

On the other hand, in the permissioned, also known as private blockchain, only a set of specific nodes have writing access to create blocks and the majority of peers have read access only. Corporations and organizations prefer this type of blockchain technology and customize it to serve their needs. Note that sometimes the blockchain is public and permissioned (consortium) and other times it is completely private (OneLedger n.d.; Schmid 2017).

9.2.4. *Blockchain of blockchains*

This concept was first introduced in the OneLedger project (Yakubov et al. 2018); it is a blockchain of various blockchains either of permissioned, permissionless or consortium types. The blockchain being composed may not be implemented using the same technology, but they are interoperable and compatible to serve the same aim.

9.3. Related works

9.3.1. *Blockchain-based PKI*

The PKI is the secure data exchange backbone over the Internet. However, it is vulnerable to the single point of failure issue where the single point is the CA. It may be the favorite target of attackers and hackers aiming to violate the end-user's security. Axon (2015) implemented a blockchain-based PKI management framework that is immutable, public and traceable. The Ethereum-based framework offers an efficient certificate revocation without the use of CRLs. It is also resilient to the man-in-the-middle attack or session hijacking because the blockchain is public, timely updated and distributed. Moreover, it eliminates the single-point-of-failure issue of PKI. The certificates are confirmed by the chain of trust validation from leaf to root CA. The revocation is done by shifting the certificate reference from the CA's smart contract white list to its blacklist.

9.3.2. *Privacy-aware blockchain-based PKI*

The previous framework does not preserve the privacy as it focuses on the traceability feature. However, Malik et al. (2018) introduced a privacy-aware blockchain-based PKI, in which the user identity may only be backtracked and exposed if a misbehavior occurs requiring node revocation and the consensus of the user under the request of authorities is obtained. Otherwise, it is protected. In other words, the privacy level is either controlled by the users or the application type using this technology. The generated keys are valid if they can be linked back to the previously used key. This key linkability is done implicitly, and the author claimed that the key linkability test returns a logical value and not the public key itself. Thus, unless misbehavior occurs or the secret keys are lost, this linkability cannot threaten the privacy. However, as the blockchain is public, a malicious node aiming to link the keys to resolve the user's identity can do this test differently. Therefore, this framework does not ensure forward privacy.

9.3.3. *Monero*

Monero (Yaga et al. 2018) is a recently introduced, yet steadily popular blockchain-based untraceable crypto-currency. It is public, secure and preserves privacy. Monero users may exchange amounts of currency without exposing its value or source. The receiver and sender identities, the source of the currency, the amount and what it is being spent on are all unknown and untraceable. In spite of that, the user may still verify the received amount of money, its validity and that it is not being spent elsewhere simultaneously, or what is known as the double spending problem.

Monero applies the ring digital signature to preserve the sender's privacy, i.e. the transaction input is signed with Schnorr-style multi-layered linkable spontaneous anonymous group signatures and its output has the transferred amount of crypto-currency, which is concealed by using Pedersen commitments and Schnorr-style Borromean ring signatures. The one-time addresses which are extracted from the public key are used to preserve the receiver's privacy. Section 9.4.2 explains more about them.

9.3.4. *Blockchain-based vehicular PKI*

Vercauteren (2008) proposed a blockchain-based PKI for vehicular networks to make pseudonym authentication and revocation efficient and fast. They chose the private blockchain type, which they proposed to be maintained and accessed by the CA, the revocation authority and the RSU, while preventing the vehicles or the OBU from having access to the blockchain. Note that the RSUs have reading rights only. In their framework, the vehicle is registered to the CA, which issues its pseudonyms that are stored as blockchain transactions. Since the vehicles have no access to the blockchain, pseudonym verification and authentication are done via the RSU. The vehicle sends the index of the pseudonym transaction in the blockchain to the RSU, which checks its existence in the blockchain and challenges the vehicle to prove its ownership of this pseudonym for the authentication to be successful.

The vehicle is also reported to the RSU if it misbehaves. The RSU then forwards the report to the RA, which issues the vehicle a revocation transaction. This solution preserves privacy and guarantees pseudonym authentication, non-repudiation and integrity. However, the described framework is more like a central database with multiple up-to-date back-ups than like a blockchain. Yet, it does reduce the CA dependability and eliminate the CRL usage.

9.4. Key concepts

9.4.1. *Ring signature*

The ring signature is used in Monero (Yaga et al. 2018) to protect the sender's privacy. It also prevents linking and tracking. Although the users are certain about the unforgeability of transactions, they are unable to identify their signers. Similarly, in our framework, we use the same algorithm to guarantee that the pseudonyms are not being linked, traced, altered or forged. The ring signature signing and verification are given below in algorithms 1 and 2 respectively:

Notation (Yaga et al. 2018)

G: The generator of points in elliptic curve (EC).

l: The order of the EC.

K_i: The public key of i.

k_i: The private key of i.

The $\mathcal{R}$ in $\alpha_i \in \mathcal{R} \, \mathbb{Z}_l$ means that α_i is randomly selected from $\{0, 1, 2, \ldots, l\text{-}1\}$.

$\mathbb{Z}_l$: is all integers (mod l).

$\mathfrak{m}$: is the message and in our case the pseudonym in the transaction's input.

R: a set of public keys.

$\mathcal{H}_n$: a hash function mapping to integers from 1 to l.

Assumptions (Yaga et al. 2018)

$R = \{K_i, j_i\} \, for \, i \in \{1,2,\ldots,n\} \, and \, j_i \in \{1,2,\ldots,m_i\}$.

$\{K_i, j_i\}$ is like a bookshelf of public keys with n shelves and on each shelf are m_i public keys.

π_i is the index of the public key on the shelf π.

Algorithm 1: Ring signature (Yaga et al. 2018)

---

1.   For each shelf $i \in \{1, \ldots, n\} \pi_i \neq m_i$

   a.   Generate a random value $\alpha_i \in \mathcal{R} \, \mathbb{Z}_l$

   b.   Seed the shelf's loop: set $c_{i,\pi_i+1} = \mathcal{H}_n(\mathfrak{m}, [\alpha_i G])$

   c.   Build the first half of the loop from seed: if $\pi_i + 1 \neq m_i$ and for $j_i = \pi_i + 1, \ldots, m_i - 1$ generate random numbers $r_{i,j_i} \in \mathcal{R} \, \mathbb{Z}_l$ and compute $c_{i,j_i+1} = \mathcal{H}_n(\mathfrak{m}, [r_{i,j_i} G + c_{i,j_i} K_{i,j_i}])$

2.   For $i \in \{1, \ldots, n\}$ generate random numbers $r_{i,m_i} \in \mathcal{R} \, \mathbb{Z}_l$. Take all r_{i,m_i}, c_{i,m_i} , and K_{i,m_i} and combine them in the connector

$$c_1 = \mathcal{H}_n(\mathfrak{m}, [r_{1,m_1} G + c_{1,m_1} K_{1,m_1}], \ldots, [r_{n,m_n} G + c_{n,m_n} K_{n,m_n}])$$

If $\pi_i = m_i$, instead of r_{i,m_i}, generate α_i and put in $\alpha_i G$ in c_1

---

3.   For each shelf. For $i \in \{1, \dots, n\}$:

a.   Build a second-half loop from connector:

if $\pi_i \neq 1$, for $j_i = 1, \dots, \pi_i - 1$ generate random numbers $r_{i,j_i} \in \mathcal{R} \, \mathbb{Z}_l$ and compute $c_{i,j_i+1} = \mathcal{H}_n(\mathfrak{m}, [r_{i,j_i}G + c_{i,j_i}K_{i,j_i}])$, noting that $c_{i,1}$ is interpreted as c_1.

b.   Tie loop end together: set r_{i,π_i} such that $\alpha_i = r_{i,\pi_i} + c_{i,\pi_i}k_{i,\pi_i}$

The signature:

$$\sigma = (c1, r_{1,1}, \dots, r_{1,m_1}, r_{2,1}, \dots, r_{2,m_2}, \dots, r_{n,m_n})$$

This signature is sent along with R the set of public keys used in the signing process and the signed message $\mathfrak{m}$.

Algorithm 2: Ring signature verification Yaga et al. (2018)

Given $\mathfrak{m}$, R and σ, the verification if performed as follows:

1.   For $i \in \{1, \dots, n\}$ and $j_i = 1, \dots, m_i$ build each loop:

$$L'_{i,j_i} = r'_{i,j_i}G + c'_{i,j_i}K_{i,j_i}$$

$$c'_{i,j_i+1} = \mathcal{H}_n(\mathfrak{m}, L'_{i,j_i})$$

Note that c'_1 is interpreted as c_1, and that it is unnecessary to compute c'_{i,m_i+1}.

2.   Compute the connector:

$$c'_1 = \mathcal{H}_n(\mathfrak{m}, L'_{1,m_1}, \dots, L'_{n,m_n}).$$

If $c'_1 = c_1$, then the signature is valid.

9.4.2. *One-time address*

To preserve the transaction receiver's output privacy, a one-time address is generated by the sender from the receiver's public key. It is put as their identifier/address in the transaction's output to avoid tracing the asset transaction history in the blockchain. Thus, only the intended receiver may read this output.

In our framework, the vehicle self-generates its own pseudonyms. Therefore, the transaction's output contains the vehicle's one-time address. We used the one-time address concept as it avoids traceability of transactions, linkability of pseudonyms and preserves privacy, which is critical in the vehicular networks. It is calculated from the vehicle's public key, the hash of the transaction and the vehicle secret key. Let H be the hash function that has parameters: K_v as the vehicle's public key, Sv as the vehicle's secret key and h_{tx} as the transaction hash.

The one-time address $= H\,(K_v, S_v, h_{tx})$

9.5. Proposed solution

9.5.1. *General description*

The proposed framework is a blockchain of two blockchains. The generated pseudonyms are saved in a permissionless public blockchain and the revoked pseudonyms are recorded in a permissioned public blockchain. The first blockchain is accessed by the registered vehicles, while the second is maintained by the RSUs, which have writing access rights and are accessed by the vehicles with reading rights only. Figure 9.5 illustrates the general proposed framework by demonstrating its three main functionalities. The first (A) is the vehicle registration phase. The second (B) is the pseudonym generation and addition to the BC_{cert} blockchain. The third (C) is the pseudonym revocation and addition to the BC_{rev} blockchain.

A vehicle is initially registered by its owner to the blockchain upon its purchase. Once registered, each vehicle is preloaded with our pseudonym management framework. This allows it to generate its own pseudonyms. The vehicle creates a transaction for each generated pseudonym and publishes it to be added to the blockchain. The transactions are assembled in blocks. They are added to the blockchain in a distributed manner by the vehicles based on a defined consensus model, without the need for the central CA or a point of trust to interfere. Our framework is privacy-aware. Thus, the public blockchain does not disclose the user's or vehicle's identities. Yet, the vehicles are still able to check the pseudonym validity without linking it to its owner or to the previously generated pseudonyms. In other words, it ensures both anonymity and unlinkability. Note that the blockchain only publishes the public key and not the private key. Being unlinkable, anonymous and untraceable are the vehicular network's essential requirements. However, maintaining the security and functionality of the network, as well as the non-repudiation and the misbehaving node revocation are other crucial requirements that need to be satisfied. In our framework, to fulfil these properties, an unlinkable ring signature is used to sign the transactions and the one-time address is used to hide the vehicle's identifier, both of which were explained in section 9.4, while the revocation process is handled by the RSUs.

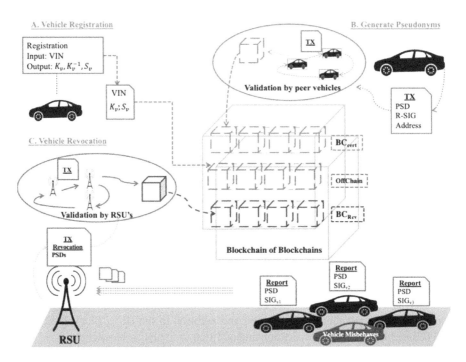

Figure 9.5. *Blockchain-based pseudonym management for vehicular networks. For a color version of this figure, see www.iste.co.uk/benarous/vehicular.zip*

9.5.2. *Registration to the blockchain*

The vehicle registration in the blockchain is done upon its purchase using the unique Vehicle Identification Number (VIN). Once registered, the vehicle obtains a secret key S_v, and a pair of public and private keys (K_v, k_v). The private key is fundamental, and it should be backed up. It is used for the ring-signatures and its owner may track all its related transactions and the generated pseudonyms. The secret key is not published in the blockchain. It is stored along with the public key in an offline chain that can only be accessed by the RSUs. It is solely used in the creation of the one-time address and is not used in the signature or encryption.

9.5.3. *Certifying process*

There is no certifying process in the traditional meaning. However, the fact that a pseudonym is inserted correctly in the blockchain and cannot be found in the revoked blockchain proves it to be valid, thus achieving the same aims ensured by the certificate without explicitly using it. When the vehicle generates its own pseudonyms, it inserts each one in a transaction containing a validity time. To keep the system distributed and eliminate the need for a central CA, each vehicle signs its own transaction without exposing its privacy using a ring signature (explained in section 4.1), which conceals the signer within a set of potential signers and attaches all of the signers' public keys to the transaction. The transaction's receiver checks the signature validity without identifying its signer. The used public keys are arbitrarily chosen from the blockchain's available public keys. Moreover, the transaction's output must include the pseudonym owner. Yet, it should be done while preserving their identity privacy and avoiding the traceability of their generated pseudonyms, for which we used the one-time addresses (explained in section 4.2).

9.5.4. Revocation process

The framework is distributed and does not require a central point of verification or revocation. The vehicles detect and report misbehaving nodes to the RSUs. The RSUs maintaining the revocation blockchain verify the received reports and revoke the pseudonym of the misbehaving vehicle. They also use the one-time address and ring-signature list of signers to identify the public key of the misbehaving node. They recompute the one-time address using the secret keys saved in the offline chain for all the signer's public keys until they find the public key from which the one-time address was extracted. Then, this key is revoked and in addition to the other valid unused pseudonyms generated by it. The RSUs insert the revoked pseudonyms and the vehicle's public key in a revocation transaction. They sign this transaction and add it to the public blockchain.

9.5.5. Transaction structure and validation

We previously mentioned two transaction types, which are valid pseudonym transaction and pseudonym revocation transaction. Each is saved in its corresponding blockchain. In what follows, we explain the structure and validation process for each type:

– The pseudonym transaction

A pseudonym transaction is created for each pseudonym generated by the vehicle. It is self-signed using the ring signature algorithm and self-addressed with a one-time usage address. Figure 9.6 illustrates a pseudonym transaction's structure. Algorithm 3.7 explains the certifying process.

```
TX: hash of TX
Input:
          Pseudonym
          Validity period
          List of Public keys of signers
          signature
Output:
          One-time address of the owner
```

Figure 9.6. *Certifying transaction structure*

Algorithm 3: Pseudonym certifying process

Notation:

V: Vehicle

TX: transaction

RING-SIG: ring signature

R: the set of public keys used in the Ring Signature

One-time-address: creates a unique address from the vehicle's public key for single usage only.

Algorithm

V: Begin

    1- Generate pseudonym

    2- Create TX {RING-SIG (Pseudonym, Validity-period, R, One-Time-Address
              (Public-key))}

    3- Publish TX

    End

The verification process of the pseudonym transaction may be executed by any vehicle in the blockchain. It consists of the signature verification, the verification that the public keys used in the ring signature are not revoked and that the pseudonym validity time is not expired. Algorithm 4.8 gives the verification process.

– *The revocation process*

The RSUs revoke the node upon the verification of malicious behavior received in the vehicle's reports. The revocation certificate structure is illustrated in Figure 9.7. It is signed by the RSU's private key, and it includes: the revoked pseudonym, the valid non-used pseudonyms and the public key of the misbehaving vehicle. Algorithm 5.9 explains the revocation process executed by the RSU. Note that the block verification process may be done by any RSU, it consists of the RSU's key validity and signature verification.

Algorithm 4: Pseudonym verification process

Notation:

V: Vehicle

RING-SIG: ring signature

R: the set of public keys used in the Ring Signature

P_K: Public key

Algorithm

V: **Begin**

1- Check for $P_K \in R$, Non-Revoked (P_K)= true.

2- Check RING-SIG

3- Check Not-expired (validity)= true.

4- Add to block.

End

TX: hash of TX
Input:

Reported Pseudonym
non-used valid pseudonyms
Public key of the owner
Signature of input by RSU

Output:

RSU's public key

Figure 9.7. *Revocation certificate structure*

Algorithm 5: Pseudonym revocation process

Notation:

V_r: reported Vehicle

Blacklist: a list of blacklisted pseudonyms

R: the set of public keys used in the Ring Signature

P_K: Public key

One-time-Address: the function that creates a unique address from the vehicle's public key for single usage only.

P@d: one-time address

Get-V_r-P_K: gets the public key of the reported vehicle from the offline chain.

Get-List-P_K-R: gets the list of transactions in which the public key is used in the ring signature.

Algorithm

RSU: **Begin**

1- Receive reports from i vehicles about V_r misbehavior.

2- Confirm misbehavior of V_r.

3- Blacklist (Pseudonym$_r$)

4- P_K=Get-V_r-P_K (R, P@d, offline-chain).

5- R'= Get-List-P_K-R (Blockchain, P_K)

6- For P@d $\in$ R'

    a.   If (One-time-Address (P_K= P@d))

                  Blacklist (pseudonym in R')

7- Blacklist (P_K)

8- Create transaction (Blacklist)

    End

9.5.6. *Block structure and validation*

The block structure follows the blockchain type and the composing transaction type which were explained above. Naturally, the block validation process is also different. Therefore, we describe them separately:

– *The certifying block*

The vehicles generate their own pseudonyms and publish them in the blockchain for validation. The vehicles assemble the pending transactions in blocks. They simultaneously execute the proof of elapsed time consensus model (see section 2.3), where the vehicle with the shortest timer gets to publish the block and chain to the blockchain by adding the hash of the previous block to it.

– *The revocation block*

The RSUs create and publish the revocation blocks after verifying and assembling the pending transactions. The RSUs take turns using the round robin consensus model (see section 2.3) to create and publish blocks.

9.5.7. *Authentication using blockchain*

In VPKI-based vehicular networks, the state message authentication between vehicles relies on the use of certificates to ensure the integrity, authenticity and non-repudiation. Note that the beacons are signed by the private key corresponding to the certified pseudonym. The authentication is done in two phases: the first is to check the certificate validity by verifying that it was issued by the CA and not altered, and also that the pseudonym is valid and not revoked. The second phase is to check the beacon signature to prove that it is signed by the pseudonym owner and that the message has not been altered.

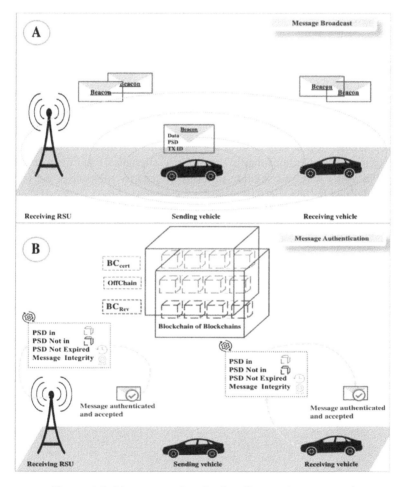

Figure 9.8. *Message authentication. For a color version of this figure, see www.iste.co.uk/benarous/vehicular.zip*

Similarly, our framework ensures that the messages are authenticated without the need to use certificates issued by the CA. When the vehicle receives a signed beacon containing the pseudonym and its reference in the blockchain, it checks that this pseudonym does exist in the pseudonym blockchain and does not exist in the revocation blockchain. Then, it verifies the pseudonym validity time and the beacon's signature to ensure the authenticity and integrity of the message. Figure 9.8 illustrates the authentication process in two sections (A and B). Section A presents the beacon broadcast and section B explains how the RSU and the vehicle use our framework to authenticate received beacons.

9.6. Analysis

We designed the framework to ensure the security and privacy essential requirements guaranteed by the current central VPKI, while also overcoming what it lacks. In what follows, we explain the ensured security properties:

– *The security*

The blockchain technology ensures the security by relying on cryptography and hashing usage. Our solution inherits the security strength of the blockchains. To compare the VPKI with our solution in terms of security robustness, we used the attack tree defined by Schceier (1999) using an Ad tool (Attack Tree, ADTool) for both solutions (see Figure 9.9). We enumerate the potential security breaches and then calculate the probability of them occuring and damaging the security, leaking and altering the data for each solution.

The occurrence probability is calculated for each leaf node using the formula defined in Sjöberg (2011), and the grade standard is shown in Table 9.1. The calculated probabilities, as well as the grades for each attack for both of our proposed framework and the VPKI are shown in Table 9.2.

We calculated the probability of occurrence P_o using formula (1) where: x is the execution difficulty, y is the detection difficulty, z is the cost. U is the utility function and $w \in [0,1]$ is the weight attached to each parameter, which is considered here to be equal to $1/3$ for each parameter. The utility function (formula 2) is calculated as in Sjöberg (2011):

$$P_o = w \, (U(x) + U(y) + U(z)) \qquad [9.1]$$

$$U(f) = C_f/f, \text{ where } C_f = 0.2 \qquad [9.2]$$

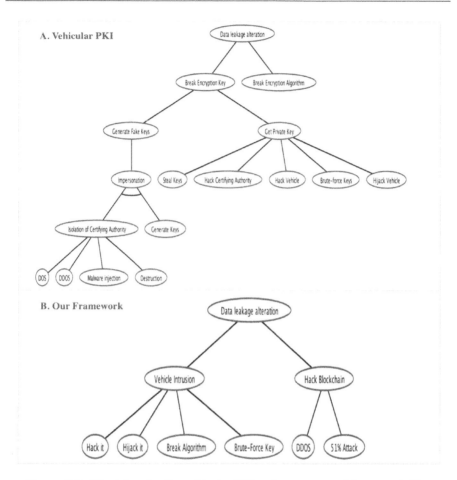

Figure 9.9. *Attack tree for the vehicular PKI and our proposed framework. For a color version of this figure, see www.iste.co.uk/benarous/vehicular.zip*

The probability P of achieving the aim at the tree root, which is to damage the security, leaking and altering the data, is calculated from the attack tree. Note that this tree is Boolean algebra-based, where the OR is considered as the sum operation and the AND is translated as the multiplication operator. For better illustration, we explain, with an example, how to calculate the probability of occurrence P of the impersonation attack and the isolation of CA from the attack tree in Figure 9.9

P (impersonation) = P (isolation of certifying authority) * P (generate Keys)

P (isolation of certifying authority) = P (DOS) + P (DDOS) + P (Malware injection) + P (destruction)

Attack cost evaluation		Technical difficulty of executing		Detection Difficulty	
Grade	Cost	Grade	Difficulty	Grade	Difficulty
5	Quite costly	5	Quite difficult	5	Quite difficult
4	Costly	4	Difficult	4	Difficult
3	Moderate cost	3	Mediate	3	Mediate
2	Cheap	2	Simple	2	Simple
1	Quite cheap	1	Quite simple	1	Quite simple

Table 9.1. *Standard grade chart*

The probability P of successfully damaging the security for both solutions indicates that the proposed framework is more secure than the centralized vehicular PKI as it has a lower probability (0.41) than that of the VPKI (0.59).

– The identity privacy

Our framework does not record the pseudonym owner identity in the public blockchain. Although the generated pseudonyms are attached to their owner's account, this link is implicit and does not expose privacy, because the user's public key is concealed in a group of potential signers when used for signing, or is seeded to the cryptographic hash function for the one-time address generation.

– The unlinkability

The use of a ring signature and one-time address prevents the linkability between the user's public key and their generated pseudonyms and also between the pseudonyms themselves. It allows the other vehicles to check that the vehicle owns the pseudonyms it uses and that they are valid and non-revoked or expired without explicitly linking them to the owner's identity. As a result, the blockchain peers cannot see the vehicle history of generated pseudonyms. It is fundamental to ensure this, otherwise an attacker who knows all of the vehicle's generated pseudonyms may track it when using them on-road.

– No single point of failure

The blockchain is distributed. All of vehicles and RSUs participate in the creation, maintenance and update of the blockchain of the blockchain framework. Thus, no CA is needed and the single point of failure problem is resolved. Furthermore, the participating peers can be considered as multiple backup and restoration points.

Our proposed framework			
Attack	*Difficulty of execution*	*Detection Difficulty*	*Attack cost evaluation*	*Probability of occurrence*
Hack it	4	3	5	0.05
Hijack it	2	1	1	0.17
Break Algorithm	5	5	5	0.04
Brute-force Key	5	5	5	0.04
DDOS	4	2	5	0.06
51% Attack	5	4	5	0.04
Probability of achieving main aim			**0.41**
VPKI			
Attack	*Difficulty of execution*	*Detection Difficulty*	*Attack cost evaluation*	*Probability of occurrence*
DOS	2	1	2	0.13
DDOS	3	2	5	0.07
Generate keys	3	3	3	0.07
Steal Key	3	2	1	0.12
Hack certifying authority	5	4	5	0.04
Hack vehicle	4	4	5	0.05
Brute-force keys	5	4	5	0.04
Break encryption Algorithms	5	4	5	0.04
Hijack vehicle	2	1	1	0.17
Malware injection	4	3	3	0.06
Destruction	4	4	4	0.05
Probability of achieving main aim			**0.59**

Table 9.2. *Probability of occurrence*

– Non-repudiation

Although we designed the framework to preserve the vehicle's privacy in the fully distributed public blockchain, the non-repudiation is another guaranteed property that ensures that the misbehaving vehicles cannot deny their committed actions and can be held responsible.

The blockchain nature ensures that the inserted elements cannot be altered or removed. Therefore, once the pseudonym is inserted in the blockchain, the vehicle can no longer deny having generated it. If it misbehaves while using this pseudonym, it gets revoked. The revocation includes the reported pseudonym, the other still valid unused pseudonyms and the vehicle's public key. The public key revocation prevents the vehicle from inserting any other pseudonyms in the blockchain. We ensured that by using an offline chain storing the public key, secret key and VIN maintained by the RSU. Note that to resolve the vehicle's owner identity, the juridical system may obtain the VIN from the RSU and investigate who it belongs to in order to identify the owner.

9.7. Comparative study

In the previous section, we highlighted our proposed framework characteristics and evaluated its security. In this section, we continue to compare the centralized vehicular PKI with our solution in terms of security properties, functionalities, complexity and characteristics, as shown in Table 9.3. We also evaluate each advantage and disadvantage of the solution.

Noting that we evaluated the implementation and design complexity by considering the code length, the distributed application's development complexity is compared to that of centralized applications and the developer's familiarity with each type. For the used security schemes, the robustness of each solution was in terms of its key security concepts it was built on. The VPKI uses elliptic curve cryptography. The blockchain also relies on this cryptography and uses ring signatures and hashing algorithms. Moreover, it utilizes the consensus model and block chaining process. Each of these algorithms adds to the overall complexity of implementation. Lastly, since users are more familiar with the VPKI HMI, they may find the blockchain framework HMI more complex to use.

9.8. Conclusion

The chapter proposed blockchain-based framework to resolve the pseudonym management issue in vehicular networks which is currently central-based VPKI. The

VPKI suffers from being a single point of failure targeted by attacks, which if compromised causes perilous security damage. The designed framework is public and distributed, ensuring both privacy and non-repudiation, which we often shorten to conditional privacy, i.e. privacy is preserved for vehicles that demonstrate correct behavior. The framework is composed of two connected blockchains: the untraceable, unlinkable permissionless public pseudonym blockchain maintained by the vehicles. The permissioned public revocation blockchain maintained by the RSUs contains an offline private chain and online public chain. The framework inherits the security strength of blockchains. It is distributed and public. So, it eliminates the need for revocation list usage. It also prevents the reliance on the CA to authenticate the vehicle's messages and all the engendered messages required by the process. Thus, the network over-head is reduced and the bandwidth usage is optimized. Moreover, it illustrated a better resiliency to attacks than the conventional vehicular PKI.

Comparison criteria		Vehicular- PKI	Our proposed framework
Main functionalities	*Registration*	*To*: trusted certifying authority *Input*: identity and VIN *Output*: Permanent certified pair of public and private keys used to request pseudonyms or their certificates	*To*: blockchain system *Input*: VIN *Output*: Pair of public and private keys, secret key
	Pseudonym generation and certification	Self-generated and certified by the trusted authority; *OR* Generated and certified by the trusted authority	Self-generated and self-signed using ring signature
	Pseudonym change	Upon expiry	Upon expiry
	Pseudonym refilling	Periodical at the certifying authority facilities *OR* On-road, on-demand after authentication to the certifying authority	Self-refilling
	Vehicle revocation	*Vehicles*: detect and report misbehaving nodes *Trusted authority*: investigate reports, revoke misbehaving node, distribute the updated CRL to vehicles	*Vehicles*: detect and report misbehaving nodes *RSU*: investigate reports, add vehicle keys to blockchain of revoked pseudonyms

Main functionalities (cont'd)	*Message authentication*	Check authority's key certificate and validity Check pseudonym certificate (integrity and validity) Check pseudonym not being revoked Check message integrity	Check pseudonym in the blockchain Check pseudonym not being revoked Check validity Check message integrity
	Message decryption	Check authority's key certificate and validity Check pseudonym certificate (integrity and validity) Check pseudonym not being revoked Decrypt the message	Check pseudonym in the blockchain Check pseudonym not being revoked Check validity Decrypt message
Security properties	*Availability*	Single point of failure	Ensured by redundancy
	Privacy	Conditional, preserved from peer vehicles, but not from authorities	Conditional, preserved unless a misbehavior occurs
	Non-repudiation	Ensured	Ensured
	Integrity	Ensured by the use of digital signatures and certificates	Ensured by digital signature and the use of blockchain
	Alteration	Only authority (or a hacker who can compromise it)	Once validated, no transaction can be altered, no data can be injected into the blockchain
	Resiliency to attacks (as explained in Table 9.2)	High	Extra high
Characteristics	*Redundancy*	Backup	All nodes save a copy of the blockchain
	Authority	Mandatory	Not needed
	Consensus	Centralized	Distributed
Complexity	*Implementation and design*	Medium	High

Complexity (cont'd)	*Security schemes used*	High	Extra high
	HMI usage	High	Extra high
	Difficulty of system breaking (as explained in Table 9.2)	High	Extra high
Evaluation	*Advantages*	Simplicity and security	Security, availability, optimization and over-head reduction, public, decentralized, authority-free
	Disadvantages	Long CRL and revocation process Single point of failure Reliance on the certificate authority to continuously provide pseudonyms/ certificates for vehicles Over-head caused by attaching the certificates to the messages, the exchange of CRL, the refilling requests	Complexity of implementation

Table 9.3. *Comparative study between our proposed framework and the vehicular PKI*

Conclusion

The aim of the work presented in this book is to provide privacy and security solutions that ensure the safe use of vehicular networks. We have guided the reader to learn about vehicular networks and their various types, technologies and challenges. These networks were initially developed to ensure the safety of their users and extend Internet services to the road. However, the cyber activity of these on-road users may compromise their privacy through tracking and exposed secrets, and may even impact their safety.

Vehicular network privacy is at risk because of the requirements imposed by the system. The wireless exchange of heartbeat messages containing the vehicle's identity and spatio-temporal data facilitates tracking by attackers. Tracking is passive, which gives the attacker the chance to track their victims for long periods of time before being detected. The attacker may use the collected data to profile their victims, blackmail them or trade their data for profit. The consequences could be more serious, such as causing road accidents.

We proposed new privacy-preserving solutions to address these issues. To do this, we first surveyed and analyzed existing solutions in the literature. Then, we described the attackers who target privacy, the types of attack they use and the means they use. Finally, we decided on the use of proof methods in order to evaluate our proposals.

Our work focused on two security issues: authentication and privacy. These two issues are contradictory by nature as most authentication methods rely on identifying data unique to each user, among which is identity. On the contrary, privacy, especially in vehicular networks, prohibits the exchange of identifying data. Because identity and location are correlated, identity exposure leads to on-road tracking and vice versa. Therefore, we needed to find solutions that ensure authentication while preserving privacy. In this regard, we proposed reputation-based anonymous authentication methods for cloud-enabled vehicular data named networks, which were introduced in Chapter 5. We also proposed another anonymous authentication method for pseudonym refilling in VANET, which we explained in Chapter 6.

To preserve location privacy, we proposed two solutions in Chapter 7. The solutions were developed for VANET users. They were crowd, infrastructure and road-map independent. They were designed to reduce vehicle tracking even when within low-density roads. They were analyzed against a global passive attacker and showed overall low ratios. In Chapter 8 we also proposed three location privacy-preserving solutions for cloud-enabled Internet of vehicles. The solutions were designed to reduce the tracking ratio, which was decreased to approximately 10% in the last scheme.

The final chapter – Chapter 9 – looked at the design of a framework that could potentially replace the centralized vehicular PKI. The framework is distributed and public, and reduces the overhead caused by the multiple queries to the authorities to request pseudonyms, check certificates or exchange certificate revocation lists. It also resolves the single point of failure issue found in the VPKI. It is privacy-aware, ensures both the unlinkability and anonymity, and also ensures the security properties of non-repudiation, integrity, availability, authenticity and revocation. When analyzed, it illustrated a higher level of security than the VPKI.

Future work should be focused on the design of an anonymous payment system for vehicular networks. The vehicles may provide each other with services and resources for free. In this case, only authentication is required to maintain traceability and the correct functioning of the network. In this regard, we already proposed an anonymous authentication method in Chapter 5. However, if these services and resources are rented, then an anonymous payment method is needed. The payment should be carried out so that:

– the service or resource provider's privacy is preserved;

– the service requester's privacy is preserved;

– the amount of money is correct.

More importantly, we should ensure that the service/resource provider gets paid the correct amount of money. At the same time; we should make sure that they provide the agreed-upon service/resource. We will think of refunding and fining policies if the contrary case occurs. Similarly, the service requester must pay for the service/resource they have benefitted from and not evade the payment.

The second objective is to redesign the blockchain-based pseudonym management framework to allow vehicles to generate pseudonyms for each other as a service. This service may be free or for profit. Initially, we need to decide on the consensus model used by the vehicle for that case. Also, because in reality the pseudonym is a pair of public and private keys, we have to ensure the forward security. Although the vehicles may generate pseudonyms for one another, they will not expose each other's secrets or read each other's encrypted messages.

Another perspective that is worth investigating is to test our privacy-preserving solutions in the IoV formed, not only with land vehicles as the main types of node, but also with unmanned aerial vehicles where the energy-constraint must be respected. It will be interesting to see whether this hybrid environment will impact the protection level provided by our solutions. Furthermore, it will be useful to study the potential performance and security challenges this environment may present.

References

3GPP (2017). ETSI TS 122 185 V14.3.0 LTE; Service requirements for V2X services (3GPP TS 22.185 version 14.3.0 Release 14).

A. Team (2006a). AVISPA v1.1 User Manual. Information Society Technologies.

A. Team (2006b). HLPSL Tutorial: A Beginner's Guide to Modelling and Analysing Internet Security Protocols. Information Society Technologies.

Ahmed, S.H., Bouk, S.H., Kim, D., Rawat, B., Song, H. (2017). Named data networking for software defined vehicular networks. *IEEE Communications Magazine*, 55(8), 60–66.

Alam, K.M., Saini, M., El Saddik, A. (2015). Toward social internet of vehicles: Concept, architecture, and applications. *IEEE Access*, 3, 343–357.

Alexiou, N., Laganà, M., Gisdakis, S., Khodaei, M., Papadimitratos, P. (2013). VeSPA: Vehicular security and privacy-preserving architecture. *Proceedings of the 2nd ACM Workshop on Hot Topics on Wireless Network Security and Privacy*. ACM, April.

Alonso, K.M. (2018). Zero to Monero: First edition. A technical guide to a private digital currency; for beginners, amateurs, and experts [Online]. Available at: https://www.getmonero.org/library/Zero-to-Monero-1-0-0.pdf.

Al-Sultan, S., Al-Doori, M., Al-Bayatti, A.H., Zedan, H. (2014). A comprehensive survey on vehicular ad hoc network. *Journal of Network and Computer Applications*, 37, 380–392.

Amro, B. (2018). Protecting privacy in VANETs using mix zones with virtual pseudonym change. *International Journal of Network Security & Its Applications (IJNSA)*, 10(1), 11 [Online]. Available at: https://ssrn.com/abstract=3679766.

Andrés, M.E., Bordenabe, N.E., Chatzikokolakis, K., Palamidessi, C. (2012). Geo-indistinguishability: Differential privacy for location-based systems. arXiv preprint arXiv:1212.1984.

AVISPA (2002). AVISPA Project [Online]. Available at: http://www.avispa-project.org/ [Accessed 19 February 2019].

AVISPA (n.d.a). MSC Example [Online]. Available at: http://people.irisa.fr/Thomas.Genet/span/sample.jpg [Accessed 19 February 2019].

AVISPA (n.d.b). AVISPA web-interface [Online]. Available at: http://www.avispa-project.org/web-interface/basic.php [Accessed 19 February 2019].

Axon, L. (2015). Privacy-awareness in Blockchain-based PKI. Working paper, University of Oxford.

Bai, F. and Krishnamachari, B. (2010). Exploiting the wisdom of the crowd: Localized, distributed information-centric VANETs. *IEEE Communications Magazine*, 48(5), 138–146.

Benaissa, K., Mellouk, A., Bitam, S. (2017). Efficient messages broadcasting within vehicular safety applications. *IEEE 28th Annual International Symposium on Personal, Indoor, and Mobile Radio Communications (PIMRC)*, October.

Benarous, L. and Kadri, B. (2017). Ensuring privacy and authentication for V2V resource sharing. *Seventh International Conference on Emerging Security Technologies (EST)*. IEEE.

Benarous, L. and Kadri, B. (2018). Privacy preserving scheme for pseudonym refilling in VANET. *International Conference on Smart Communications in Network Technologies (SaCoNeT)*. IEEE.

Benarous, L., Kadri, B., Bouridane, A. (2017). A survey on cyber security evolution and threats: Biometric authentication solutions. In *Biometric Security and Privacy*, Jiang, R., Al-maadeed, S., Bouridane, A., Crookes, D., Beghdadi, A. (eds). Springer, Cham.

Beresford, A.R. and Stajano, F. (2003). Location privacy in pervasive computing. *IEEE Pervasive Computing*, 1, 46–55.

Bitam, S., Mellouk, A., Zeadally, S. (2015). VANET-cloud: A generic cloud computing model for vehicular Ad Hoc networks. *IEEE Wireless Communications*, 22(1), 96–102.

Bonomi, F. (2013). The smart and connected vehicle and the Internet of Things. Invited talk, Workshop on Synchronization in Telecommunication Systems.

Boualouache, A. (2016). Security and privacy in vehicular AD-HOC networks. Dissertation, University of Sciences and Technology Houari Boumediene (USTHB), Bab Ezzouar.

Boualouache, A. and Moussaoui, S. (2014). S2si: A practical pseudonym changing strategy for location privacy in VANETs. *International Conference on Advanced Networking Distributed Systems and Applications*. IEEE.

Boualouache, A. and Moussaoui, S. (2017). TAPCS: Traffic-aware pseudonym changing strategy for VANETs. *Peer-to-Peer Networking and Applications*, 10(4), 1008–1020.

Boualouache, A., Senouci, S.-M., Moussaoui, S. (2016). Vlpz: The vehicular location privacy zone. *Procedia Computer Science*, 83, 369–376.

Bouk, S.H., Ahmed, S.H., Kim, D., Song, H. (2017). Named-data-networking-based ITS for smart cities. *IEEE Communications Magazine*, 55(1), 105–111.

Burmester, M., Magkos, E., Chrissikopoulos, V. (2008). Strengthening privacy protection in VANETs. *IEEE International Conference on Wireless and Mobile Computing, Networking and Communications*, 12–14 October.

Burrows, M., Abadi, M., Needham, R.M. (1989). A logic of authentication. *Proceedings of the Royal Society of London A. Mathematical and Physical Sciences*, 426(1871), 233–271.

Buterin, V. (2014). A next-generation smart contract and decentralized application platform. White paper, 3(37).

Buttyán, L., Holczer, T., Vajda, I. (2007). On the effectiveness of changing pseudonyms to provide location privacy in VANETs. *European Workshop on Security in Ad-hoc and Sensor Networks*. Springer, Berlin, Heidelberg.

Buttyán, L., Holczer, T., Weimerskirch, A., Whyte, W. (2009). SLOW: A practical pseudonym changing scheme for location privacy in VANETs. *IEEE Vehicular Networking Conference (VNC)*, 28–30 October.

Chaum, D.L. (1981). Untraceable electronic mail, return addresses, and digital pseudonyms. *Communications of the ACM*, 24(2), 84–90.

Chaurasia, B.K., Verma, S., Tomar, G.S., Bhasker, S.M. (2009). Pseudonym based mechanism for sustaining privacy in VANETs. *First International Conference on Computational Intelligence, Communication Systems and Networks*. IEEE.

Chen, M., Mau, D.O., Zhang, Y., Taleb, T., Leung, V.C.M. (2014). VENDNET: VEhicular Named Data NETwork. *Vehicular Communications*, 1(4), 208–213.

Chen, M., Tian, Y., Fortino, G., Zhang, J., Humar, I. (2018). Cognitive internet of vehicles. *Computer Communications*, 120, 58–70.

Cisco White Paper (2019). Encrypted traffic analytics [Online]. Available at: https://www.cisco.com/c/dam/en/us/solutions/collateral/enterprise-networks/enterprise-network-security/nb-09-encrytd-traf-anlytcs-wp-cte-en.pdf [Accessed 3 March 2019].

Compagna, L. (2005). SAT-based model-checking of security protocols. PhD Thesis, Universita di Genova and University of Edinburgh.

Contreras-Castillo, J., Zeadally, S., Guerrero-Ibañez, J.A. (2018). Internet of vehicles: Architecture, protocols, and security. *IEEE Internet of Things Journal*, 5(5), 3701–3709.

Crosby, M., Nachiappan, P.P., Verma, S., Kalyanaraman, V. (2015). BlockChain technology beyond bitcoin. Sutardja Center for Entrepreneurship & Technology Technical Report, University of California, Berkeley.

Cuervo, E. and Shakimov, A. (n.d.). Privacy and networks CPS 96 [Online]. Available at: https://studylib.net/doc/15143690/privacy-and-networks-cps-96-eduardo-cuervo-amre-shakimov [Accessed 2 March 2019].

Da Cunha, F.D., Boukerche, A., Villas, L., Viana, A.C., Loureiro, A.A.F. (2014). Data communication in VANETs: A survey, challenges and applications. Dissertation, INRIA Saclay.

Danezis, G. (2003). Mix-networks with restricted routes. *International Workshop on Privacy Enhancing Technologies*. Springer, Berlin, Heidelberg.

Dib, O., Brousmiche, K.-L., Durand, A., Thea, E., Hamida, E.B. (2018). Consortium blockchains: Overview, applications and challenges. *International Journal On Advances in Telecommunications*, 11(1&2), 51–64.

Dini, G. (2018) Lecture notes public key infrastructures security in networked computing systems. Department of Ingegneria dell'Informazione, University of Pisa.

Dok, H., Echevarria, R., Fu, H. (2009). Privacy issues for vehicular ad-hoc network. *International Conference on Future Generation Communication and Networking*. Springer, Berlin, Heidelberg.

Dressler, F., Klingler, F., Sommer, C., Reuven, C. (2018). Not all VANET broadcasts are the same: Context-aware class-based broadcast. *IEEE/ACM Transactions on Networking*, 26(1), 17–30.

Eckhoff, D. and Sommer, C. (2016). Marrying safety with privacy: A holistic solution for location privacy in VANETs. *IEEE Vehicular Networking Conference (VNC)*.

Eckhoff, D., German, R., Sommer, C., Dressler, F., Gansen, T. (2011). SlotSwap: Strong and affordable location privacy in intelligent transportation systems. *IEEE Communications Magazine*, 49(11), 126–133.

EconomicsDiscussion.net (n.d.). The five types of games in game theory. *Economicsdiscussion* [Online]. Available at: http://www.economicsdiscussion.net/game-theory/5-types-of-games-in-game-theory-with-diagram/3827 [Accessed 23 February 2019].

Egan, M. and Mather, T. (2004). *The Executive Guide to Information Security: Threats, Challenges, and Solutions*. Addison-Wesley Professional, Indianapolis.

Emara, K.A.A.E.-S. (2016). Safety-aware location privacy in vehicular ad-hoc networks. Doctoral Dissertation, Technische Universität München, Munich.

Emara, K., Woerndl, W., Schlichter, J. (2015). CAPS: Context-aware privacy scheme for VANET safety applications. *Proceedings of the 8th ACM Conference on Security & Privacy in Wireless and Mobile Networks*. ACM.

ETSI (2018). Intelligent Transport Systems (ITS); Security; Pre-standardization study on pseudonym change management. ETSI TR 103 415 V1.1.1.

Fadlullah, Z.M., Taleb, T., Schöller, M. (2010). Combating against security attacks against mobile ad hoc networks (MANETs). *Security of Self-Organizing Networks: MANET, WSN, WMN, VANET*, 173, 1–13.

Freudiger, J., Raya, M., Felegyhazi, M., Papadimitratos, P. (2007). Mix-zones for location privacy in vehicular networks. *ACM Workshop on Wireless Networking for Intelligent Transportation Systems (WiN-ITS)*.

Freudiger, J., Shokri, R., Hubaux, J.-P. (2009). On the optimal placement of mix zones. *International Symposium on Privacy Enhancing Technologies Symposium*. Springer, Berlin, Heidelberg.

Friesland, K. (2018). 10 worst internet privacy scandals to date. Technadu [Online]. Available at: https://www.technadu.com/worst-internet-privacy-scandals/30236/ [Accessed 14 March 2019].

Gao, T. and Deng, X. (2018). A pseudonym ring building scheme for anonymous authentication in VANETs. *International Conference on Broadband and Wireless Computing, Communication and Applications*. Springer, Cham.

Geers, K. (2011). *Strategic Cyber Security*. NATO CCD COE Publications, Estonia.

Gerla, M. (2012). Vehicular cloud computing. *11th Annual Mediterranean Ad Hoc Networking Workshop (Med-Hoc-Net)*. IEEE.

Gerla, M., Lee, E., Pau, G., Lee, U. (2014). Internet of vehicles: From intelligent grid to autonomous cars and vehicular clouds. *IEEE World Forum on Internet of Things (WF-IoT)*, 6–8 March.

Glancy, D.J. (2012). Privacy in autonomous vehicles. *Santa Clara Law Review*, 52, 1171.

Glouche, Y., Genet, T., Heen, O., Houssay, E., Saillard, R. (2006–2017). SPAN [Online]. Available at: http://people.irisa.fr/Thomas.Genet/span/ [Accessed 19 February 2019].

Gope, P., Lee, J., Quek, T.Q.S. (2018). Lightweight and practical anonymous authentication protocol for RFID systems using physically unclonable functions. *IEEE Transactions on Information Forensics and Security*, 13(11), 2831–2843.

Gu, Q. and Liu, P. (2007). Denial of service attacks. *Handbook of Computer Networks: Distributed Networks, Network Planning, Control, Management, and New Trends and Applications*, 3, 454–468.

Gu, L., Zeng, D., Guo, S. (2013). Vehicular cloud computing: A survey. *IEEE Globecom Workshops (GC Wkshps)*, December.

Guo, J. and Balon, N. (2006). Vehicular ad hoc networks and dedicated short-range communication. Paper, University of Michigan.

Guo, N., Ma, L., Gao, T. (2018). Independent mix zone for location privacy in vehicular networks. *IEEE Access*, 6, 16842–16850.

Gupta, A. (2022). VANET simulation in MATLAB [Online]. Available at: https://www.github.com/earthat/VANET-Simulation-in-MATLAB [Accessed 21 February 2019].

Hartenstein, H. and Laberteaux, K. (2010). *VANET: Vehicular Applications and Inter-Networking Technologies*. Wiley, Chichester.

Heinze, J. (2016). How the rise of driverless cars will transform the advertising industry. *CarTech* [Online]. Available at: https://www.connectedcar-news.com/news/2016/jul/04/how-rise-driverless-cars-will-transform-advertising-industry/ [Accessed 27 March 2019].

Hotz, H. (2006). A short introduction to game theory (Lecture Notes) [Online]. Available at: https://www.theorie.physik.uni-muenchen.de/lsfrey/teaching/archiv/sose_06/softmatter/talks/Heiko_Hotz-Spieltheorie-Vortrag.pdf [Accessed 25 April 2022].

How secure is my password? (n.d.). How secure is my password? [Online]. Available at: https://howsecureismypassword.net/ [Accessed 10 April 2019].

Hu, Y.-C., Perrig, A., Johnson, D.B. (2006). Wormhole attacks in wireless networks. *IEEE Journal on Selected Areas in Communications*, 24(2), 370–380.

Huang, L., Matsuura, K., Yamane, H., Sezaki, K. (2005). Enhancing wireless location privacy using silent period. *IEEE Wireless Communications and Networking Conference*, 2.

Huang, D., Williams, S.A., Shere, S. (2012). Cheater detection in vehicular networks. *IEEE 11th International Conference on Trust, Security and Privacy in Computing and Communications*, 25–27 June.

Hussain, R., Kim, S., Oh, H. (2009). Towards privacy aware pseudonymless strategy for avoiding profile generation in VANET. *International Workshop on Information Security Applications*. Springer, Berlin, Heidelberg.

Hussain, R., Rezaeifar, Z., Oh, H. (2015). A paradigm shift from vehicular ad hoc networks to VANET-based clouds. *Wireless Personal Communications*, 83(2), 1131–1158.

Irisa (2006). SPAN [Online]. Available at: http://people.irisa.fr/Thomas.Genet/span/ [Accessed 18 April 2018].

Isograph (n.d.). Attack tree [Online]. Available at: https://www.isograph.com/software/attacktree/ [Accessed 20 February 2019].

Javadi, M.M. (2006). User Guide MobiSim v3 – A framework to manage mobility models. Masoudmoshref [Online]. Available at: http://masoudmoshref.com/old/myworks/documentpages/mobisim/UserGuide.pdf.

Jiang, W., Li, F., Lin, D., Bertino, E. (2017). No one can track you: Randomized authentication in vehicular ad-hoc networks. *IEEE International Conference on Pervasive Computing and Communications (PerCom)*, 13–17 March.

Kang, J., Yu, R., Huang, X., Jonsson, M., Bogucka, H., Gjessing, S., Zhang, Y. (2016). Location privacy attacks and defenses in cloud-enabled internet of vehicles. *IEEE Wireless Communications*, 23(5), 52–59.

Kang, J., Yu, R., Huang, X., Zhang, Y. (2018). Privacy-preserved pseudonym scheme for fog computing supported internet of vehicles. *IEEE Transactions on Intelligent Transportation Systems*, 19(8), 2627–2637.

Kargl, F., Waldschmidt, C., Al-Momani, A. (2016). Physical layer-based message authentication in VANETs. GI/ITG KuVS Fachgespräch Inter-Vehicle Communication 2016, 31 March–1 April, Humboldt-Universität zu Berlin.

Kerrache, C.A., Calafate, C.T., Cano, J.-C., Lagraa, N., Manzoni, P. (2016). Trust management for vehicular networks: An adversary-oriented overview. *IEEE Access*, 4, 9293–9307.

Khacheba, I., Yagoubi, M.B., Lagraa, N., Lakas, A. (2017). Location privacy scheme for VANETs. *International Conference on Selected Topics in Mobile and Wireless Networking (MoWNeT)*. IEEE.

Khacheba, I., Yagoubi, M.B., Lagraa, N., Lakas, A. (2018). CLPS: Context-based location privacy scheme for VANETs. *International Journal of Ad Hoc and Ubiquitous Computing*, 29(1–2), 141–159.

Khodaei, M. (2012). Secure Vehicular Communication Systems: Design and Implementation of a Vehicular PKI (VPKI). Dissertation, School of Electrical Engineering, Stockholm.

Khodaei, M. and Papadimitratos, P. (2016). Evaluating on-demand pseudonym acquisition policies in vehicular communication systems. *Proceedings of the First International Workshop on Internet of Vehicles and Vehicles of Internet*. ACM.

Khodaei, M., Jin, H., Papadimitratos, P. (2014). Towards deploying a scalable & robust vehicular identity and credential management infrastructure. *IEEE Vehicular Networking Conference (VNC)*, Paderborn.

Kim, O.T.T., Nguyen, V.D., Hong, C.S. (2014). Which network simulation tool is better for simulating vehicular ad-hoc network? *Proceedings of the Korean Information Science Society*, 930–932.

Kumar, V., Mishra, S., Chand, N. (2013). Applications of VANETs: Present & future. *Communications and Network*, 5(01), 12.

Kurihara, T. (2013). 1609.2-2013 – IEEE standard for wireless access in vehicular environments. Security services for applications and management messages. VT – IEEE Vehicular Technology Society.

Laurendeau, C. and Barbeau, M. (2006). Threats to Security in DSRC/WAVE. *International Conference on Ad-Hoc Networks and Wireless*. Springer, Berlin, Heidelberg.

Lawson, P., McPhail, B., Lawton, E. (2015). The connected car: Who is in the driver's seat? A study on privacy and onboard vehicle telematics technology. Study, British Columbia Freedom of Information and Privacy Association, Vancouver [Online]. Available at: https://fipa.bc.ca/wp-content/uploads/2018/01/CC_report_lite.pdf.

Lequerica, I., Longaron, M.G., Ruiz, P.M. (2010). Drive and share: Efficient provisioning of social networks in vehicular scenarios. *IEEE Communications Magazine*, 48(11), 90–97.

Li, M., Sampigethaya, K., Huang, L., Poovendran, R. (2006). Swing & swap: User-centric approaches towards maximizing location privacy. *Proceedings of the 5th ACM Workshop on Privacy in Electronic Society*. ACM.

Liao, J. and Li, J. (2009). Effectively changing pseudonyms for privacy protection in VANETs. *10th International Symposium on Pervasive Systems, Algorithms, and Networks*. IEEE.

Lim, H.-J. and Chung, T.-M. (2012). Privacy treat factors for VANET in network layer. In *Soft Computing in Information Communication Technology*, Luo, J. (ed.). Springer, Berlin, Heidelberg.

Litman, T. (2018). Autonomous vehicle implementation predictions implications for transport planning. Report, Victoria Transport Policy Institute.

Liu, X., Zhao, H., Pan, M., Yue, H., Li, X., Fang, Y. (2012). Traffic-aware multiple mix zone placement for protecting location privacy. *Proceedings IEEE INFOCOM*, 10 May.

Liu, Y., Wang, Y., Chang, G. (2017). Efficient privacy-preserving dual authentication and key agreement scheme for secure V2V communications in an IoV paradigm. *IEEE Transactions on Intelligent Transportation Systems*, 18(10), 2740–2749.

Liu, B., Zhou, W., Zhu, T., Xiang, Y., Wang, K. (eds) (2018a). Location privacy-preserving mechanisms. In *Location Privacy in Mobile Applications*. Springer, Singapore.

Liu, J., Li, Q., Sun, R., Du, X., Guizani, M. (2018b). An efficient anonymous authentication scheme for Internet of Vehicles. *IEEE International Conference on Communications (ICC)*, 20–24 May.

Lord, K.M. and Sharp, T. (eds) (2011). *America's Cyber Future: Security and Prosperity in the Information Age*, vol. 1. Center for a New American Security, Washington, DC.

Lozupone, V. (2018). Analyze encryption and public key infrastructure (PKI). *International Journal of Information Management*, 38(1), 42–44.

Lu, R., Lin, X., Luan, T.H., Liang, X., Shen, X. (2011). Anonymity analysis on social spot based pseudonym changing for location privacy in VANETs. *IEEE International Conference on Communications (ICC)*, 5–9 June.

Lu, R., Lin, X., Luan, T.H., Liang, X., Shen, X. (2012). Pseudonym changing at social spots: An effective strategy for location privacy in VANETs. *IEEE Transactions on Vehicular Technology*, 61(1), 86–96.

Lucero, S. (2016). Cellular vehicle-to-everything (C-V2X) connectivity. IHS Technology, Internet Everything.

Lukács, A. (2016). What is privacy? The history and definition of privacy. University of Szeged, Faculty of Law and Political Sciences, Department of Labour Law and Social Security [Online]. Available at: http://publicatio.bibl.u-szeged.hu/10794/7/3188699.pdf.

Lutterotti, P., Pau, G., Jiang, D., Gerla, M., Delgrossi, L. (2008). C-VeT, the UCLA vehicular testbed: An open platform for vehicular networking and urban sensing. *International Conference on Wireless Access for Vehicular Environments (WAVE 2008)*, 182.

Luxembourg University (n.d.). Attack tree, ADTool [Online]. Available at: http://satoss.uni.lu/members/piotr/adtool/ [Accessed 20 February 2019].

Ma, Z., Kargl, F., Weber, M. (2008). Pseudonym-on-demand: A new pseudonym refill strategy for vehicular communications. *IEEE 68th Vehicular Technology Conference*, 24 October.

Maglaras, L., Al-Bayatti, A.H., He, Y., Wagner, I., Janick, H. (2016). Social internet of vehicles for smart cities. *Journal of Sensor and Actuator Networks*, 5(1), 3.

Malik, N., Nanda, P., Arora, A., Xiangjian, H., Puthal, D. (2018). Blockchain based secured identity authentication and expeditious revocation framework for vehicular networks. *17th IEEE International Conference on Trust, Security and Privacy in Computing and Communications/12th IEEE International Conference on Big Data Science and Engineering (TrustCom/BigDataSE)*, 1–3 August.

Mandylionlabs (n.d.). Brute force calculator [Online]. Available at: http://www.mandylionlabs.com/index15.htm [Accessed 10 April 2019].

Mathews, S. (2014). An effective strategy for pseudonym generation & changing scheme with privacy preservation for VANET. *International Conference on Electronics and Communication Systems (ICECS)*. IEEE.

MATLAB (n.d.). MATLAB [Online]. Available at: https://uk.mathworks.com/products/matlab.html [Accessed 21 February 2019].

Mehmood, A., Natgunanathan, I., Xiang, Y., Poston, H., Zhang, Y. (2018). Anonymous authentication scheme for smart cloud-based healthcare applications. *IEEE Access*, 6, 33552–33567.

Mejri, M.N., Ben-Othman, J., Hamdi, M. (2014). Survey on VANET security challenges and possible cryptographic solutions. *Vehicular Communications*, 1(2), 53–66.

Memon, I., Chen, L., Arain, Q.A., Memon, H., Chen, G. (2018). Pseudonym changing strategy with multiple mix zones for trajectory privacy protection in road networks. *International Journal of Communication Systems*, 31(1), e3437.

Meraihi, R., Senouci, S.-M., Meddour, D.-E., Jerbi, M. (2008). Vehicle-to-vehicle communications: Applications and perspectives. In *Wireless Ad Hoc and Sensor Networks*, Labiod, H. (ed.). ISTE Ltd, London, and John Wiley & Sons, New York [Online]. Available at: https://doi.org/10.1002/9780470610893.ch12.

Mitnick, K.D. and Simon, W.L. (2011). *The Art of Deception: Controlling the Human Element of Security*. John Wiley & Sons, New York.

MobiSim (n.d.). MobiSim [Online]. Available at: http://masoudmoshref.com/old/myworks/documentpages/mobility_simulator.htm [Accessed 21 February 2019].

Mousavi, S.M., Rabiee, H.R., Mochref, M., Dabirmoghaddam, A. (2007). MobiSim: A framework for simulation of mobility models in mobile ad-hoc networks. *Third IEEE International Conference on Wireless and Mobile Computing, Networking and Communications (WiMob 2007)*, October.

Nakamoto, S. (2008). Bitcoin: A peer-to-peer electronic cash system. *Decentralized Business Review*, 21260 [Online]. Available at: https://www.debr.io/article/21260.pdf.

National (n.d.). 10 astonishing technologies that power Google's self-driving cars [Online]. Available at: https://www.national.co.uk/tech-powers-google-car/ [Accessed 20 December 2018].

NetAnim (n.d.). NetAnim 3.105 [Online]. Available at: https://www.nsnam.org/wiki/ NetAnim_3.105 [Accessed 21 February 2019].

NS2 (n.d.). The Network Simulator – ns-2 [Online]. Available at: https://www.isi.edu/nsnam/ ns/ [Accessed 21 February 2019].

NS3 (n.d.). ns-3.29 [Online]. Available at: https://www.nsnam.org/releases/ns-3-29/ [Accessed 21 February 2019].

NS3 Tutorial (2019). NS3 Project [Online]. Available at: https://www.nsnam.org/ docs/release/3.29/tutorial/ns-3-tutorial.pdf [Accessed 21 February 2019].

OMNeT (n.d.). What is OMNeT++? [Online]. Available at: https://omnetpp.org/intro/ [Accessed 21 February 2019].

OneLedger (n.d.). OneLedger [Online]. Available at: https://oneledger.io/en/ [Accessed 14 November 2018].

OpenStreetMap (n.d.). Welcome to OpenStreetMap! [Online]. Available at: https://www. openstreetmap.org/ [Accessed 21 February 2019].

Palanisamy, B. and Liu, L. (2011). MobiMix: Protecting location privacy with mix-zones over road networks. *IEEE 27th International Conference on Data Engineering*, 11–16 April.

Palanisamy, B., Liu, L., Lee, K., Singh, A., Tang, Y. (2012). Location privacy with road network mix-zones. *8th International Conference on Mobile Ad-hoc and Sensor Networks (MSN)*. IEEE.

Pan, Y. and Li, J. (2012). An analysis of anonymity for cooperative pseudonym change scheme in one-dimensional VANETs. *Proceedings of the 2012 IEEE 16th International Conference on Computer Supported Cooperative Work in Design (CSCWD)*, 23–25 May.

Pan, Y. and Li, J. (2013). Cooperative pseudonym change scheme based on the number of neighbors in VANETs. *Journal of Network and Computer Applications*, 36(6), 1599–1609.

Pan, Y., Shi, Y., Li, J. (2017). A novel and practical pseudonym change scheme in VANETs. *International Conference on Innovative Mobile and Internet Services in Ubiquitous Computing*. Springer, Cham.

PAT RESEARCH (n.d.). Top companies for self-driving vehicles [Online]. Available at: https://www.predictiveanalyticstoday.com/top-companies-autonomous-cars-self-driving-car/ [Accessed 19 December 2018].

Petit, J., Schaub, F., Feiri, M., Kargl, F. (2015). Pseudonym schemes in vehicular networks: A survey. *IEEE Communications Surveys & Tutorials*, 17(1), 228–255.

Pfleeger, C.P. and Pfleeger, S.L. (2006). *Security in Computing*, 4th edition. Prentice Hall, Hoboken.

Pfleeger, C.P., Pfleeger, S.L., Margulies, J. (2015). *Security in Computing*, 5th edition. Prentice Hall, Upper Saddle River.

PrimePages (n.d.). Random small primes [Online]. Available at: https://primes.utm.edu/lists/small/small.html [Accessed 10 April 2019].

Raazi, S.M.K.-U.-R., Pervez, Z., Lee, S. (eds) (2011). Key management schemes of wireless sensor networks: A survey. In *Security of Self-Organizing Networks: MANET, WSN, WMN, VANET*, 1st edition. Auerbach Publications, New York.

Rawashdeh, Z.Y. and Mahmud, S.M. (2011). Communications in vehicular networks. In *Mobile Ad-Hoc Networks: Applications*, Wang, X. (ed.). InTech, Rijeka.

Raya, M. and Hubaux, J.-P. (2007). Securing vehicular ad hoc networks. *Journal of Computer Security*, 15(1), 39–68.

Sampigethaya, K., Huang, L., Li, M., Poovendran, R., Matsuura, K., Sezaki, K. (2005). CARAVAN: Providing location privacy for VANET. Paper, Department of Electrical Engineering, Washington University, Seattle.

Sampigethaya, K., Li, M., Huang, L., Poovendran, R. (2007). AMOEBA: Robust location privacy scheme for VANET. *IEEE Journal on Selected Areas in Communications*, 25(8), 1569–1589.

Schaub, F., Kargl, F., Ma, Z., Weber, M. (2010). V-tokens for conditional pseudonymity in VANETs. *2010 IEEE Wireless Communication and Networking Conference*, April.

Schmid, P. (2017). The Blockchain: What is it? And why is it important to risk management and insurance? Speech, RIMS, New York.

Schneier, B. (1999). Attack trees. *Dr. Dobb's Journal*, 24(12), 21–29.

Schoettle, B. and Sivak, M. (2014). A survey of public opinion about autonomous and self-driving vehicles in the U.S., the U.K., and Australia. Report, University of Michigan, Ann Arbor, Transportation Research Institute, USA [Online]. Available at: https://deepblue.lib.umich.edu/bitstream/handle/2027.42/108384/103024.pdf?sequence=1 &isAllowed=y.

Sen, J. (2010). A survey on wireless sensor network security. arXiv preprint arXiv:1011.1529.

Sen, S., Clark, J.A., Tapiador, J.E. (2010). Security threats in mobile ad hoc networks. In *Security of Self-Organizing Networks: MANET, WSN, WMN, VANET*, 1st edition, Raazi, S.M.K.-U.-R., Pervez, Z., Lee, S. (eds). Auerbach Publications, New York.

Seuwou, P., Patel, D., Ubakanma, G. (2014). Vehicular ad hoc network applications and security: A study into the economic and the legal implications. *International Journal of Electronic Security and Digital Forensics*, 6(2), 115–129.

Sivasakthi, M. and Suresh, S.R. (2013). Research on vehicular ad hoc networks (VANETs): An overview. *International Journal of Applied Science and Engineering Research*, 2(1), 23–27.

Sjöberg, K. (2011). Standardization of wireless vehicular communications within IEEE and ETSI. *IEEE VTS Workshop on Wireless Vehicular Communications*, 9 November.

Song, J.-H., Wong, V.W., Leung, V.C. (2010). Wireless location privacy protection in vehicular ad-hoc networks. *Mobile Networks and Applications*, 15(1), 160–171.

Statista (2016). IoT number of connected devices [Online]. Available at: https://www.statista.com/statistics/471264/iot-number-of-connected-devices-worldwide/ [Accessed 22 September 2018].

Stolfo, S.J., Bellovin, S.M., Hershkop, S., Keromytis, A., Sinclair, S., Smith, S.W. (eds) (2008). *Insider Attack and Cyber Security: Beyond the Hacker*, vol. 39. Springer Science & Business Media, New York.

Sumo (n.d.). Eclipse SUMO – Simulation of Urban MObility [Online]. Available at: https://www.dlr.de/ts/en/desktopdefault.aspx/tabid-9883/16931_read-41000/ [Accessed 21 February 2019].

Sun, Y., Zhang, B., Zhao, B., Su, X., Su, J. (2015). Mix-zones optimal deployment for protecting location privacy in VANET. *Peer-to-Peer Networking and Applications*, 8(6), 1108–1121.

Sun Tzu (1910). *Sun Tzŭ on the Art of War: The Oldest Military Treatise in the World*. Luzac & Company, London.

Sun Tzu Said (2022). Sun Tzu's Art of War [Online]. Available at: https://suntzusaid.com/ [Accessed 26 March 2019].

Sunshine (n.d.). Scientific notation: Table of large numbers [Online]. Available at: http://sunshine.chpc.utah.edu/Labs/ScientificNotation/ManSciNot1/table.html [Accessed 10 April 2019].

T.A. Team (2006). HLPSL tutorial [Online]. Available at: http://www.avispa-project.org/package/tutorial.pdf [Accessed 19 April 2018].

Valency Networks (2008). Man in the middle attack. *Valency Networks* [Online]. Available at: http://www.valencynetworks.com/articles/cyber-attacks-explained-man-in-the-middle-attack.html [Accessed 27 February 2019].

VanetMobiSim (n.d.). VanetMobiSim [Online]. Available at: http://vanet.eurecom.fr/ [Accessed 21 February 2019].

Veins (n.d.). Veins [Online]. Available at: https://veins.car2x.org/ [Accessed 21 February 2019].

Vercauteren, F. (2008). Discrete logarithms in cryptography. ESAT/COSICKU Leuven ECRYPT Summer.

Wang, X., Mao, S., Gong, M.X. (2017). An overview of 3GPP cellular vehicle-to-everything standards. *GetMobile: Mobile Computing and Communications*, 21(3), 19–25.

Wang, S., Yao, N., Gong, N., Gao, Z. (2018a). A trigger-based pseudonym exchange scheme for location privacy preserving in VANETs. *Peer-to-Peer Networking and Applications*, 11(3), 548–560.

Wang, X., Jiang, J., Wang, B., Xia, Z. (2018b). A VANET anonymous authentication mechanism for multi-level application scenarios. *International Conference on Cloud Computing and Security*, 6–8 June.

Warren, S.D. and Brandeis, L.D. (1890). The right to privacy. *Ethical Issues in the Use of Computers*, 4(5), 172–183.

Waymo (n.d.). Self-driving vehicles [Online]. Available at: https://waymo.com/journey/ [Accessed 19 December 2018].

Weerasinghe, H., Fu, H., Leng, S. (2010). Anonymous service access for vehicular ad hoc networks. *Sixth International Conference on Information Assurance and Security*. IEEE.

Westin, A.F. (1967). *Privacy and Freedom*. Atheneum, New York.

Whaiduzzaman, M., Sookhak, M., Gani, A., Buyya, R. (2014). A survey on vehicular cloud computing. *Journal of Network and Computer Applications*, 40, 325–344.

Xingjun, S. and Huibin, X. (2014). An effective scheme for location privacy in VANETs. *Journal of Networks*, 9(8), 2239.

Yaga, D., Mell, P., Roby, N., Scarfone, K. (2018). NISTIR 8202 – Blockchain technology overview. National Institute of Standards and Technology, US Department of Commerce.

Yakubov, A., Shbair, W., Wallbom, A., Sanda, D., State, R. (2018). A blockchain-based PKI management framework. *The First IEEE/IFIP International Workshop on Managing and Managed by Blockchain (Man2Block) Colocated with IEEE/IFIP NOMS 2018*, 23–27 April, Tapei.

Yang, F., Wang, S., Li, J., Liu, Z., Sun, Q. (2014). An overview of internet of vehicles. *China Communications*, 11(10), 1–15.

Ying, B. and Makrakis, D. (2015). Pseudonym changes scheme based on candidate-location-list in vehicular networks. *IEEE International Conference on Communications (ICC)*, June.

Ying, B., Makrakis, D., Mouftah, H.T. (2013). Dynamic mix-zone for location privacy in vehicular networks. *IEEE Communications Letters*, 17(8), 1524–1527.

Ying, B., Makrakis, D., Hou, Z. (2015). Motivation for protecting selfish vehicles' location privacy in vehicular networks. *IEEE Transactions on Vehicular Technology*, 64(12), 5631–5641.

Yu, R., Zhang, Y., Gjessing, S., Xia, W., Yang, K. (2013). Toward cloud-based vehicular networks with efficient resource management. arXiv preprint arXiv:1308.6208.

Yue, X., Chen, B., Wang, X., Duan, Y., Gao, M., He, Y. (2018). An efficient and secure anonymous authentication scheme for VANETs based on the framework of group signatures. *IEEE Access*, 6, 62584–62600.

Zeadally, S., Hunt, R., Chen, Y.-S., Irwin, A., Hassan, A. (2012). Vehicular ad hoc networks (VANETS): Status, results, and challenges. *Telecommunication Systems*, 50(4), 217–241.

Zheng, Z., Xie, S., Dai, H.-N., Chen, X., Wang, H. (2017). An overview of blockchain technology: Architecture, consensus, and future trends. *IEEE International Congress on Big Data (BigData Congress)*, 25–30 June.

Index

Other titles from

in

Networks and Telecommunications

2021

LAUNAY Frédéric
NG-RAN and 5G-NR: 5G Radio Access Network and Radio Interference

2020

PUJOLLE Guy
Software Networks: Virtualization, SDN, 5G and Security (2nd edition revised and updated)
(Advanced Network Set – Volume 1)

GONTRAND Christophe
Digital Communication Techniques

2019

LAUNEY Frédéric, PEREZ André
LTE Advanced Pro: Towards the 5G Mobile Network
Harmonic Concept and Applications

TOUNSI Wiem
Cyber-Vigilance and Digital Trust: Cyber Security in the Era of Cloud Computing and IoT

2018

ANDIA Gianfranco, DURO Yvan, TEDJINI Smail
Non-linearities in Passive RFID Systems: Third Harmonic Concept and Applications

BOUILLARD Anne, BOYER Marc, LE CORRONC Euriell
Deterministic Network Calculus: From Theory to Practical Implementation

LAUNAY Frédéric, PEREZ André
LTE Advanced Pro: Towards the 5G Mobile Network

PEREZ André
Wi-Fi Integration to the 4G Mobile Network

2017

BENSLAMA Malek, BENSLAMA Achour, ARIS Skander
Quantum Communications in New Telecommunications Systems

HILT Benoit, BERBINEAU Marion, VINEL Alexey, PIROVANO Alain
Networking Simulation for Intelligent Transportation Systems: High Mobile Wireless Nodes

LESAS Anne-Marie, MIRANDA Serge
The Art and Science of NFC Programming
(Intellectual Technologies Set – Volume 3)

2016

AL AGHA Khaldoun, PUJOLLE Guy, ALI-YAHIYA Tara
Mobile and Wireless Networks
(Advanced Network Set – Volume 2)

BATTU Daniel
Communication Networks Economy

BENSLAMA Malek, BATATIA Hadj, MESSAI Abderraouf
Transitions from Digital Communications to Quantum Communications:
Concepts and Prospects

CHIASSERINI Carla Fabiana, GRIBAUDO Marco, MANINI Daniele
Analytical Modeling of Wireless Communication Systems
(Stochastic Models in Computer Science and Telecommunication Networks
Set – Volume 1)

EL FALLAH SEGHROUCHNI Amal, ISHIKAWA Fuyuki, HÉRAULT Laurent,
TOKUDA Hideyuki
Enablers for Smart Cities

PEREZ André
VoLTE and ViLTE

2015

BENSLAMA Malek, BATATIA Hadj, BOUCENNA Mohamed Lamine
Ad Hoc Networks Telecommunications and Game Theory

BENSLAMA Malek, KIAMOUCHE Wassila, BATATIA Hadj
Connections Management Strategies in Satellite Cellular Networks

BERTHOU Pascal, BAUDOIN Cédric, GAYRAUD Thierry, GINESTE Matthieu
Satellite and Terrestrial Hybrid Networks

CUADRA-SÁNCHEZ Antonio, ARACIL Javier
Traffic Anomaly Detection

LE RUYET Didier, PISCHELLA Mylène
Digital Communications 1: Source and Channel Coding

PEREZ André
LTE and LTE Advanced: 4G Network Radio Interface

PISCHELLA Mylène, LE RUYET Didier
Digital Communications 2: Digital Modulations

2014

ANJUM Bushra, PERROS Harry
Bandwidth Allocation for Video under Quality of Service Constraints

BATTU Daniel
New Telecom Networks: Enterprises and Security

BEN MAHMOUD Mohamed Slim, GUERBER Christophe, LARRIEU Nicolas, PIROVANO Alain, RADZIK José
Aeronautical Air–Ground Data Link Communications

BITAM Salim, MELLOUK Abdelhamid
Bio-inspired Routing Protocols for Vehicular Ad-Hoc Networks

CAMPISTA Miguel Elias Mitre, RUBINSTEIN Marcelo Gonçalves
Advanced Routing Protocols for Wireless Networks

CHETTO Maryline
Real-time Systems Scheduling 1: Fundamentals
Real-time Systems Scheduling 2: Focuses

EXPOSITO Ernesto, DIOP Codé
Smart SOA Platforms in Cloud Computing Architectures

MELLOUK Abdelhamid, CUADRA-SANCHEZ Antonio
Quality of Experience Engineering for Customer Added Value Services

OTEAFY Sharief M.A., HASSANEIN Hossam S.
Dynamic Wireless Sensor Networks

PEREZ André
Network Security

PERRET Etienne
Radio Frequency Identification and Sensors: From RFID to Chipless RFID

REMY Jean-Gabriel, LETAMENDIA Charlotte
LTE Standards
LTE Services

MELLOUK Abdelhamid, HOCEINI Said, TRAN Hai Anh
Quality-of-Experience for Multimedia: Application to Content Delivery Network Architecture

NAIT-SIDI-MOH Ahmed, BAKHOUYA Mohamed, GABER Jaafar, WACK Maxime
Geopositioning and Mobility

PEREZ André
Voice over LTE: EPS and IMS Networks

2012

AL AGHA Khaldoun
Network Coding

BOUCHET Olivier
Wireless Optical Communications

DECREUSEFOND Laurent, MOYAL Pascal
Stochastic Modeling and Analysis of Telecoms Networks

DUFOUR Jean-Yves
Intelligent Video Surveillance Systems

EXPOSITO Ernesto
Advanced Transport Protocols: Designing the Next Generation

JUMIRA Oswald, ZEADALLY Sherali
Energy Efficiency in Wireless Networks

KRIEF Francine
Green Networking

PEREZ André
Mobile Networks Architecture

2011

BONALD Thomas, FEUILLET Mathieu
Network Performance Analysis

2008

CHADUC Jean-Marc, POGOREL Gérard
The Radio Spectrum

GAÏTI Dominique
Autonomic Networks

LABIOD Houda
Wireless Ad Hoc and Sensor Networks

LECOY Pierre
Fiber-optic Communications

MELLOUK Abdelhamid
End-to-End Quality of Service Engineering in Next Generation Heterogeneous Networks

PAGANI Pascal *et al.*
Ultra-wideband Radio Propagation Channel

2007

BENSLIMANE Abderrahim
Multimedia Multicast on the Internet

PUJOLLE Guy
Management, Control and Evolution of IP Networks

SANCHEZ Javier, THIOUNE Mamadou
UMTS

VIVIER Guillaume
Reconfigurable Mobile Radio Systems

Printed and bound by CPI Group (UK) Ltd, Croydon, CR0 4YY

27/10/2024

14580735-0003